Building and Sustaining Coaching Culture

David Clutterbuck, David Megginson and Agnieszka Bajer

Chartered Institute of Personnel and Development

Published by the Chartered Institute of Personnel and Development
151 The Broadway, London SW19 1JQ

This edition first published 2016

Designed and typeset by Exeter Premedia Services, India
Printed in Great Britain by Ashford Colour Press

British Library Cataloguing in Publication Data
A catalogue of this publication is available from the British Library

ISBN 9781843983767
eBook ISBN 9781843984467

CIPD

Chartered Institute of Personnel and Development

151 The Broadway, London SW19 1JQ
Tel: 020 8612 6200
Email: cipd@cipd.co.uk
Website: www.cipd.co.uk
Incorporated by Royal Charter.
Registered Charity No. 1079797

Shelfie

A **bundled** eBook edition is available with the purchase of this print book.

CLEARLY PRINT YOUR NAME ABOVE IN UPPER CASE

Instructions to claim your eBook edition:
1. Download the Shelfie app for Android or iOS
2. Write your name in **UPPER CASE** above
3. Use the Shelfie app to submit a photo
4. Download your eBook to any device

Building and Sustaining a Coaching Culture

David Clutterbuck, David Megginson and Agnieszka Bajer

The Chartered Institute of Personnel and Development is the leading publisher of books and reports for personnel and training professionals, students, and all those concerned with the effective management and development of people at work. For details of all our titles, please contact the publishing department:

tel: 020 8612 6204

email: publish@cipd.co.uk

The catalogue of all CIPD titles can be viewed on the CIPD website:

www.cipd.co.uk/bookstore

An e-book version is also available for purchase from:

www.ebooks.cipd.co.uk

Contents

List of figures, tables and exhibits   viii
About the authors   xi
Preface   xii
Acknowledgements   xiii
About the book   xvii

PART 1   A FRESH VIEW ON COACHING CULTURE

Chapter 1   So, What is a Coaching Culture After All?
What is culture and why bother?   3
What culture looks and feels like   4
Defining culture   5
The essence of coaching and mentoring   7
So what is a coaching culture?   7
Coaching culture model   9
Stages of coaching culture development   13
Business case for a coaching culture   15
Summary   18

Chapter 2   Systemic View on a Coaching Culture
A much needed mindset shift   19
A bit of background on systems theory   21
Key systems of a coaching culture   21
Coaching culture on the edge of chaos   23
Managing polarities while developing coaching culture   26
Problems . . . a curse or a blessing in disguise?   27
Working smarter, not harder   30
Summary   35

PART 2   THE ABCS OF COACHING CULTURE PLANNING AND
IMPLEMENTATION

Chapter 3   Getting Set and Ready
Is a coaching culture for you?   39
To invest or not to invest?   45
Getting initial support from key influencers   47
The ABCs of coaching culture planning and implementation   49
Who should be involved in the coaching culture planning   51
process?
Summary   53

Chapter 4   Knowing Where You Want To Get To
            What is a coaching culture vision and why is it important?   55
            What makes a coaching culture vision effective?   56
            Creating an effective coaching culture vision   57
            Summary   62

Chapter 5   What's Your Starting Point and How Will You Measure
            Progress?
            Why perform baseline and context assessment?   63
            Coaching culture audit   65
            Tools and templates   68
            Summary   79

Chapter 6   Charting the Course
            Critical components of a successful coaching culture   81
            strategy
            Coaching culture strategy workshop and beyond   88
            Summary   97

PART 3   LAYING THE FOUNDATIONS

Chapter 7   Making Effective Use of External Coaches
            Evolution of external coaching   101
            Benefits and drawbacks of using external executive   102
            coaches
            Key steps to making effective use of external coaches   102
            Summary   122

Chapter 8   Developing Internal Capacity for Coaching
            Is coaching by managers really so important?   123
            Instilling coaching culture within the work teams   133
            Internal semi-professional or professional coaching pool   137
            Making effective use of internal coaches   138
            Summary   143

Chapter 9   Team Coaching – Fad or Future?
            Why focus on teams?   145
            So what is a team?   145
            Why team coaching?   146
            What is team coaching?   147
            The role and competencies of a team coach   149
            How does team coaching work?   152
            Team coaching supervision   156
            The future of team coaching   157
            Summary   163

Chapter 10 Formal and Informal Mentoring
    A very brief history of mentoring   165
    Developmental mentoring defined   166
    How is developmental mentoring different from   167
    developmental coaching?
    Applications of mentoring   168
    Different forms of mentoring   170
    Formal mentoring, informal mentoring – or both?   172
    Making formal mentoring work – international good   173
    practice
    Making informal mentoring work   176
    Summary   181

PART 4   MOVING BEYOND THE BASICS

Chapter 11 The Unsung Heroes of Coaching Culture
    The key roles   186
    Summary   196

Chapter 12 Marketing Coaching and Mentoring
    Why marketing?   197
    Coaching and mentoring marketing fundamentals   197
    Elements of an effective marketing plan   199
    Summary   207

Chapter 13 Cross-Cultural Issues
    Coaching – a western approach or a universal transcultural   210
    tool?
    Skills and characteristics of an effective cross-cultural   211
    coach
    Developing multicultural skills   213
    Does developing a coaching culture help leverage cultural   214
    differences?
    Does one size fit all?   216
    Summary   218

    Epilogue   219

    Resources and Bibliography   223

    Index   235

List of figures, tables and exhibits

CHAPTER 1

Table 1.1	Definitions of organisational culture	6
Figure 1.1	The developmental conversation model	8
Table 1.2	Definitions of coaching culture	8
Figure 1.2	Coaching culture model	10
Figure 1.3	Stages of coaching culture development	13

CHAPTER 2

Table 2.1	A mindset shift: from linear to systemic approach	20
Figure 2.1	Levels of systems in organisations	22
Table 2.2	Characteristics of CAS and implications for a coaching culture	24
Figure 2.2	Example of a 'why tree'	31
Table 2.3	Levels of thinking exercise	36

CHAPTER 3

Table 3.1	Coaching culture relevance indicators	40
Figure 3.1	Supportive climate dimensions	42
Table 3.2	Supportive climate dimensions and key indicators	44
Figure 3.2	Expected returns matrix	45
Exhibit 3.1	Example of articulating a business need for a coaching culture in a hospitality business	47
Figure 3.3	The ABC-DE of coaching culture planning and interpretation	50
Exhibit 3.2	Improvements achieved in Scania	53

CHAPTER 4

Table 4.1	Characteristics of an effective coaching culture vision	56
Figure 4.1	Coaching culture visioning process	57

CHAPTER 5

Table 5.1	Examples of drivers and barriers towards creating a coaching culture	64
Exhibit 5.1	Template for a structured interview/focus group	68
Exhibit 5.2	One-to-one interview with top management	69
Exhibit 5.3	Assessing the quality of the coaching relationship	70
Exhibit 5.4	Assessing the team leader as coach	71
Exhibit 5.5	Coaching culture visible manifestations questionnaire	73

Exhibit 5.6   Development stages of coaching culture   73
Exhibit 5.7   Audit report table of contents   76
Exhibit 5.8   Benefits of transition coaching for new EY partners   79
              measured by net engagement revenue

CHAPTER 6

Figure 6.1   Charting the course in the context of the ABC-DE   82
              model of coaching culture planning and
              implementation
Figure 6.2   Main areas of coaching and mentoring culture strategy   82
Figure 6.3   Effective coaching culture strategy workshop access   89
Exhibit 6.1   Sample agenda of a coaching culture strategy   91
              workshop
Exhibit 6.2   Example of a coaching culture strategy document   94
              contents page
Exhibit 6.3   Examples of questions from coaching culture   94
              workshop strategy
Exhibit 6.4   Coaching and mentoring modalities in a professional   95
              services firm

CHAPTER 7

Figure 7.1   Key steps to making effective use of external coaches   103
Exhibit 7.1   Sample coaching policy and guidelines in a public   104
              organisation
Figure 7.2   Key elements in establishing and maintaining an   105
              appropriate pool of coaches
Exhibit 7.2   RFP for the provision of executive coaching services   107
Exhibit 7.3   Sample post-session reflection instructions   109
Exhibit 7.4   Typical supervision-oriented session   110
Exhibit 7.5   Example of externally resourced coaching engagement   113
              steps
Exhibit 7.6   Process for leveraging individual coaching for   115
              organisation development process

CHAPTER 8

Exhibit 8.1   Stages of the coaching and feedback development   129
              programme in a Greek bank
Exhibit 8.2   The six levels of coaching and feedback development   130
              programme evaluation
Exhibit 8.3   Reaction to the coaching and feedback development   131
              programme
Exhibit 8.4   Before and after results of the coaching and feedback   131
              development programme
Exhibit 8.5   Sustainability of results   133
Table 8.1   Programme elements and characteristics   141

CHAPTER 9

Table 9.1   Team coaching definitions   148
Figure 9.1   Key steps in team coaching conversation   152
Exhibit 9.1   Examples of questions to establish readiness for team   153
              coaching
Exhibit 9.2   Engagement index score   159
Exhibit 9.3   Pyramid's Change Initiative Development Model   159
Table 9.2   Team coaching programme elements   161
Exhibit 9.4   Anthony Owens team coaching meta-model   161
Table 9.3   Team coaching meta-model   161

CHAPTER 10

Table 10.1   Similarities between developmental coaching and   167
              developmental mentoring
Table 10.2   Main differences between formal and informal   172
              mentoring

CHAPTER 12

Figure 12.1   Marketing coaching and mentoring fundamentals   198
Table 12.1   Examples of aligning marketing with coaching culture   199
              strategy

EPILOGUE

Figure E.1   The house of care   221

About the authors

David Clutterbuck is one of the pioneers of coaching and mentoring. Co-founder with David Megginson of the European Mentoring and Coaching Council (EMCC), the primary body representing coaching and mentoring in Europe, he is author or co-author of more than 60 books. Visiting professor at three UK universities, he leads the practitioner network, Coaching and Mentoring International.

David Megginson is Emeritus Professor of HRD at Sheffield Business School. He is a joint founder, with David Clutterbuck, of the European Mentoring and Coaching Council and an author and co-author of many books on coaching and mentoring.

Agnieszka Bajer is a highly sought-after organisation development consultant, facilitator, speaker and executive coach. In her professional career of over 20 years, she has held a number of leadership positions in international organisations. Currently she is a Senior Manager at PwC Cyprus, where she leads the leadership development and coaching practice. Agnieszka is one of the founding members of EMCC Greece.

Preface

When two of us started to explore coaching culture around 15 years ago, there was neither significant literature on the topic, nor a great deal of experience, from which to extract good practice. After considerable research, we pulled together what knowledge we were able to gather and produced the first substantive and evidence-based book on the topic in 2005: *Making Coaching Work: Creating a Coaching Culture*. We have been gratified since to see people from around the world either using our diagnostics to measure their organisations' progress towards a coaching culture or developing new insights and practical approaches.

In this new volume, we (now a trio of authors) have attempted to bring the topic up to date, incorporating new cases, and a new understanding of what works well and less well. We have placed greater emphasis on the complexity of culture change and on recommendations of good practice.

As in the previous book, we have used the term 'coaching culture' as shorthand for a coaching and mentoring culture. Our observation of organisations' experience reinforces our perception that integrating coaching and developmental mentoring is an essential part of the culture change that organisations aspire to. When managers in organisations become mentors, they have a safe environment in which they can practise non-directive, person-centred developmental approaches, while still feeling valued for their own knowledge and experience; being a mentor develops their confidence in their ability to be a developer of others more generally.

We have also learned that the work team plays a much more significant role in achieving a coaching culture than previously realised. Corporate coaching strategies are important in creating the framework for a coaching culture, but it is primarily in the work team that coaching behaviours can become the norm. While it is clear from research evidence that there are contextual problems – such as conflict of interest and role – in the line manager being the coach to the team, most of these problems seem to disappear if the focus is on creating a coaching culture (in which the team may also coach their manager!).

A question we are often asked is: Can you give examples of organisations that have fully achieved a coaching culture? Our answer is always no, because it's so difficult to maintain a consistent coaching climate. What we do see is increasing numbers of organisations that have most of the pillars in place and have enough pockets of excellence to point to coaching as an expected norm. But even strong cultures are vulnerable to a change of leadership to people with different values or to an influx of large numbers of people who don't 'get' the coaching culture.

We also have many questions still unanswered. For example, we suspect, based on comparisons between organisations at different points on the journey towards a coaching culture, that organisational structure, talent selection and management, diversity management and a number of other factors can promote or impede progress. When we have clarity on those topics, no doubt it will be time for another update!

David Clutterbuck, David Megginson and Agnieszka Bajer

Acknowledgements

We are profoundly grateful for our unique circle of colleagues, collaborators, clients and contributors with whom we had the privilege to work with over the past couple of years and who offered their invaluable insights and support in creating this book.

The passion and commitment to developing coaching cultures that we have witnessed while interviewing people responsible for coaching and mentoring, coaching champions, sponsors, as well as coaches and mentors in various organisations has provided us with ongoing inspiration while we were working on the book.

Over the course of the two years it took to complete this book, we talked to dozens of people who shared their experiences in developing a coaching culture. We heard hundreds of stories and, unfortunately, we were not able to include all of them in this book. We are grateful to all these people for the time, openness and willingness to share their thoughts.

The following individuals contributed to the stories featured in the book:

'STORIES FROM THE FIELD' CONTRIBUTORS

Dr Hilary Armstrong, Director, Changeworks Pty Ltd

Hilary has been working as a consultant and thought leader for 25 years. In her own company, Changeworks Pty Ltd, she develops and designs programmes on collaborative and networked leadership that connect social network analysis, diversity of thinking, robust conversations, executive coaching and ethical reflection to create organisational cultures in which optimism, innovation, engagement and accountability are developed.

Shola Awolesi, Global Leadership Development Manager, Save the Children

Shola manages Save the Children's flagship leadership programme in London and works in partnership with key stakeholders around the globe to design and deliver Save the Children's High Potentials programme, the SMDP.

Shola is a coach who works closely with managers and leaders in charities and the public sector to improve performance. She manages Save the Children's network of pro-bono coaches and is working internally to develop a coaching culture.

Tim Bright, Partner at OneWorld Consulting, Istanbul

Tim has 25 years' experience in executive search, coaching, mentoring and HR consulting in Europe, Asia and the US. He is the Managing Partner of OneWorld Consulting's team of consultants and works with clients at all stages of the talent lifecycle.

Sanem Celikyilmaz, Leadership & Talent Development Manager, Vodafone Turkey

Sanem has worked in various HR roles since 2003. Since 2011, she has been in the role of Leadership & Talent Development Manager in Vodafone Turkey, where she is responsible for a range of leadership and talent development initiatives and competency development programmes.

Elena Chelokidi, ACC, President Elect of ICF Russia 2016–2017

Elena is a coach passionate about promoting coaching in business and in the society. She is an organisation development consultant and provides masterclasses for coaches and HR managers. Elena is also involved in translating and publishing books and she is a volunteer coach for a non-profit organisation.

Claire Davey, Head of Coaching & Leadership Development, Deloitte (UK & Switzerland)

Claire has worked in the UK and internationally as an executive coach and development consultant for global organisations within professional services, the financial sector, education, telecommunications and elite sport. She is currently responsible for driving the coaching agenda for Deloitte, developing partners and directors, and identifying opportunities to further enhance leadership effectiveness and presence.

Neslihan Eroğlu, HR Manager, Brisa Bridgestone Sabancı, Turkey

Neslihan has extensive experience in HR; her career has also included audit, sales and operation roles. She has been in her role of HR Manager at Brisa Bridgestone Sabancı since 2010 and she is responsible for all HR functions such as talent management, learning and development, recruitment, employee branding and compensation and benefits.

Victoriya Sergeevna (S) Evtyuhova, Director of secondary school No 5 in Krasniy Sulin

Victoriya is an Erickson International University (Moscow) certified coach and an honorary worker of the general education of the Russian Federation. She is the initiator of the innovative project 'Coaching in education', which aims at creating a coaching culture at schools.

Dr Colleen Harding, Head of Organisational Development, Bournemouth University

Dr Colleen Harding is Head of Organisational Development at Bournemouth University in the UK. Colleen holds a Doctorate in Coaching and Mentoring from Oxford Brookes University and is Assistant Editor of the *International Journal of Evidence-Based Coaching and Mentoring*.

Nicki Hickson, Director of Coaching, EY UK & Ireland

Nicki has a BA (Hons) degree in Psychology and Physiology from Oxford University and a Masters in Human Resource Management and Business. She has spent 20 years working in the UK and internationally as an HR professional in multinational blue chip companies, and has more recently specialised in learning and development and coaching at EY (Ernst & Young). Nicki is accredited at Senior Practitioner level with the European Mentoring and Coaching Council (EMCC) and has been doing formal executive coaching for the past ten years.

Olympia Mitsopoulou Kolyris, founder of Atom Wave, Switzerland

Olympia is a solution-focused coach, trainer and facilitator who designs corporate coaching and mentoring programmes for sustainable change. She believes waves of change in organisations can happen only if we work at an individual level ('atomo' in Greek means 'individual').

Toby Lindsay, Executive Director, Twelve Winds Consulting and Cohort Director, Elizabeth Garrett Anderson Programme, University of Birmingham

Toby has been working in the field of people and organisation development for the best part of 20 years through developing and leading his own businesses and working alongside others coaching, consulting and facilitating. He is tenacious, strategic and fun (more often than not) and works with presence and commitment.

Po Lindvall, MSc, PhD Candidate and EMCC-accredited Master Practitioner coach and mentor

Lindvall has more than 25 years' experience in coaching managers, executives, sports coaches and top athletes, and was the first VP Research on the Executive Board of EMCC 2012–15.

Darelyn 'DJ' Mitsch, MCC

Darelyn 'DJ' Mitsch is a thought leader in the business coaching field and one of the first 25 coaches in the world to earn a Master Certified Coach designation from the International Coach Federation (ICF). Past president of ICF Global, she is the CEO of Pyramid Resource Group and Founder of Pyramid's Leadership and Healthcare Coaching Institutes.

Jane Molloy, Director, Learning A Living Ltd.

An ICF-accredited coach (PCC), facilitator and consultant with over 25 years' experience working in leadership and organisational development, Jane led in-house L&D teams in FTSE 100 companies in retail and financial services before moving into organisational development consulting, first with thought-leading consultancy firms, then setting up her own business in 2004.

Anthony Owens, Leadership and Organisational Development Consultant, Health Education England (Yorkshire and Humber)

Anthony is a coach and supervisor who works with organisations and local economies to develop sustainable and strategically aligned coaching cultures to deliver better care.

Kate Stevens, Talent Development, EY UK & Ireland

Kate has a BSc in Psychology from Durham University and an MSc in Occupational Psychology from the University of Nottingham. She is a chartered occupational psychologist and has worked in both client-facing and in-house consulting roles, more recently specialising in talent development and coaching at EY, with a strong focus on delivering career coaching and career and family transition coaching within EY UK & Ireland.

Maria Symeon, Global Coaching Leader, PwC

Maria has over 15 years' experience in organisation development. She has worked extensively in the areas of executive coaching, leadership development and talent management in the UK and across the PwC Network. She maintains an active executive coaching portfolio consisting of PwC Partners.

Dr Julie-Anne Tooth, Executive Coach, Australia

Julie-Anne has been coaching and developing leaders for more than 25 years. She has helped shape the professional coaching industry through the publication of her PhD research in the book, *Experiencing Executive Coaching* (Scholars Press 2014) and her involvement in the Standards Australia 'Coaching in organizations' (2011) project. In her work she develops the coaching skills of leaders and delivers coaching programmes that enhance leadership capability and organisational cultures.

Contributors also included several members of the **EY Americas Executive Coaching** practice, all of whom have extensive experience in the coaching profession and are Certified Professional Coaches through the International Coaching Federation.

Moreover, we want to thank the following individuals: **Maria Georgiou, Director at PwC Cyprus**, who was the first to read the manuscript and offered her valuable feedback; **Maria Vilanidou, a Marketing Communications Strategist**, who shared her expertise and ideas on marketing coaching and mentoring; **Georgia Pavlou**, who was responsible for the graphic design of figures included in the book; and **Amanda Barber**, EA to David Clutterbuck, who offered valuable help in putting the manuscript together.

We would also like to express our personal thanks to the people who have supported us in this endeavour:

David Megginson

Personal thanks to Ian Jenner for sharing the journey, and to all the members of the MSc Coaching and Mentoring at Sheffield Hallam University for their insights and experiments.

Agnieszka Bajer

Lise Lewis, the President of European Mentoring and Coaching Council, is the person who introduced me to my esteemed co-authors and made this amazing collaboration possible. I'm incredibly grateful for having had the opportunity to work with the two living legends of coaching and mentoring – David Clutterbuck and David Megginson.

Writing this book would not have been possible without the limitless patience and support of my wonderful husband, Nassos Papazoglou, who has been gracefully putting up with my writing for almost two years and has never questioned why I had to spend yet another weekend in front of my computer.

I'm also deeply indebted to my colleagues at PwC, who have been continuously encouraging and supporting me to complete this project. I'm especially thankful to my boss, Philippos Soseilos – Partner at PwC Cyprus – for giving me the space to pursue my professional dreams.

Finally, I want to thank my dear friend, Hara Granath, for always being a role model of courage and determination and to my family and friends for putting up with my preoccupation with this book.

About the book

This book is for everyone who is passionate about coaching and who has an interest in creating an environment that supports learning and growth. You will find the book useful if you are:

- **a human resources manager** who wants to maximise the positive impact of coaching and mentoring in your organisation
- **a leader or a manager** who is interested in facilitating growth and achieving better results through creating an environment where people continuously grow and develop
- **an organisation development consultant** (internal or external) who wants to effectively support their clients on the journey towards a coaching culture
- **a coach or a mentor** (internal or external) who would like to explore how your work fits into the larger landscape of coaching and mentoring in the organisation(s) you work with
- **a faculty member** who teaches courses on human resource management, organisation development or coaching and mentoring
- **a student** who would like to deepen your knowledge on the subject of coaching and mentoring culture.

HOW THIS BOOK IS ORGANISED

We have arranged this book in four parts. Here are the brief descriptions of the chapters within them.

PART ONE: A FRESH VIEW ON COACHING CULTURE

This part of the book examines how our view on coaching culture has evolved over the past decade.

Chapter 1: So, What is a Coaching Culture After All?

Here we examine the notion of organisational culture, offer a variety of definitions of coaching culture (both by academics and practitioners) and present a model of coaching culture, accompanied by a few examples of what a coaching culture might look like in practice. We explore how a coaching culture develops and what the business case for a coaching culture might be.

Chapter 2: Systemic View on Coaching Culture

This chapter addresses the issue of building a coaching culture from the systemic perspective. We review theories that we believe are relevant to cultivating a coaching culture and look at various practices and tools that can be used to adopt a systemic perspective on coaching and a coaching culture.

PART TWO: THE ABCs OF COACHING CULTURE PLANNING AND IMPLEMENTATION

In Part Two we answer the question: 'Ok, so where do I start?' This section considers the practices of organisations that have had success in cultivating a coaching culture and we reflect on what works and what doesn't when it comes to planning and implementing a coaching culture strategy.

Chapter 3: Getting Set and Ready

This chapter discusses the necessary preparation before proceeding with any major steps towards building or strengthening a coaching culture within an organisation. It helps readers reflect on whether (and how) a coaching culture can benefit their organisation and to plan the groundwork before making any significant investment.

Chapter 4: Knowing Where You Want To Get To

Here we explore creating a vision of a coaching culture. You will find useful information on what a coaching culture vision is, how to create it and who to involve to ensure ongoing support for coaching or mentoring initiatives in the future.

Chapter 5: What's Your Starting Point and How Will You Measure Progress?

This chapter provides tips on how to identify the starting point for a coaching culture and how to measure progress. We offer suggestions as to what are the important areas to look at. You will also find tools that can be useful in establishing the baseline and measuring progress towards a coaching culture.

Chapter 6: Charting the Course

Chapter 6 is about creating an effective coaching and mentoring strategy and ensuring that the right conditions are in place so that the coaching strategy can be implemented in the most efficient and effective way.

PART THREE: LAYING THE FOUNDATIONS

Part Three focuses on four key drivers that have been frequently reported to lead to the development or enhancement of coaching culture in many organisations: external coaching; internal coaching; team coaching; and mentoring. This section of the book sets out to explore how to leverage these four areas for the benefit of the organisation and its people.

Chapter 7: Making Effective Use of External Coaches

Chapter 7 gives a detailed overview of how to ensure that the pool of external coaches that an organisation is using produces maximum value and makes a positive impact on the organisation's culture.

Chapter 8: Developing Internal Capacity for Coaching

Here we talk about how to develop internal capacity for coaching, focusing on three primary modalities of internal coaching: manager as a coach; coaching within work teams; and internal professional coaching.

Chapter 9: Team Coaching – Fad or Future?

As most organisations report that the majority of their employees work in teams, this chapter explores how team coaching can be effectively used to improve teams' performance and support the shift towards a coaching culture.

Chapter 10: Formal and Informal Mentoring

Here we show how the use of formal and informal mentoring can contribute to the development of a coaching culture within an organisation. We present the wide variety of mentoring types and how they can support the efforts to shape desired behaviours in the workplace.

PART FOUR: MOVING BEYOND THE BASICS

When organisations go beyond the initial stages of coaching culture development, they tend to look at how to further build the momentum and tap into the power of coaching. At this point issues such as people and infrastructure, marketing coaching and making it culturally congruent come to the surface and get examined in more detail.

Chapter 11: The Unsung Heroes of Coaching Culture

Here we have a look at the key roles that are necessary to build and maintain a strong coaching culture in an organisation. Our focus is mainly on HR, coaching or mentoring managers, executive sponsors and champions of coaching.

Chapter 12: Marketing Coaching and Mentoring

Marketing plays a significant role in developing a coaching culture and this chapter describes the foundations and essential elements of an effective coaching and mentoring marketing plan.

Chapter 13: Cross-Cultural Issues

This chapter explores whether coaching is appropriate in all cultural contexts, what the skills and characteristics of effective cross-cultural coaches and mentors are, how cross-cultural competencies get developed and whether a coaching culture can help leverage cultural differences.

PART ONE

A FRESH VIEW ON COACHING CULTURE

CHAPTER 1

So, What is a Coaching Culture After All?

'If you get the culture right, most of the other stuff will just take care of itself.'
Tony Hsieh, Founder and CEO of Zappos.com

OVERVIEW

This chapter sets out to explore what organisational culture is and why it is so important. It then moves on to present our definition and model of coaching culture, giving examples of what a coaching culture may look like on each level. It also describes the four distinct stages of coaching culture development and looks at the business case for developing a coaching culture. Finally, it describes how leading organisations define a coaching culture.

WHAT IS CULTURE AND WHY BOTHER?

We have asked the above question a number of times during various workshops and it always leads to the same result: a heated debate. What is interesting is that nobody ever questions or disagrees with the two basic assumptions implied in it, that:

- culture exists, and
- there are valid reasons we should bother.

It seems that culture and the experience of its impact are such an integral part of human existence that questioning it would be as unthinkable as questioning gravity.

The intuitive belief most people hold about the power of culture to make or break organisations has been widely supported by research and repeatedly documented in academic literature. Most management theorists and researchers agree that culture can be one of the key determinants of how successful the company will be. Empirical research has produced a large number of findings demonstrating the impact of culture on performance (Cameron and Ettington 1998; Denison 1990; Trice and Beyer 1993; Kotter and Heskett 1992).

Edgar Schein (1992), the American guru of culture and leadership, said that 'culture is the key to organisational excellence and the function of leadership is the creation and management of culture'. Dutch cultural expert Geert Hofstede wrote: 'In general, we find that outstandingly successful organisations usually have strong and unique cultures ... Unsuccessful organisations have weak indifferent sub-cultures or old sub-cultures that become sclerosed and can actually prevent the organisation's adaptation to changed circumstances' (Hofstede 1980, p394).

Culture is important because it determines:

- decision-making processes and criteria (how decisions are made and what is considered to be the 'right decisions' for the organisation)
- what is deemed to be appropriate behaviour and acceptable ways of interacting with others
- how people perceive their responsibilities and deal with tasks that are assigned to them
- the promptness and efficiency with which the organisation performs its key functions
- an organisation's agility and adaptability to change
- the way the organisation perceives and interacts with the main stakeholders outside of the organisation.

WHAT CULTURE LOOKS AND FEELS LIKE

Before looking at culture definitions, it might be helpful to see what culture looks and feels like. The story below is based on an experiment performed by Stephenson in 1967. Although it had nothing to do with organisational culture per se, it is relevant to the subject.

Five rhesus monkeys were placed in a cage with a few bananas hanging from the ceiling.

A ladder was conveniently placed underneath. Whenever one of the monkeys attempted to climb the ladder to reach for the bananas, ALL the monkeys were sprayed with ice-cold water.

After a while, the monkeys eventually made the link between the attempt to reach for the bananas and being collectively punished with ice-cold water. Finally, it was no longer necessary to use the ice-cold water – no monkey would even go near the ladder.

The researcher then replaced one of the monkeys with a new one. Not being aware of the ice-cold water treatment, the new monkey immediately attempted to climb the ladder to reach for the bananas. However, within a fraction of a second, the other monkeys would attack it and continue beating it up until it stopped trying.

One by one, the monkeys who experienced ice-cold water treatment were replaced with new ones. Every time a new member would attempt to reach for the bananas, it would get a beating from the rest, including the monkeys who never experienced the cold water.

Eventually, the cage was populated by five new monkeys, none of which had the experience of the ice-cold water. When the researcher introduced a new monkey, the other monkeys attacked the newcomer the moment it approached the ladder.

What is fascinating in this story is that even though none of the monkeys knew about the collective punishment with ice-cold water, somehow they learnt that reaching for the banana was off limits. They became the guardians of a norm the purpose of which they didn't understand. It's not surprising that the story has gone viral on social media – we can all relate to it at a deep, personal level. Most of us had the experience of being introduced to a new cultural context – a new organisation, a new team, or even just our partner's family – and suffering the consequences of unintentionally violating the unwritten cultural norms of that group. Many of us eventually assimilated into the group's culture and started behaving a certain way without questioning the reasons, simply because it was 'the way we do things round here' (Deal and Kennedy 1988).

The fact that culture can drive behaviour in such a powerful and consistent way is impossible to ignore. More and more organisations nowadays are conscious of the link between their culture and performance. Leveraging or transforming culture in a way that supports organisational mission, vision and objectives is considered a must by a lot of organisations.

DEFINING CULTURE

Management science began investigating the subject of culture in organisations as early as the 1930s. The Hawthorn studies at Western Electric Company were the first attempt to use the concept of culture in the context of the work environment. However, it wasn't until the late 1970s and early 1980s that the researchers approached the subject of culture in organisations in a more systematic way, drawing heavily on anthropology and sociology. What sparked this interest was the impressive success of Japanese companies and curiosity as to whether culture could be one of the contributing factors.

The term 'organisational culture' was popularised in the early 1980s. The rapid rise of interest in this aspect of business management was triggered by four seminal books on the subject:

- Ouchi (1981) *Theory Z: How American Business Can Meet the Japanese Challenge.*
- Pascale and Athos (1981) *The Art of Japanese Management: Applications for American Executives.*
- Deal and Kennedy (1981) *Corporate Cultures: The Rites and Rituals of Corporate Life.*
- Peters and Waterman (1982) *In Search of Excellence: Lessons from America's Best Run Companies.*

Since then, organisational culture has been the subject of research by a number of distinguished management theorists. While there seems to be universal agreement that culture is a powerful force shaping an organisation's performance, there is a surprising lack of consensus on its definition. Even at the beginning of the more systematic organisational culture research, Barney noted that: 'Few concepts in organisational learning literature have as many competing definitions as organisational culture' (Barney 1986, p657).

In spite of these differences, it's possible to identify a few ideas where the literature converges:

- Culture is created over time through the interaction of people and their environment. This is clearly expressed by Schein when he portrays culture as "a pattern of basic assumptions – invented, discovered, or developed by a given group as it learns to cope with its problems of external adaptation and internal integration – that has worked well enough to be considered valid and, therefore, to be taught to new members as the correct way to perceive, think, and feel in relation to those problems" (Schein 1992).
- Culture creates consistent patterns of meaning and behaviour that bind people together and make them unique as a group. This idea has been expressed by Hofstede (1980), Martin and Siehl (1992), Schein (1992), Van den Berg and Wilderom (2004), Wagner and Hollenbeck (2010) and many others.
- Culture is a combination of visible and invisible elements that exist on multiple levels. Arguments supporting this can be found in the work of a number of academics, for example, Martin and Siehl (1983), Uttal (1983), Denison (1990).

The above points of consensus show that the majority of researchers perceive culture as a unique, shared set of beliefs and assumptions that were adopted by its members over time and which lead to consistent patterns of meaning and behaviour. They encompass both the visible (artefacts, behaviours) and the invisible (assumptions, beliefs) aspects of culture. These common points guide our approach to a coaching culture; we consider the visible manifestations, as well as the underlying driving forces, as critical to describe and understand what a coaching culture is.

In addition, we will build on our bounded functionalism approach to creating a coaching culture (Clutterbuck and Megginson 2005). This approach sees culture as a contribution to organisational effectiveness and, therefore, seeks to align culture with the needs of the organisation and its stakeholders. It also assumes that organisational culture can be transformed to an extent that allows a coaching culture to take root and flourish.

We are far from claiming that it is possible to overcome all the obstacles towards creating a coaching culture if leaders follow all the tenets presented in this book. Transforming organisational culture is a complex task and there are various forces at play. The suggestions presented in this book are based on what we have seen work in various organisations. However, each organisation is unique and, therefore, our approach should be seen as a useful toolbox rather than a fail-proof recipe for a coaching culture.

Table 1.1 Definitions of organisational culture

Hofstede (1980)	'The collective programming of the mind that distinguishes the members of one organization from another. This included shared beliefs, values and practices that distinguished one organization to another.'
Ouchi (1981)	'The organisational culture consists of a set of symbols, ceremonies and myths that communicate the underlying values and beliefs of the organisation to its employees.'
Martin & Siehl (1983)	Glue that holds together an organisation through shared patterns of meaning. Three component systems: context or core values, forms (process of communication, eg jargon), strategies to reinforce content (eg rewards, training programmes).
Uttal (1983)	'Shared values and beliefs that interact with an organization's structures and control systems to produce behavioral norms.'
Denison (1990)	Refers to culture as 'the underlying values, beliefs and principles that serve as a foundation for an organisation's management system as well as the set of management practices and behaviours that both exemplify and reinforce those basic principles.'
Schein (1992)	Organisational culture implies 'a pattern of basic assumptions – invented, discovered, or developed by a given group as it learns to cope with its problems of external adaptation and internal integration – that has worked well enough to be considered valid and, therefore, to be taught to new members as the correct way to perceive, think, and feel in relation to those problems.'
Trompenaars (1993)	'Culture is the way in which a group of people solves problems and reconciles dilemmas.'
Taylor (2005)	'Culture is created from the messages that are received about how people are expected to behave in the organization.'
Ven den Berg & Wilderom (2004)	'Shared perceptions of organisational work practices within organisational units that may differ from other organisational units.'
Wagner (2010)	'An informal, shared way of perceiving life and membership in the organisation that binds members together and influences what they think about themselves and their work.'
Hawkins (2012)	'Culture resides in the habituated ways of connecting that an organisation repeats. Culture resides not just inside the organisation, but more importantly in the relationship patterns with all the key stakeholders.'

THE ESSENCE OF COACHING AND MENTORING

There are too many definitions of coaching and mentoring out there to include a representative selection in this chapter. These definitions and models of coaching vary considerably:

- from ones that are highly directive and nearer instruction, to highly non-directive, not even giving feedback
- from short-term task and performance focus to longer-term personal transformation
- from individual focus to team focus.

The same is true, with much overlap, of mentoring. Our view is that a coaching culture embraces that diversity of approaches, seeking to create environments with multiple ways of stimulating creative understanding and positive change.

Peter Hawkins observed: 'What is the essence of coaching, once we strip away all the theories and models, the different schools and methodologies, and the mushrooming multi-billion dollar business? At its heart, coaching provides some skills and disciplines to aid generative conversations. These are conversations that generate new thinking, previously unknown to the other party, which arises out of the quality of the relationship' (Hawkins 2012).

A pragmatic way of defining what we mean by coaching (and mentoring) is to focus therefore on the nature of the conversations that underlie the process. This is illustrated in our model of developmental conversations in Figure 1.1.

Developmental conversations, such as coaching and mentoring, help people understand their inner context (what's going on for them internally) and their external context (their personal and professional environments).

The coach (or mentor) helps to gain crucial insights into each of these worlds and to have a conversation that links them, with a view to achieving better decisions and, consequently, better results.

SO WHAT IS A COACHING CULTURE?

The term 'coaching culture' has been used with increased frequency in the past 15 years. However, in spite of its growing popularity, there is still little clarity as to what a coaching culture really is. While there have been a few more books published on the subject recently, the literature on coaching culture remains scarce – especially by contrast with the vast number of publications on coaching and mentoring in general.

In our previous book, *Making Coaching Work*, we defined a coaching culture as one where: 'Coaching is the predominant style of managing and working together, and where a commitment to grow the organisation is embedded in a parallel commitment to grow the people in the organisation' (Clutterbuck and Megginson 2005).

Recent books published on the subject offer alternative definitions. Jones and Gorell define a coaching culture as one where 'people are empowered and where coaching happens at every level. . . . It adds to the bottom line performance. It is the recognised tool that touches every part of the employee life-cycle' (Jones and Gorell 2014).

Peter Hawkins states that: 'A coaching culture exists in an organisation when a coaching approach is a key aspect of how the leaders, managers, and staff engage and develop all their people and engage their stakeholders, in ways that create increased individual, team, and organisational performance and shared value for all stakeholders' (Hawkins 2012).

An older but well-established definition by Hart (2003) talks about coaching culture as: 'An organisational setting in which not only formal coaching occurs, but also, most or a large segment of individuals in the organisation practice coaching behaviours as a means of relating to, influencing and supporting each other.'

Figure 1.1 The developmental conversation model

The developmental conversation

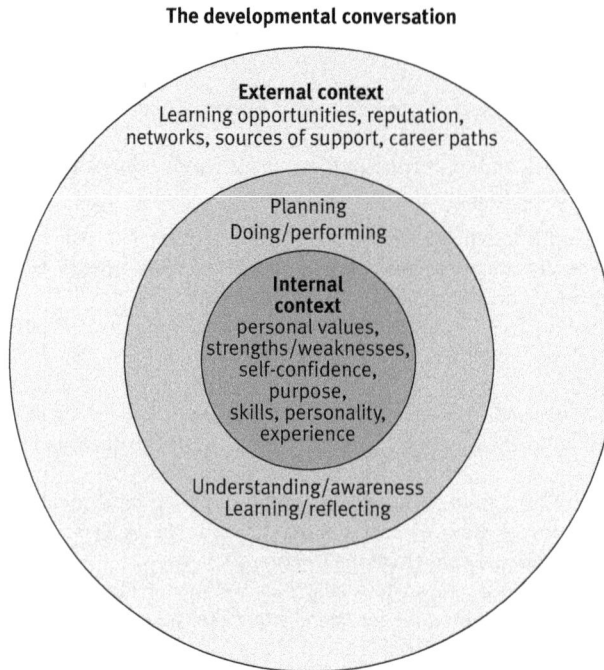

Table 1.2 Definitions of coaching culture

Hart (2003)	'An organisational setting in which not only formal coaching occurs, but also, most or a large segment of individuals in the organisation practice coaching behaviours as a means of relating to, influencing and supporting each other.'
Hardingham (2004)	'A culture where people coach each other all the time as a natural part of meetings, reviews and one-to-one discussions of all kinds.'
Clutterbuck & Megginson (2005)	'Coaching is the predominant style of managing and working together, and where a commitment to grow the organisation is embedded in a parallel commitment to grow the people in the organisation.'
BlessingWhite (2009)	A coaching culture is 'built on organizational and leadership beliefs and practices that reflect coaching as a strategic business driver and critical talent management tool.'
Keddy & Johnson (2011)	'Supporting each other's development and quality of thinking is at the forefront. ... everyone who wants to be coached and when it is appropriate and practical, is offered coaching.'
Hawkins (2012)	'A coaching culture exists in an organisation when a coaching approach is a key aspect of how the leaders, managers, and staff engage and develop all their people and engage their stakeholders, in ways that create increased individual, team, and organisational performance and shared value for all stakeholders.'
Jones & Gorell (2014)	'... people are empowered and where coaching happens at every level. ... It adds to the bottom line performance. It is the recognised tool that touches every part of the employee life-cycle.'

All these definitions touch upon essential elements of a coaching culture. They present a coaching culture as a way of working and interacting at every level of the organisation and at each stage of the employee life-cycle to develop and support others, as well as to improve bottom-line results. While potentially describing what a coaching culture might look like in a lot of cases, this approach to defining it does not explicitly address the deeper levels of a coaching culture, such as beliefs, assumptions and mindsets.

Coaching culture – just like any other kind of culture – resides both at the visible and the invisible level. What transpired from our work and the hundreds of conversations that we held about creating and sustaining a coaching culture over the years is that it is not just about having people engage in coaching conversations and use coaching skills on a regular basis. It is also – and perhaps even more importantly – about people adopting a coaching philosophy, principles, beliefs and mindsets and applying them to all professional activities and interactions. For example, no amount of coaching skills training and application will ever lead to creating a strong coaching culture if people don't internalise the underlying principles of coaching, such as attentiveness, curiosity, openness and trust. While what a coaching culture looks like will vary depending on the organisation, what it is rooted in seems to be stable and consistent across the board.

Based on these observations, we realised that the heart or the DNA of a coaching culture lies in the invisible elements and that these elements are common to most organisations, irrespective of the industry and the nature of their business.

Working with a number of organisations on developing a coaching culture, holding hundreds of conversations with executives and HR professionals, facilitating LinkedIn discussions and reviewing the existing literature on the subject allowed us to gather a considerable amount of data on what a coaching culture seems to be. After distilling all that data, we were able to capture the essence of a coaching culture in the following definition:

> A coaching culture is one where the principles, beliefs and mindsets driving people's behaviour in the workplace are deeply rooted in the discipline of coaching.

The use of the word 'discipline' in our definition is quite deliberate. It originates from the Latin word *disciplina* and means 'instruction', 'teaching' or 'a branch of knowledge'. Probably nobody would argue that in recent decades, coaching (and mentoring) has earned the right to be referred to as a discipline in that sense.

But there is also another meaning of the word 'discipline', which is 'to train oneself or someone else to do something in a controlled and habitual way'. This second take on 'the discipline of coaching' refers to a consistent practice of coaching and following its principles, which can lead in turn to developing new habits in individuals and the organisation.

Our definition doesn't describe specific habits, behaviours or practices. Frustrating as it might be, it is simply impossible to foresee how a coaching culture will manifest itself in each organisation. The form and shape it eventually takes depends on a myriad of factors, such as wider organisational and national culture, business strategy, the industry it belongs to, the products and services it offers, its competition and the markets it operates in and so forth.

COACHING CULTURE MODEL

To bring our definition to life, we have developed a coaching culture model (Figure 1.2), inspired by Ed Schein's *Three Levels of Culture* (Schein 1985).

Figure 1.2 Coaching culture model

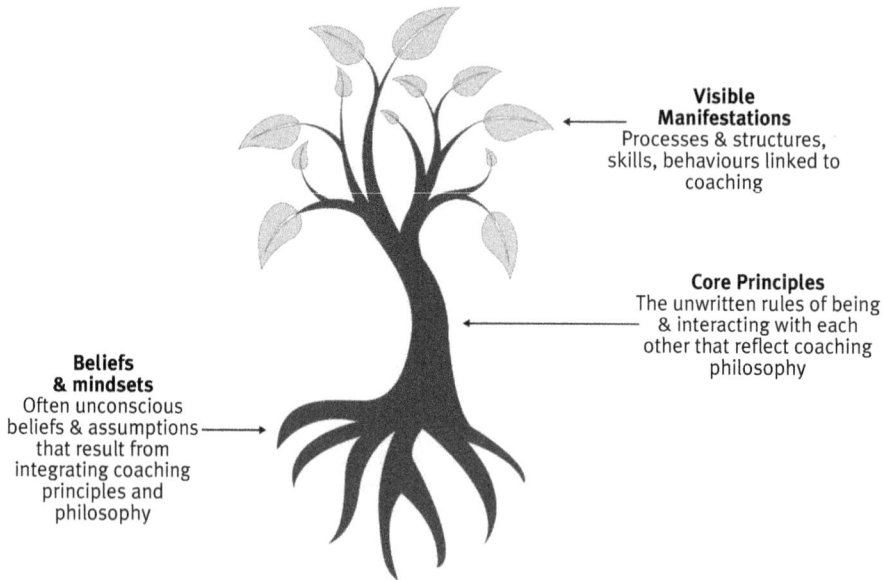

Visible Manifestations
Processes & structures, skills, behaviours linked to coaching

Core Principles
The unwritten rules of being & interacting with each other that reflect coaching philosophy

Beliefs & mindsets
Often unconscious beliefs & assumptions that result from integrating coaching principles and philosophy

Our model is represented by a tree, with its crown, branches and foliage in full view, its trunk providing support for the crown and connecting it with the roots, which are invisible under the ground. We picked a tree to symbolise a coaching culture not only because it is a living organism that evolves and grows – just like culture does – but also because it belongs to and interacts with a larger ecosystem. For a coaching culture to take root, it needs to grow in fertile ground and a supportive climate. We will describe that ground and climate in Chapter 3.

Our work with various organisations has enabled us to collect a large variety of examples at each level of the coaching culture model, some of which are presented below.

VISIBLE MANIFESTATIONS OF A COACHING CULTURE

Visible manifestations of a coaching culture are the tangible and observable aspects of a coaching culture, such as *processes, structures, skills* and *behaviours*.

Processes and structures

A few typical examples of processes and structures that support coaching and mentoring in the organisation are:

- a pool of internal or external coaches
- internal and external coaching policy and guidelines
- coaching and mentoring supervision
- competency framework that includes coaching
- developing others and coaching part of the performance evaluation criteria
- coaching culture steering committee
- head of coaching and mentoring
- work team processes which use peer coaching to encourage collaboration and enhance teamwork practices.

Skills

People have the skills required to coach and mentor others. A few examples of these skills are:

- listening effectively
- establishing trust
- summarising and paraphrasing
- giving feedback
- questioning
- setting expectations
- identifying outcomes and clarifying goals
- building relationships
- enabling insight and learning
- use of coaching and mentoring models and techniques
- observing.

Behaviours

Probably the most noticeable manifestation of a coaching and mentoring culture in an organisation are behaviours. Below are a few typical examples of behaviours that can be associated with a coaching culture:

- engaging in dialogue when people face difficulties or challenges to help them think through the choices and options
- getting involved in the process of inquiry and exploration to identify the best possible solution to a problem
- supporting, but also challenging, team members with the aim of helping them to grow and develop
- frequently providing and seeking feedback and seeing it as an opportunity to improve
- actively listening to each other to support understanding and insight
- inquiring about counterpart's concerns and needs
- admitting mistakes and learning from them
- suspending assumptions and judgement and freely engaging with others' thinking
- openly admitting to lack of skill or knowledge and asking for help
- expressing opinions with openness and honesty
- taking time to reflect.

CORE PRINCIPLES

A coaching culture is underpinned by a set of core principles. In organisations where a coaching culture is well established, these principles often become the unwritten rules of being and interacting with each other. Core principles are not entirely hidden from sight, but they are not as readily discernible as the outward manifestations of culture described above. This is the reason why in our model we see them as the trunk of the tree, which supports the visible manifestations of culture. Core principles can develop into a wide range of behaviours, depending on the organisation, the nature of its business, environment and its needs. A few examples of these principles are:

Attentiveness

When interacting with others, people give them their undivided attention. They are fully present to the other person by creating a distraction-free environment, both internally and externally. This facilitates deep listening, connection, and understanding, which are the foundations of effective communication.

Collaboration

Achieving a goal requires collaboration with others. This includes agreement on collective goals, sharing information, knowledge and ideas, integrating perspectives and mutual support to achieve the desired outcomes. This joint effort results in creating valuable synergies, where the whole becomes bigger than the sum of its parts.

Curiosity

Asking good questions is as important as finding good answers. When faced with a problem, a challenge or a learning opportunity, people avoid zooming in on one 'right answer'. Instead, they engage in a dialogue,[1] where assumptions are avoided and the subject is explored with an open mind and curiosity. Interaction of this kind taps into people's potential to co-create meaning, value and solutions by engaging in collective exploration and inquiry.

Ethicality

When faced with a dilemma, people engage in conversations on the ethical aspects of the situation. Ethical issues are part of business discussions and decisions are governed by the accepted principles of right and wrong. Expedience and other forms of 'the end justifying the means' are regularly challenged.

Growth

Each person has potential to grow and develop and it is their responsibility to tap into that potential, both in themselves and in others. People continuously challenge and stretch themselves and others. This results in continuous learning, which is valued more than being right or an expert at something.

Openness and honesty

People openly share what they think, how they feel and what their intentions are. Feedback is given in a generous and open way and personal perceptions are valued and respected. People respectfully support each other in minimising blind spots and challenging limiting beliefs. The same amount of honesty is present when individuals self-reflect.

Reflection

True learning only takes place when people reflect on their experiences. Making a conscious effort to synthesise, abstract and articulate key lessons from experiences in the workplace is encouraged both on an individual and collective level. Learning that occurs as a result of that reflection is often shared to increase joint problem-solving capacity in the future.

Respect

Respect is reflected by having positive feelings of esteem for others and valuing them irrespective of position, hierarchical power, or potential differences in opinions, interests

---

[1] In Ancient Greece διάλογος (which literally means 'through word') referred to Socrates-style conversations, which proceeded by means of questions and answers. These conversations created a freeflowing of meaning, which allowed its participants to discover insights that otherwise wouldn't be attainable to them individually. This form of conversation has been largely lost in modern society until it was re-introduced through coaching.

or culture. Respect is considered the right of each individual, rather than something that has to be earned.

BELIEFS AND MINDSETS

These are the prevalent beliefs and mindsets that are taken for granted by most members of the group. This collective conviction that they are true can only come from direct experience and repeated success of implementing the principles described above to an extent that it becomes almost impossible to question them. A few examples of these mindsets and beliefs are:

- Extraordinary results can only be achieved through creating synergies.
- The whole is always bigger than the sum of its parts.
- Collaborative effort is more effective and sustainable than personal heroics.
- The path to good solutions leads through inquiry.
- The obvious answers are usually not the most accurate ones.
- It's safe to express personal opinions and points of view.
- Reflecting on experiences aids learning and supports problem-solving.
- Abilities can be developed through hard work and dedication.
- We get the best out of people through challenging and supporting them.
- Human potential is unlimited.

STAGES OF COACHING CULTURE DEVELOPMENT

Like any living organism, a coaching culture cannot achieve its mature stage overnight. In *Making Coaching Work* (Clutterbuck and Meginson 2005), we identified four distinct stages of coaching culture development. These four stages, which we named *nascent*, *tactical*, *strategic* and *embedded*, are still relevant today.

Linking the stages of culture development with our coaching culture model resulted in the graphical representation illustrated in Figure 1.3.

Figure 1.3 Stages of coaching culture development

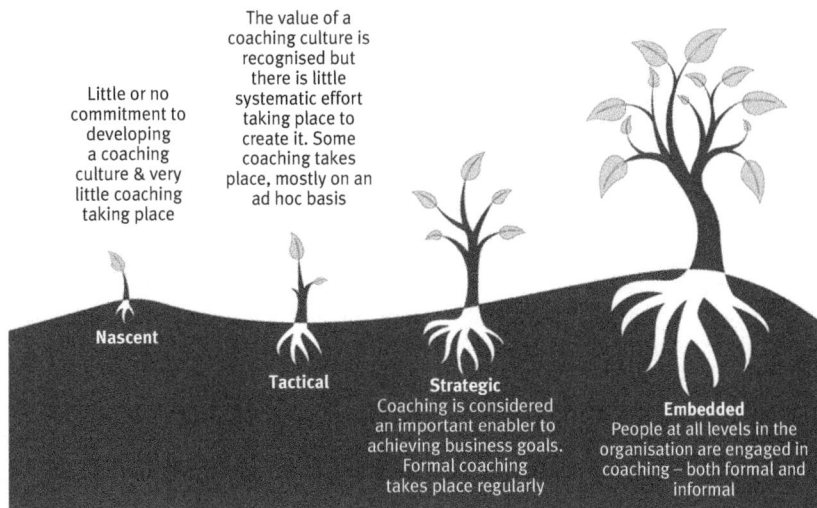

Little or no commitment to developing a coaching culture & very little coaching taking place

Nascent

The value of a coaching culture is recognised but there is little systematic effort taking place to create it. Some coaching takes place, mostly on an ad hoc basis

Tactical

Strategic
Coaching is considered an important enabler to achieving business goals. Formal coaching takes place regularly

Embedded
People at all levels in the organisation are engaged in coaching – both formal and informal

AT THE *NASCENT* STAGE

'The organisation shows little or no commitment to creating a coaching culture. While some coaching may happen, it is highly inconsistent in both frequency and quality. Top managers present poor role models and coaching behaviours tend to be abandoned in the face of more urgent, if less important, demands on managers' time. Any executive coaching provided is uncoordinated and typically the result of severe performance problems with a few individuals or a status boost for senior managers incapable of (or unwilling to engage in) self-development. People tend to avoid tackling difficult behavioural or ethical issues, out of embarrassment, ineptitude, fear, or a combination of all three' (Clutterbuck and Megginson 2005).

AT THE *TACTICAL* STAGE

'The organisation has recognised the value of establishing a coaching culture, but there is little understanding of what that means, or what will be involved. Top management sees the issue as primarily one for HR. There are systems in place to train coaches and/or mentors, and there are numerous discrete HR systems such as succession planning and appraisal, but the links between these and the coaching process are at best tenuous. There is a broad understanding among individual contributors and managers of the potential benefits of coaching, but the commitment to coaching behaviours as integral to management style is low. People recognise the need to tackle difficult behavioural or ethical issues, but will only do so in environments where they feel very safe' (Clutterbuck and Megginson 2005).

AT THE *STRATEGIC* STAGE

'There has been considerable effort expended to educate managers and employees in the value of coaching and to give people the competence (and, therefore, confidence) to coach in a variety of situations. Managers are rewarded/punished for delivery/non-delivery of coaching, typically linked to formal appraisal of direct reports. Top management has accepted the need to demonstrate good practice and most, if not all, set an example by coaching others. They spend time getting across to employees how coaching behaviours support the key business drivers. However, while the formal coaching process works well (in part because it is measured), the informal process creaks at the joints. There are plans to integrate coaching and mentoring with the wider portfolio of HR systems and, at a mechanical level, these largely work. People are willing to confront difficult behavioural or ethical issues on an ad hoc basis and there are good role models for doing so with both resolution and compassion' (Clutterbuck and Megginson 2005).

AT THE *EMBEDDED* STAGE

'People at all levels are engaged in coaching, both formal and informal, with colleagues both within the same function and across functions and levels. People also use the skills of learning dialogue and coaching with various stakeholders outside of the organisation.

   'Some senior executives are mentored by more junior people and there is widespread use of 360° feedback at all levels to provide insights into areas where the individual can benefit from coaching help. Much, if not most, of this coaching and mentoring is informal, but people are sufficiently knowledgeable and skilled to avoid most of the downsides to informal mentoring. Coaching and mentoring are so seamlessly built into the structure of HR systems that they occur automatically. The skills of learning dialogue are sufficiently widespread that people are able to raise difficult or controversial issues, knowing that their motivations will be respected and that colleagues will see it as an opportunity to improve, either personally, or organisationally, or both' (Clutterbuck and Megginson 2005)

   We offer a diagnostic tool that can be used to assess which level of coaching culture development an organisation is at in Chapter 5: What's Your Starting Point?

BUSINESS CASE FOR A COACHING CULTURE

It is easy to think that developing a coaching culture can benefit every organisation, especially when looking at the numerous research findings indicating that coaching and organisational culture have such a strong positive impact on business performance. Recent examples are the International Coach Federation study, which found that coaching can be indicative of increased employee engagement[2] and boost financial performance,[3] and the 2014 Great Place to Work survey, which revealed two main drivers of best companies' growth: a steady focus on company culture and an investment in employee development programmes.

This has been supported by a number of respected writers in the field of coaching, a good example of which is the quote below:

'When you create a culture of coaching, the result may not be directly measurable in dollars. But we have yet to find a company that can't benefit from more candour, less denial, richer communication, conscious development of talent, and disciplined leaders, who show compassion for people' (Sherman and Freas 2004).

However, we need to acknowledge that there might be organisations for which investing in a coaching culture doesn't make much business sense, at least not at the moment. In *Making Coaching Work* (Clutterbuck and Megginson 2005), there is an example of a call centre with a high turnover of staff, which might decide that short-term incentives, work–life balance and effective recruitment are a more rational and viable strategy. Determining whether a coaching culture is the right fit for an organisation is a key step. We offer guidance on how to do that in Chapter 3: Getting Set and Ready.

A very common request that we get from organisations, which are contemplating introducing a coaching culture is to share some data and statistics that would illustrate how developing a coaching culture helps organisations thrive. While we understand the need to validate the assumption that a coaching culture can be beneficial for some organisations, we also want to stress that an effective business case for a coaching culture is never generic. Instead, it is firmly rooted in the individual circumstances of the organisation and identifies how a coaching culture will support it in achieving its mission, vision and strategic objectives.

STORIES FROM THE FIELD

In this chapter, you will find a small collection of four stories narrated by organisations from the public, private and non-governmental sector. They share their thoughts on coaching culture and its perceived benefits. This small selection of a larger number of organisations featured in this book is intended as a sample of current views on what a coaching culture is and why it is considered to be something worth investing in.

PwC

PwC (previously known as PricewaterhouseCoopers) is a multinational professional services network. It is one of the Big Four auditors, along with Deloitte, EY and KPMG, providing assurance (including financial audit), tax, consulting and advisory services to companies.

PwC has always been focused on developing its people to deliver on its brand promise and coaching has long been acknowledged as one of the most powerful ways to enable people to rise to their potential and play an increasingly bigger role in the firm's success.

---

[2] 65% of employees from companies with strong coaching cultures rated themselves as highly engaged.

[3] 60% of respondents from organisations with strong coaching cultures reported their 2013 revenue to be above average, compared with their peer group.

The purpose of coaching in PwC is to help the business and those who support it to accelerate the development and recognition of PwC professionals in the context of working and learning so that the firm may be distinctive as an organisation and deliver on PwC's brand promise.

The philosophy, mindsets and skills of coaching are part of the Whole Leader and Relationships areas of PwC Professional (the firm's competency framework) and have a key role in strengthening PwC.

PwC defines coaching as 'a relationship-based productive conversation in which people learn.' It sees coaching as an authentic dialogue that takes place both with people within the firm and its clients.

PwC considers a coaching culture to be one where coaching is:

- seen as an essential day-to-day business skill to be used both with people within the firm and with its clients, thereby helping bring the PwC Experience to life
- recognised and rewarded as a core business skill.

EY – UK & Ireland

EY (previously known as Ernst & Young) is a global professional services organisation with over 200,000 people. They are a purpose-led organisation and the development of a highly skilled and motivated workforce is a foundational strategy to fulfil their purpose: building a better working world.

To support the development of a highly skilled and motivated workforce, EY has a unique global career development framework called EYU. This stands for 'EY and You', reflecting the mutual commitment EY has to support its people and the ownership each individual is expected to take over their career.

Coaching is a key pillar of EYU and is a fundamental part of the way EY people work, both internally and in deepening their client relationships. Coaching brings together the learning and experiential elements of EYU to help its people achieve their potential and build an inclusive, performance-based culture that demonstrates its values.

At EY, coaching is defined as any meaningful conversation that helps the individual develop new skills and insights and transforms learning and experiences into practice. Coaching occurs formally through one-to-one interventions with defined goals, timelines and sponsorship, and informally through the everyday use of coaching skills in meaningful conversations with EY people and their clients.

EY invests in coaching based on the findings from research conducted internally and externally on positive, anticipated outcomes and return on investment (ROI):

- Creating a culture of on-the-job coaching helps attract and retain the younger generations.
- Coaching maximises the benefits of formal learning by helping people embed learning and develop their skills.
- Providing on-the-job coaching boosts engagement of those already having valuable experiences.
- Coaching helps leaders adapt to new challenges and develop the skills and capabilities they need to succeed.
- Coaching helps people understand how to effectively adapt to organisational change.
- Using coaching skills in client interactions helps deliver better service to our clients.
- Coaching leads to significant financial benefits for organisations.

Save the Children International

Save the Children (SC) is a child rights organisation with a mandate rooted in the United Nations Convention on the Rights of the Child. As part of the global Save the Children movement, it works in 120 countries worldwide, funding programmes and advocating to change children's lives.

Their work spans both ongoing development programmes and emergency responses, including in the UK. The organisation aims to inspire breakthroughs in the way the world treats children and sets an ambitious goal of doing whatever it takes to ensure that all children survive, learn and are protected by 2030.

Because of the scale of this ambition, SC needs to find the best ways to support its leaders to grow and develop, to have all hands on deck and everyone work to their full potential. Coaching was introduced in 2009 as part of this effort and now SC has a pool of over 100 volunteer executive coaches who work with the organisation's leaders.

When asked about her definition of coaching culture, Shola Awolesi, the Global Leadership Development Manager and the person responsible for coaching within SC, told us that 'a coaching culture is a culture which encourages two-way dialogue, where managers, staff and peers are able to have open conversations that help people to think and that create the time and space for people to come up with their own solutions. A coaching culture is one where people understand what coaching means and what it can achieve and where the organisation ensures that there are processes, systems or resources that make that possible.'

Municipal General Education School No 5 – Krasny Sulin, Russia

General Education School No 5 in Krasny Sulin in Russia is the first school in Russia which is implementing systemic coaching in the educational process in all areas of pedagogical interaction. The school has 25 employees (15 of whom are teachers) and seven qualified internal coaches.

According to Victoriya Evtuchova, the Director of General Education School No 5 in Krasny Sulin in Russia, the main purpose of education is supporting children to grow and be capable of self-development and self-realisation in the rapidly changing society. This calls for major changes in how schools operate and particularly to how teachers' professional and personal development is approached. Victoriya believes that the most important skill in terms of student-oriented education is the teacher's mastery in implementing innovative approaches, such as coaching. She describes a coaching culture at her school as one where coaching mindset, philosophy and tools are regularly used to:

- manage the school and its projects
- support teachers in their personal and professional growth and development
- bring innovation into lesson plans
- stimulate pedagogical interaction in class
- prepare students for state exams
- manage school projects
- support student personality development
- work with parents to facilitate the creation of supportive environment at students' homes.

SUMMARY

Culture matters because it is a powerful set of forces that drives individual and collective behaviour and, ultimately, performance and results. However, there is no universally 'right' or 'wrong' culture – the only way to evaluate it is to look at whether it supports or hinders the organisation in fulfilling its mission, realising its vision and meeting strategic objectives. In many cases, a coaching culture does provide that support, but not always.

For a coaching culture to take root, it's not enough to make sure that there are coaching conversations happening – people also need to start thinking differently about things such as problem-solving, collaboration and development. Moreover, the organisation's ecosystem has to be 'friendly' enough to support this new way of thinking, feeling and acting.

The way a coaching culture manifests itself will largely depend on the individual circumstances of the organisation. What a coaching culture looks and feels like in PwC will be different from what people experience in Vodafone.

Finally, a coaching culture takes time and effort to develop. We've identified four distinct stages of culture development and describe each at the culture visible manifestations level.

?

FIELDWORK

Reflect on your organisation or an organisation you are familiar with and answer the questions below:

- Are there any visible manifestations of a coaching culture that can be observed when people work and interact with others?
- Are any of the core principles of coaching culture widely accepted as true in the organisation?
- What mindsets seem to be prevalent in the organisation?
- How might the current mindsets support or hinder potential efforts to create or strengthen a coaching culture?
- What mindset shifts might be necessary for a coaching culture to take root?

CHAPTER 2

Systemic View on a Coaching Culture

'You think that because you understand "one", you must also understand "two". After all, "one" and "one" make "two". But you forget that you must also understand that word in the middle – "and".'
Sufi teaching story

OVERVIEW

This chapter illustrates a shift of mindset that we have observed in the last few years and contrasts linear and systemic thinking in organisations. It also gives a brief introduction to complexity theory and its relevance to building and sustaining a coaching culture. Finally, it presents practices and tools that can be used to adopt a systemic perspective towards coaching and a coaching culture.

A MUCH NEEDED MINDSET SHIFT

In the VUCA (volatile, uncertain, complex and ambiguous) world that we live in, the shortcomings of traditional, top–down approaches to change, scientific management methods and linear thinking have become more evident than ever. This creates an increasing openness and curiosity about alternative ways of managing organisational change.

In our first book on coaching culture, we observed that 'coaches, with their emphasis on one-to-one relationships, are a bit like social teenagers. They can focus obsessively on a relationship and pay precious little attention to the wider society' (Clutterbuck and Megginson 2005).

Since then, coaching and mentoring have experienced a subtle – and yet already visible – shift of mindset. More and more HR professionals, business executives, coaches and mentors have started adopting an increasingly systemic approach, gradually moving away from an individual-focused, linear way of thinking about managing and developing people. This shift in some cases results in a radically different worldview, one that strikes us as much more effective when it comes to a number of organisation development practices, including building a coaching culture.

FROM LINEAR TO SYSTEMIC THINKING

A good indication of whether a linear or systemic approach is being adopted is the kind of assumptions that guide one's thinking. A situation that illustrates some of these assumptions at play is one many readers will be familiar with – when the annual employee survey indicates that line managers don't spend sufficient time and energy on coaching their team members.

Following a linear line of thinking in this situation leads to the conclusion that either team members or managers 'are at fault'; one of the assumptions frequently present in linear thinking is that there is single responsibility for failure. This results in zooming in on people involved, to determine which side is the weak link. And when the weak link is identified, we zoom in even further to figure out what exactly is wrong with them: is it the lack of skills, willingness or self-confidence? Another assumption linked to linear mindset is that there is one, right solution and it will be possible to predict the outcomes. This often leads to large-scale interventions that follow a relatively rigid process designed to deliver specific, foreseeable outcomes.

In a lot of companies this approach results in line managers being subjected to the old training ritual of 'sheep dipping': sending a large population of people on a short, usually generic coaching or management skills course and expecting all their 'ailments' to be magically cured on their return to work. Unfortunately, the impact of the environment in which people operate is significantly more powerful than any individual manager's skills, behaviours or personality. Even if managers have the best intentions to use their newly acquired knowledge and skills in the workplace, the system will quickly make them 'course correct' and return to the old patterns of behaviour.

Systemic thinking, on the other hand, is founded on the assumption that there are many important factors that are usually interlinked and contribute to any situation or problem. Instead of just zooming in, a systemic thinker zooms in *and* out. They look *both* at the individual *and* at their context, carefully exploring the nature of interactions between the top or senior management, managers and team members – focusing on business needs and pressures, objectives and the nature of interactions with the outside world. After taking that broader view and being able to see the proverbial forest for the trees, a systemic thinker asks: 'How do all these elements and factors contribute to the problem?' It might be that managers don't spend enough time coaching their team members because they spend an inordinate amount of time travelling between sites, participating in meetings, producing reports or revising budgets. If this is the case, coaching training will not solve the problem.

This subtle shift happening in the world of coaching is very encouraging. Even more so is the fact that there are organisations that incorporate elements of complex systems theory in their approach to building a coaching culture.

Table 2.1 A mindset shift: from linear to systemic approach

FROM ⟹ TO

Linear approach	Systemic approach
Single responsibility for failure/success	Multiple contributions to failure/success
Problems need to be fixed	Visible problems are usually just a symptom of deep, underlying issues
Focus on the parts that comprise the whole (zooming in)	Focus both on the individual parts and the whole (zooming in and out)
Adapting to change	Generating change

Tight controls	Broad guidelines combined with encouragement and enablement to take initiative
Structured processes	Evolving processes
Predicted outcomes	Emerging and evolving outcomes
People need 'fixing'	People are competent
Either . . . or	Both . . . and . . .
Complicated (consisting of many independent elements that can be addressed piece by piece)	Complex (resulting from networks of multiple, interactive causes that cannot be individually distinguished and addressed in a piecemeal manner)
Working within boundaries	Working across boundaries

A BIT OF BACKGROUND ON SYSTEMS THEORY

Although popularised relatively recently, the philosophy behind systems theory is thousands of years old and was documented in ancient texts, such as the Chinese Tao Te Ching, more than 2,500 years ago.

Modern systems thinking is a body of knowledge and tools that draws from many diverse fields such as psychology, biology, ecology and engineering. It has been successfully applied to consulting, management (eg Senge 1990, Stapley 2006) and coaching (eg Cavanagh 2006, O'Neill 2007) in the past decades.

One of the pioneers of systems thinking was a biologist, Ludwig von Bertalanffy, who developed general systems theory between the 1920s and 1960s. He held a view that the world is a series of systems within systems, much like a set of Russian dolls. Figure 2.1 gives a graphical representation of systems within systems that are at play and need to be taken into consideration when aiming to cultivate a coaching culture within an organisation.

KEY SYSTEMS OF A COACHING CULTURE

There are at least three levels to be considered in the context of developing a coaching culture (as illustrated in Figure 2.1): the individual, the team and the organisation. Each of these levels consists of internal and external systems that are interacting with each other, resulting in numerous feedback loops. Understanding these sub-systems allows those responsible at each of the three levels to make choices and to develop structures, processes and behaviours which support the coaching culture.

INDIVIDUAL LEVEL

For the individual, internal systems include how they understand their strengths and weaknesses, their motivations and values, how they use their energy and the assumptions they make about themselves. External systems include their team(s), their close personal relationships inside and outside work, the organisational culture, and assumptions they make about other people and other people make about them. The feedback loops include, for example, how their assumptions and behaviours create behaviour in others and vice versa, as well as how the individual learns.

TEAM LEVEL

For the team, internal and external systems are pretty much a mirror of those for the individual, but with the added complication of interpersonal dynamics. So internal systems include team strengths and weaknesses and how the team collectively manages these. In a well-managed, well-integrated team, everyone is aware of each other's strengths and weaknesses, work is arranged to achieve the maximum use of strengths, and the team follows a strategy to import selected competences and find new ways to leverage strengths. In less functional teams, the feedback loops are disjointed and tend to cause noise in the system. Again, an important feedback loop between the internal and external systems is how the team learns.

Figure 2.1 Levels of systems in organisations

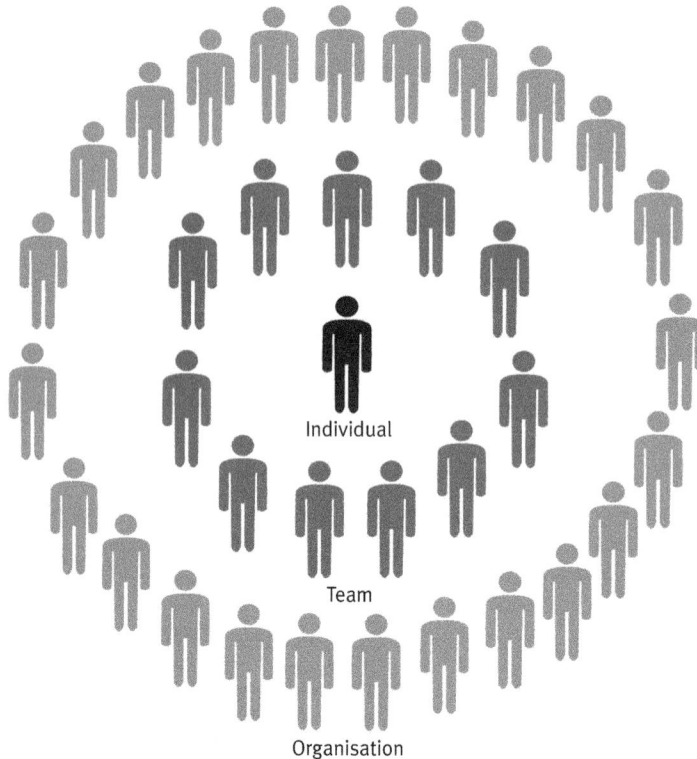

Individual

Team

Organisation

ORGANISATION LEVEL

For the organisation, internal systems include the cultural and historical legacy, the structure of the hierarchy, the internal political backcloth, key assumptions about the way the organisation functions and so on. The external context relates to changing markets and technology, interfaces with society, availability of resources (including financial and human capital), strategic alliances and so on. Feedback loops include expectations and relationships with customers, suppliers and other stakeholders, reputation management, and how the organisation learns.

Excellent organisations are characterised by their openness to feedback and their constant search for information that will help them thrive in the future.

An effective approach to creating a coaching culture needs to take all the above systems and their interactions into consideration. We find that successful initiatives aiming at supporting a coaching culture usually target all three levels.

COACHING CULTURE ON THE EDGE OF CHAOS

A theory that gained a lot of interest because of its holistic approach to understanding the dynamic and fluid nature of organisations is the complex adaptive systems (CAS) theory.

The term 'complex system' refers to a system that consists of many interrelated elements with non-linear relationships that make them very difficult to understand and predict. A complex adaptive system (CAS) is a system made up of a number of autonomous systems which are able to adapt and evolve within a changing environment. An organisation, a team, human body, a flock of birds, an ecosystem or a city are all examples of a CAS.

Complexity scientists suggest that living systems (and that includes all types of organisations) migrate to a state of dynamic stability called the 'edge of chaos'. As described by Shona Brown and Kathleen Eisenhardt:

> '... the edge of chaos lies in an intermediate zone where organisations never quite settle into a stable equilibrium but never quite fall apart, either. This intermediate zone is where systems of all types – biological, physical, economic, and social – are at their most vibrant, surprising, and flexible. The power of a few simple structures to generate enormously complex, adaptive behaviour whether flock behaviour among birds, resilient government (as in democracy) or simply successful performance by major corporations is at the heart of the edge of chaos. The edge of chaos captures the complex, uncontrolled, unpredictable but yet adaptive (in technical terms, self-organised) behaviour that occurs when there is some structure but not very much. The critical managerial issue at the edge of chaos is to figure out what to structure, and, as essential, what not to structure' (Brown and Eisenhardt 1998).

Individuals and organisations 'on the edge' are characterised by openness, creativity and a high level of comfort with disequilibrium. They are flexible enough to evolve and reinvent themselves, but stable enough to stay true to their essence.

Staying on the edge of chaos is like walking a tightrope – it requires a significant amount of concentration and conscious effort. Complex adaptive systems can easily go off-balance – either to the disruptive side (resulting in the disintegration and collapse of the system), or the stability side (leading to stagnation, rigidity and bureaucracy).

It is clear that a coaching culture and its possible visible manifestations, such as constructive challenge, creative exploration, openness to new ideas and focus on continuous growth and development, can support an organisation in striking the right balance and staying 'on the edge'.

However, the links between complex adaptive systems theory and a coaching culture don't stop here. Complexity theory is also relevant to the process of developing a coaching culture itself – the most successful organisational approach to building a coaching culture seems to balance 'on the edge' as well, combining the right amount of structure with appropriate flexibility, adaptability and co-evolution.

Complexity scientists have identified several characteristics that distinguish CAS from systems that are either locked in rigid order, or are too chaotic for any stability to emerge. Some of these characteristics can be quite relevant to building and sustaining a coaching culture within an organisation. Table 2.2 describes these characteristics and their implications for a coaching culture.

Table 2.2 Characteristics of CAS and implications for a coaching culture

Common characteristics of CAS	Description	Coaching culture on the edge
Emergence	Like a swarm of bees or a flock of birds, CAS are made up of many individual agents who take decisions and act based on information in their local environment to form a functioning mechanism	No rigid, centralised, 'one size fits all' approach to coaching and mentoring. Core values of the organisation support a coaching culture and its core principles. There are local coaching agents with good understanding of local business environment and culture. Coaching is linked and customised to local business needs and culture. Coaching is well integrated into everyday work team practices.
Co-evolution	CAS interact with their environment and both co-influence and change each other	Evolving needs of individuals, teams, the organisation and its wider environment are being monitored to make coaching and other organisational development initiatives highly relevant and effective. Bottom–up input and suggestions for improvement are strongly encouraged and taken on board. Impact of coaching is evaluated and improvements are continuously made. Processes are never static – they evolve and change to suit coaching users' and providers' needs. Individual and team coaching is seen as a way to develop individuals and teams but also to gain valuable input for the development of the organisation in general (see Stories from the Field: Co-evolution: Organisational Learning from Individual and Team Coaching, p32).
Requisite variety	The greater the variety in the system, the stronger it is	A wide variety of coaching and mentoring approaches are available: self-coaching, peer coaching, individual coaching, team coaching, line manager as a coach, formal and informal mentoring, reverse mentoring, and so on. A variety of internal and external coaches are being used.
Connectivity	The quality of relationships between the agents of the system is critical to the system's survival. Interactions and relationships are	Coaches and mentors who work with or within the organisation are well connected and committed to each other's and coaching/mentoring practice's development and growth (through creating communities of practice, meetings, conferences, newsletters, online groups, and so on).

	where vital feedback is exchanged and an opportunity for the system to evolve presents itself	Coaches, coaching clients and coaching sponsors are well connected and discuss expectations, progress and results of coaching.
		Building quality relationships with all the stakeholders in and outside of the organisation is considered to be top priority.
		Coaching is used as a tool to leverage learning through creating learning 'alliances', such as team-based learning (see Chapter 8: Developing Internal Capacity for Coaching).
		People collaborate across horizontal and hierarchical boundaries to identify high-leverage solutions.
Simplicity of rules	CAS are governed by simple rules	Coaching and mentoring programmes have simple and clear guidelines.
		Coaching and mentoring relationships are guided by a clear code of ethics.
		Coaching training for non-professional coaches, such as line managers, offers a few powerful tools that are relevant to their work, implementable and easy to remember.
		There is a simple and clear guide for coaching clients on how to make the best use of coaching.
		Coaching philosophy and practices are translated into a language that is easy to understand and remember.
Iteration	Often referred to as butterfly or snowball effect. Small changes in the system, which pass through repeated small-scale experiments a few times, can have a huge impact down the road	Key influencers are identified and brought on board to promote coaching.
		Coaching initiatives are first rolled out as a pilot, with a built-in learning mechanism that provides input for future improvements.
		Small improvements and adjustments are continuously made to all forms of coaching.
		Large emphasis is placed on the continuous development of coaching skills (through supervision and CPD).
		Leverage points are identified and used to build or sustain a coaching culture (see Working Smarter, Not Harder, p29).
		Organisation is open to experimentation around various coaching and mentoring modalities.

		Coaching interventions are developed through iterative experimentation – they start from a 'basic' version and are improved along the course of implementation.
Sub-optimal	CAS don't need to be perfect to thrive. If they had a motto, it would be: 'done is better than perfect'	Coaching and mentoring strategy aims at meeting the organisation where it currently is (in terms of coaching and mentoring culture development stage) and building it from the ground up.
		There is acceptance that a learner coach or mentor is better than no coach at all.
		Skills are built and improvements are made gradually and expectations are realistic.
		The lack of 'ideal' conditions, such as committed executive sponsorship or absolute readiness for coaching, does not stop coaching champions from looking for appropriate ways of introducing coaching to the organisation.
Nested systems	There are systems within systems (like Russian dolls) and they all influence each other	Links of coaching and mentoring with other HR systems in the organisation are identified.
		HR systems are aligned so that they support each other, for example coaching is part of performance appraisal and management.
		Coaches working with or within the organisation are familiar with systems theory and use systemic approach in coaching.
		Individuals seek feedback and are aware of their impact on their colleagues and teams, taking personal responsibility for making a positive contribution.

One of the aims of this chapter is to provide the reader with a few useful practices and tools to use to successfully adopt a systemic approach to developing a coaching culture. These practices and tools are:

- polarity management
- systems thinking model
- root-cause analysis
- identifying high-leverage points in the system.

MANAGING POLARITIES WHILE DEVELOPING COACHING CULTURE

As mentioned before, staying 'on the edge' requires careful balancing between polarities: order and chaos, structure and flexibility, micro and macro, centralisation and decentralisation, continuity and change. This approach doesn't come naturally to most

Westerners, who tend to view polarities as opposing forces rather than interconnected, interdependent and complementary parts of a whole, such as ying and yang[1] (Choi 2010).

This lack of familiarity – or comfort – with paradox and duality leads a lot of organisations to work hard on solving problems, which aren't problems at all – they are polarities to be managed.

Polarity management involves moving from focusing on one pole as the problem and the other as the solution ('either . . . or' thinking), to valuing both poles ('both . . . and' thinking). Good polarity management gets the best of both poles while avoiding the drawbacks of either.

Effective polarity management is particularly relevant in approaching issues which are characterised by high complexity, diversity, speed of change and resistance to change (Johnson 1998). Transforming organisational culture meets all the criteria above.

Some of the common polarities we often notice in organisations working on building a coaching culture are:

- structure and flexibility
- consistency and customisation
- individual learning and organisation learning
- theory and practice
- individual needs and strategic alignment
- efficiency and effectiveness.

Interestingly, in a study of consistently high-performing companies in the 1990s, one of us identified that a common characteristic was the attention that top management paid to maintaining a constantly shifting balance between opposites, such as control and autonomy, or values and rules, or evolutionary and revolutionary change (Goldsmith and Clutterbuck 1997).

Another example of effective management of polarities is a university with a strong commitment to coaching, which proclaimed values of learner-centredness and the coachee setting the agenda. At the same time, the university wanted to make sure that it would benefit from the process and that there would be return on investment from hiring external coaches. Instead of seeing the above dilemma as an 'either . . . or' proposition, the university decided to manage that polarity by having organisation development staff attend half of the first meeting between coach and coachee to seek to ensure that the goals of the organisation were factored into the objectives of coaching.

There are a number of available tools to manage polarities effectively. For more information on polarity management, read Barry Johnson's *Polarity Management: Identifying and Managing Unsolvable Problems*, or go to www.polaritypartnerships.com.

PROBLEMS . . . A CURSE OR A BLESSING IN DISGUISE?

There is a line in Hamlet which says: 'There is nothing good or bad but thinking makes it so.' Linear thinking makes problems seem bad. They are perceived as something to be avoided, and – if that is no longer an option – to be fixed. Systems thinking looks at problems differently – it views them as useful clues pointing in the direction of underlying issues. The aim of uncovering those underlying issues is to find solutions that can offer a true, sustainable change instead of a quick fix with a short lifespan.

---

[1] In Chinese philosophy, yin and yang describes how opposite or contrary forces are actually complementary, interconnected, and interdependent in the natural world, and how they give rise to each other as they interrelate to one another. Many tangible dualities (such as light and dark, fire and water, expanding and contracting) are thought of as physical manifestations of the duality symbolised by yin and yang. Source: Wikipedia.

Understanding what a problem is pointing to is a bit like peeling an onion: each removed layer uncovers deeper, more meaningful information until we get to the very heart of the matter. There is a useful model[2] (Goodman 2002) that suggests that the following levels of meaning are worth exploring when faced with an issue:

- event level – focusing on what happened
- patterns level – focusing on whether it has happened before
- structures level – focusing on what is causing the pattern that is being observed
- mental models level – focusing on the kind of thinking that contributes to the existing structures.

To see how this could be relevant to developing a coaching culture, we will use the following example:

> George is Head of Learning and Development in a large professional services firm. A development centre for the firm's high-potential managers was recently organised and it clearly indicated that the vast majority of managers should further develop their coaching skills. As creating a coaching culture is high on the firm's priorities list, George easily obtained approval and the budget for a four-day coaching course.

EVENT LEVEL

The most superficial event level is one where we simply perceive what happened.

In George's case, he noticed that eight out of thirty managers nominated for the training cancelled at the last minute or didn't show up for training without any notice.

THE PATTERN LEVEL

Going beyond the superficial level of events, we start noticing patterns
The questions that will help George look for patterns are: 'Has this happened before?' or 'Is this problem similar to other problems that we had in the past?' Asking these questions might lead George to discover that there were other cases of cancellations or no-shows in the past. George might also notice that they were almost always from the same part of the business.

Why go to the pattern level?

Observing patterns allows us to forecast and in some cases prevent certain events
If George knows that managers from a particular business unit have a tendency of cancelling last minute or not showing up at all, he might decide to discuss this with their line manager and build their commitment to reduce last-minute cancellations or no-shows. He might even introduce a new policy on cancellations.

THE STRUCTURE LEVEL

Below the pattern level lies the structure level. Structures can be:

- physical – such as buildings and other infrastructure, office lay-out, equipment, etc
- organisational – business units, departments, teams
- processes and procedures – performance management system, quality management systems, policies, operational processes, etc.

---

[2] Goodman, M. (2002) *The Iceberg Model*. Hopkinton, MA: Innovation Associates Organizational Learning. Available at: http://www.ascd.org/ [Accessed 9 February 2016].

When George investigates, 'What is causing the pattern I'm observing?' he discovers that managers from the business unit in question have much higher utilisation targets than the rest of the firm. This means that to meet their personal utilisation targets, they need to be working on client projects almost around the clock. They simply can't afford to 'waste' four days on training – they would never be able to catch up with their targets if they did!

Why go to the structure level?

Understanding structures allows us to change or redesign them
In his position as Head of Learning and Development, George will sometimes have to react to events at a superficial level. However, if he is serious about creating a coaching culture in his organisation, he will have to find a way of addressing issues at the structure level as well. A systemic approach to creating a coaching culture means that George will have to reach out across the boundaries of his role and department and cooperate with others to solve problems and remove obstacles to creating a coaching culture. In this case, George might decide to raise the issues with management and suggest that a number of approved training hours should be counted towards people's utilisation targets across the firm.

THE MENTAL MODEL LEVEL

Mental models are ideas, images, values, attitudes and generalisations that guide people's thoughts, behaviours and actions and allow structures to function as they do. They can be generalisations, such as 'Coaching is a waste of time' or more complex theories about how things work. They shape how we perceive things, think and act. For example, if people believe that coaching is a waste of time, they will act differently than if they believe that coaching is a thought-provoking partnership which inspires growth and learning and contributes to their career progression.

Why go to the mental model level?

A real and sustainable systemic transformation can only happen through discovering, challenging and changing mental models
By engaging with all the stakeholders, George might discover that managers in the particular business unit are seen and valued as experts in their field, responsible for delivering high-quality services to clients, but not for growing and developing people. They are rewarded for being as productive and as efficient as possible, and their results are mostly measured in billable hours and quality of client deliverables. Getting to the level of mental models, especially the tacit ones, will be much more difficult, however. Assuming that George has relationships of trust with key stakeholders and can engage them in deep, meaningful conversations, he might find that some of the active mindsets are:

- 'Managers' value is directly proportional to their subject matter expertise'
- 'At the end of the day, it's only financial results that count towards a promotion to Senior Manager'
- 'Managers' role is to deliver client-facing work' or
- 'We don't have the time for all that people nonsense'.

Using the systemic thinking model described above allows us to see obstacles experienced in developing coaching in a completely different light. Instead of seeing them as something undesirable, we start viewing them as valuable sources of information. When we look carefully enough and go beyond the superficial, we start noticing clues pointing to the heart of the problem. This allows us to design effective solutions that cut to the heart of the issue, instead of merely dealing with the symptoms.

WORKING SMARTER, NOT HARDER

The task of building and sustaining a coaching culture can seem daunting, especially considering what we have already said about the complexity of issues that need to be addressed and the rigidity of mental models that people hold.

A lot of organisations get discouraged midway into their coaching strategy implementation – some of them even go back to where they used to be a few years before. It's not entirely surprising: the amount of effort that seems to be required to overcome the system's resistance to change can make the most zealous proponents of coaching feel disenchanted at best.

Systems thinking, however, offers an opportunity to find ways to work smarter, not necessarily harder. The whole point of going to structure and mental model level is to identify the *root causes* of problems and challenges linked to building a coaching culture. Identifying those root causes opens up a possibility of higher impact, with less energy.

IDENTIFYING ROOT CAUSES

The technique of five whys was originally developed by Sakichi Toyoda and was used within the Toyota Motor Corporation during the evolution of its manufacturing methodologies. Also known as a 'why tree', it's one of the simplest and most user-friendly methods of root-cause analysis. By repeatedly asking 'why', layers of issues and symptoms that hide the root cause are peeled away.

The process starts off with stating the symptom(s) of a problem. Subsequently, a series of 'why' questions are asked about the problem to uncover the root cause. Five whys is just a rule of thumb – unless there is reasonable evidence to confirm the root cause, it's advisable to continue the exploration. Figure 2.2 gives an example of a simple why tree. The complexity of the why tree depends on the number of branches (possible answers to a question) and is virtually unlimited, although for expediency reasons you will want to limit yourself to the few key ones.

HIGH-LEVERAGE POINTS AND SOLUTIONS THAT WORK

Archimedes is believed to have said: 'Give me a lever long enough and a fulcrum on which to place it, and I shall move the world.' Almost 2,300 years later in his seminal book *The Fifth Discipline*, Peter Senge put the idea of leverage into the context of business and systems thinking:

> 'To me, bottom line of systems thinking is leverage – seeing where actions can lead to significant, enduring improvements. Often, leverage follows the principle of economy of means: where the best results come not from large-scale efforts but small, well-focused actions. Our non-systemic ways of thinking are so damaging specifically because they consistently lead us to focus on low-leverage changes: we focus on symptoms where the stress is greatest. We repair or ameliorate the symptoms. But such efforts only make matters better in the short run, at best, and worse in the long run.'

In other words, symptomatic solutions push on low-leverage points, where a lot of energy is expended with little or no result in the long run. High-leverage solutions, on the other hand, resolve the root causes of the issues.

In our previous example, George faced last-minute training participation cancellations and 'no-shows'. Focusing on cancellations and trying to incentivise or penalise people to prevent a similar situation from occurring in the future would be just pushing on a low-leverage point. While requiring high effort, this solution would probably not bring the desired results in the long run.

Figure 2.2 Example of a 'why tree'

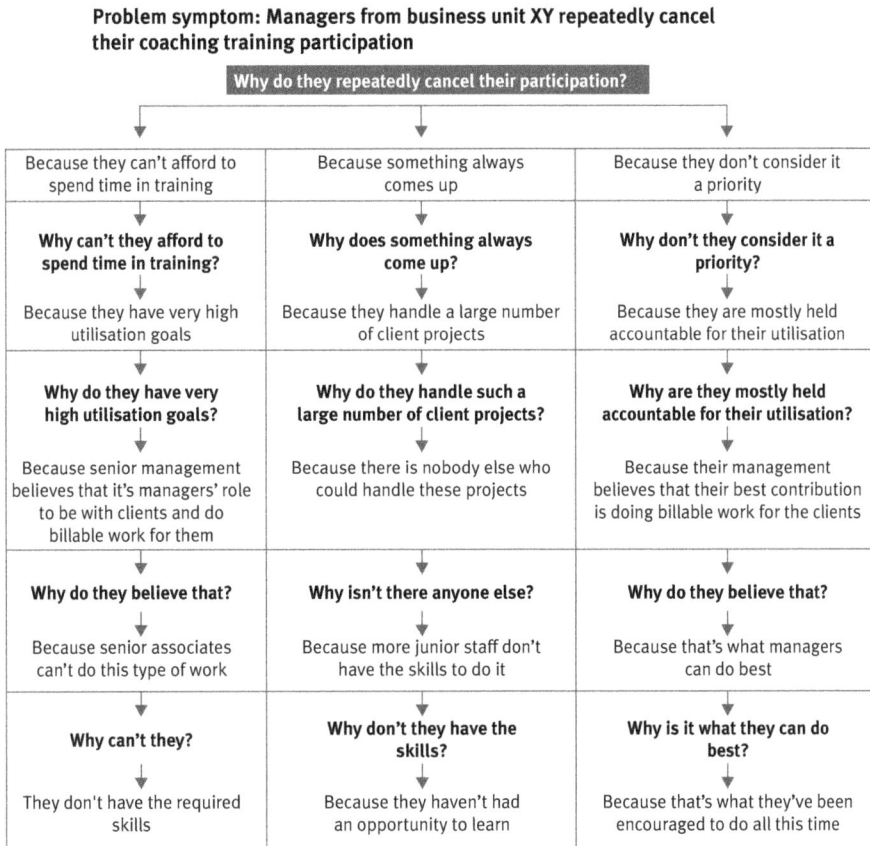

Problem symptom: Managers from business unit XY repeatedly cancel their coaching training participation

Why do they repeatedly cancel their participation?		
Because they can't afford to spend time in training	Because something always comes up	Because they don't consider it a priority
Why can't they afford to spend time in training?	**Why does something always come up?**	**Why don't they consider it a priority?**
Because they have very high utilisation goals	Because they handle a large number of client projects	Because they are mostly held accountable for their utilisation
Why do they have very high utilisation goals?	**Why do they handle such a large number of client projects?**	**Why are they mostly held accountable for their utilisation?**
Because senior management believes that it's managers' role to be with clients and do billable work for them	Because there is nobody else who could handle these projects	Because their management believes that their best contribution is doing billable work for the clients
Why do they believe that?	**Why isn't there anyone else?**	**Why do they believe that?**
Because senior associates can't do this type of work	Because more junior staff don't have the skills to do it	Because that's what managers can do best
Why can't they?	**Why don't they have the skills?**	**Why is it what they can do best?**
They don't have the required skills	Because they haven't had an opportunity to learn	Because that's what they've been encouraged to do all this time

High-leverage points, on the other hand, can only be found in the deeper levels of the model and through identifying the root cause of the issue. In George's case, the root cause was junior staff's lack of skills to deliver client-facing work. The structures that led to this problem were managers' personal utilisation targets. These, in turn, were supported by a number of active mental models, such as: 'Managers' value is directly proportional to their subject matter expertise', or 'Managers' role is to deliver client-facing work'.

Therefore, George's high leverage will be at the meeting point of the following two issues: the capability of junior staff to deliver client-facing work and managers' personal utilisation targets.

A possible solution could be changing managers' objectives – lowering their personal utilisation targets – and introducing a new objective – increasing utilisation of junior staff in client-facing work. To support managers in achieving their objectives, George could also design and implement a work team process where managers support and coach junior staff to undertake some of the client-facing duties.

To enable the above solution, George would have to unearth and challenge the mental models held by senior management that led to the problem in the first place. As Einstein said: 'We cannot solve our problems with the same thinking that created them.'

It's also probably clear from the examples above that George couldn't possibly implement these high-leverage solutions on his own. To identify and implement high-leverage solutions, people need to collaborate across horizontal and hierarchical boundaries. This highlights the fact that building and sustaining a coaching culture is a collective venture which requires deep commitment and collaboration of a number of key stakeholders willing to engage in open-minded experimentation to make things work.

We have gone into significant depth on the issue of complex systems and systems thinking in this chapter because our observations on what works and what doesn't indicate that a linear or localised approach to developing a coaching culture can be costly and largely ineffective.

Organisations are complex systems and, as such, even a small change to one part of the organisation will inevitably have an impact on the remaining parts. When coaching culture initiatives don't fit with or don't address the larger system, people may resist or even reject them in the same manner that the immune system may reject a much needed transplant.

From our experience, the key elements of the larger system to keep in mind when working on developing a coaching culture are:

- external context (eg industry, markets, competition)
- organisational context (eg mission, vision, strategy, key objectives, politics, agendas, interests)
- team context (eg team purpose, values, team dynamics)
- individual context (eg people's values, motives, mental models).

STORIES FROM THE FIELD

SYSTEMIC APPROACH TO BUILDING A COACHING CULTURE IN DELOITTE UK

Deloitte UK is part of one of the largest professional services networks in the world. It provides audit, tax, consulting, enterprise risk and financial advisory services, and it is one of the 'Big Four' professional services firms along with PwC, EY and KPMG.

Developing a coaching culture has always been very high on the people agenda for Deloitte, as it recognises the vital role this plays in keeping it at the leading edge of its sector.

When asked how Deloitte's thinking about developing a coaching culture has changed over the past couple of decades, Claire Davey, Head of Coaching and Leadership Development in the UK and Switzerland, said:

'The shift is evident from the evolution of coaching practice and its application within our firm. When we began, people perceived coaching as remedial in nature, but this changed as they started to realise coaching was there to support high performance. Receiving coaching became a token of recognition and a confirmation that the firm saw their potential. Providing highly effective coaching to individuals was only the first step. We knew the impact we could have on the business if we could enable teams to become greater than the sum of their parts, and we wanted to realise the potential for this. That led us on to the next stage, where we added team coaching to our portfolio of available modalities. Where we're at now is a very interesting and exciting point, where we experiment with what coaching the organisation might look like.'

This clear shift from linear to systemic thinking that Claire describes is visible in how the firm approaches building a coaching culture. Deloitte works on doing this at multiple levels and by engaging multiple stakeholders and systems – individuals, teams and the organisation as a whole.

Interestingly, Deloitte's approach closely matches most – if not all – characteristics of complex adaptive systems. We focus here on co-evolution, simplicity of rules and iteration, which have helped Deloitte strengthen its coaching culture. We also give an example of how going to the level of structures has resulted in creating stronger levers for coaching culture development.

Co-evolution: organisational learning from individual and team coaching

An interesting example of co-evolution is the systemic research that Deloitte now performs annually in the spirit of organisational development. The firm runs a series of surveys, focus groups, in-depth interviews and workshops spanning the spectrum of the coaching network to 'harvest organisational learning' (to use Peter Hawkins' term) from individual and team coaching (Hawkins 2012).

'It's a time-consuming process but we decided to continue to invest in it as the benefits far outweigh the cost. There is a lot of valuable information from the OD perspective that can enable our business in the future', said Claire. 'It's important that this information is objective so we can gain the maximum benefit from the process. At the same time, it has to fit with who we are as an organisation and recognise the culture that's already in place. To achieve this, we partner with our external supervisor so we get the right balance of objectivity and understanding of our ecosystem.'

Deloitte uses iterative experimentation in this process; the methodology evolves based on experiences and lessons learnt from the previous implementation. The most recent approach draws data from coaching needs analysis information and a joint workshop with internal and external coaches and supervisors, who map themes and patterns emerging from coaching engagements they were involved in. Confidentiality is safeguarded both by the population that participates in the process (coaches who are bound by the rule of confidentiality and code of ethics) and by focusing on themes and patterns and not individual cases.

What Deloitte learns from this process are current themes around issues and challenges faced by people in the firm. The interaction of testing, learning and refinement provides for a natural evolution of processes and development of ideas within the organisation, and is one of the many positives that Deloitte gains from this approach. The knowledge and understanding it provides of emerging themes within the organisation allows Deloitte to search for the best possible ways to build on the positive patterns and address the issues, modify its coaching model and approach, decide when to use a different approach (for example, experiential learning), or even make a structural or process change if necessary. Until now, the outcomes of this process were looked at mostly through the talent management and HR lens, but there is now a growing appetite for this information from the senior leadership, who realise that the organisational intelligence collected through coaching (through systemic research) can provide valuable input for managing the business, improving the quality of services to the clients and further improving the bottom line.

Iteration – butterfly effect in developing a coaching culture

Two good examples of how Deloitte has experienced a 'butterfly effect' in developing a coaching culture are set out here: senior partner coaching training and experimentation with a new coaching modality.

Senior partner coaching training

In 2014, Deloitte ran a pilot to train senior partners as executive coaches. The objective was to provide an exceptional experience to an extremely influential group of people, who would then hopefully become strong champions of coaching.

The training was centred on a neuroscience and brain-based approach. The provider was carefully selected to ensure credibility and quality of delivery; apart from the usual criteria such as coaching accreditation and experience as a coach and a facilitator, Deloitte selected someone who had previously been used in the organisation and had a good understanding of the business. The training initially helped partners to understand the theory and the science behind the approach, learn the necessary coaching skills and practise them in a safe environment. The pre-requisite for participating was having a real-life challenge – professional or personal – that would be used as the subject of peer coaching sessions.

The impact of this intervention on the participating group was extremely positive; it clearly demonstrated the impact of coaching (all partners found solutions to their challenges through peer coaching) and it achieved its purpose of equipping them with the necessary skills to coach.

The result was that a group of highly respected and powerful individuals, with strong and convincing voices, started role-modelling and promoting coaching in the organisation. Claire told us: 'The messages they were giving and their impact were really strong – and almost viral. There was a rush of people coming in and asking me how they could do that; how they could learn to coach as well.'

Deloitte partner Keith Leslie was one of these people. He noted the benefits senior partner coaching training had across the organisation, commenting: 'Professionally, it has been very powerful. It has enabled me to step up a gear in my relationships with my most senior clients, and gave me a specific capability and standing to offer coaching as an intervention when we face internal colleague challenges.'

Experimenting with a new coaching modality

When we were interviewing Claire, she recalled an incident that led to an ongoing iteration of coaching within Deloitte. One of the internal executive coaches announced that she did not wish to continue with one-to-one executive coaching. Instead, she wanted to use her coaching skills for a greater impact and . . . coach the organisation. There was no specific 'banner' that this type of coaching could be put under; however, it became apparent that it was fully aligned with the business needs and created a new dimension to coaching culture. Also, the positive impact that this type of coaching could potentially have on the organisation was promising.

Eventually, it was agreed that the coach would start her experiment, remaining in the formal supervision. The success of the experiment is clear not only because the coach is now using her coaching expertise, without being commissioned, to help leaders within the organisation while performing her day job – managing the business, co-creating and implementing business strategy and interacting with partners – but also because other senior coaches are now adopting a similar approach.

According to Claire: 'It's a completely different, emergent type of coaching, happening on the fringes – it's innovative and that's what makes it exciting and rewarding when you see it succeed. It is the openness to experiments like this that allows a coaching culture to thrive. To do it, we need to balance carefully "on the edge" of chaos and avoid holding things too tightly; we need to know the boundaries and the edges of our awareness, whilst at the same time allowing things to emerge and evolve systemically.'

Simplicity as an important driver in developing a coaching culture

As mentioned earlier in this chapter, one of the characteristics of complex adaptive systems is that they are governed by simple rules. In a coaching culture, this, amongst other things, translates itself into creating simple guidelines on how to embed coaching skills into the organisational culture, using a language that is easy to understand and providing user-friendly tools to make coaching more accessible and easier.

Claire told us that: 'Often it's the word "coaching" that stands in the way of growing coaching culture. For me, what's important is that the principles are there and that people access them and integrate them in their day-to-day interactions with their colleagues and clients, rather than whether we call it "coaching" or "coaching philosophy".' To this end, the focus is on behaviours that can be used in individual situations to deliver the same positive experiences that are at the centre of a coaching culture.

Deloitte created a field guide with ten suggested behaviours or 'moves' that people can use to turn interactions into exceptional experiences. All the moves match Deloitte's coaching philosophy perfectly and are presented in a simple, accessible format: a booklet that easily fits into a pocket, where each move is accompanied by useful coaching questions.

These include encouraging people to see a situation from the other person's perspective, reframing issues and revealing new angles to challenge assumptions, encouraging collaboration to achieve results, encouraging people to take accountability for problems and issues, and addressing the difficult issues that people avoid talking about.

Taken as a whole, the behaviours recognise the individual and facilitate their growth, offering a good balance of challenge and support to enable them to move out of their comfort zone.

Implementing systemic thinking to bring about culture change – going to the structure level

As we have already said, to make a sustainable systemic change, it is often necessary to go to the level of structures and mental models. Claire illustrates this by saying: 'We could spend all the time and money in the world on coaching and it wouldn't make the desired impact if performance reviews and reward systems didn't support our efforts. In order to bring about the desired change, there has to be a robust framework with powerful levers in place.'

Debbie Stevenson, Deloitte's Head of HR, adds: 'Performance management is changing. It's less about an annual review of past performance and more about regular check-ins between individuals and their team leaders. These check-in conversations are forward-looking, build on individuals' strengths, and support career development. Coaching conversations are increasingly an essential part of every leader's job.'

At the time of our conversation, it was still too early in the implementation of this approach to say how it had contributed to the cultivation of a coaching culture; however, Claire had already noticed that it was encouraging people to have better performance conversations, where people asked for input, clarified expectations and gave feedback more regularly.

SUMMARY

The most common misconception about how to develop a coaching culture in an organisation is that it can be done by focusing solely on 'fixing' individuals. In spite of the fact that millions are spent annually on training, many organisations report that results are not entirely satisfactory. The systemic perspective explains why, although necessary, training alone is not sufficient to develop a coaching culture. Systems within which people operate, such as their team or the organisation at large, are much more powerful than even the most motivated individual. Companies that had success in creating a coaching culture were able to balance 'on the edge', effectively managing polarities and addressing systems at all three levels: individual, team and organisation. Creating a coaching culture can be a daunting task, accompanied by numerous challenges and problems. Systemic thinking, however, offers a different perspective on problems. Without them, we wouldn't be able to understand how the system works. Problems can also lead to identifying high-leverage solutions, where a small amount of effort (such as in the butterfly effect) can produce a big impact.

FIELDWORK

?

Levels of thinking

Identify a disruptive event, or a problem that is linked to creating a coaching culture in your company (or a company you are familiar with). Put the description of this event into the table below and work your way down through the patterns, structures and mental models.

Table 2.3 Levels of thinking exercise

Event level
What happened?
Pattern level
Has this happened before?   *Is this problem similar to other problems we had in the past?*
Structure level
What is causing the pattern that I'm observing?
Mental model level
What kind of thinking led to the structures that contributed to the problem?   *How can I find that out?*

Tree of Whys

Now try the Tree of Whys method, starting from the description of the problem and then working your way down the tree, repeating the 'why' questions as many times as necessary.

Reflection

- Did these two exercises help to broaden your perspective? If so, how can you use this perspective going forward?
- Are there any leverage points that you were able to identify through your analysis? If yes, what are they?
- Can you think of any high leverage solutions that would effectively address the root cause of the problem and support building a coaching culture in your organisation?
- Who would you have to involve? What boundaries would you have to surpass?

PART TWO

THE ABCS OF COACHING CULTURE PLANNING AND IMPLEMENTATION

CHAPTER 3

Getting Set and Ready

'The secret of getting ahead is getting started.'
Mark Twain

OVERVIEW

In this chapter, we talk about the necessary preparation before taking any steps towards building or strengthening a coaching culture within an organisation. First, our aim is to help you decide whether investing in a coaching culture is a wise decision for your organisation. Secondly, we talk about the importance of getting the right people on board, both in terms of sponsorship but also hands-on involvement in the coaching culture planning process.

We also outline the ABC-DE model of strategic coaching culture planning that describes the necessary steps to create a robust and dynamic coaching culture strategy.

IS A COACHING CULTURE FOR YOU?

At first glance, this might seem a strange question to ask. After all, wouldn't every organisation want to have a coaching culture? Most publications on the subject claim that it can benefit an organisation in a number of ways and on many different levels, from increasing employee engagement to generating breakthrough innovations and much stronger competitive advantage. While all these claims can potentially be true, we believe that some organisations might benefit more from investing their time and resources elsewhere.

Developing a coaching culture is not an easy task. It demands a significant amount of commitment, effort and resources. Consequently, the decision as to whether (and how) to invest in building a coaching culture needs to be a well-considered one. And most importantly, it has to make sound business sense.

Having assisted numerous organisations in making this kind of decision for decades, we have been able to identify two main factors that can bring clarity on the issue:

- **Relevance** – the extent to which a coaching culture is expected to support an organisation in achieving its primary objectives
- **Supportive climate** – the organisational context and whether it can support the development of a coaching culture.

RELEVANCE

In 2005, in *Making Coaching Work* we said: 'Coaching will never move beyond a "nice to have", HR-driven initiative at the margin, unless it contributes, and is seen to contribute, to a core business issue that is of central concern to top management and a wide range of other stakeholders in the organisation' (Clutterbuck and Megginson 2005). Today, this statement rings truer than ever. It is clear that there is no point in even trying to develop a coaching culture if it is not perceived to be strategically relevant.

There is a broad consensus that any significant investment should aim to support the organisation's ability to fulfil its mission, achieve its vision and contribute to the achievement of strategic objectives. Therefore, the first thing to look at is whether key stakeholders acknowledge that creating or strengthening this type of culture does indeed have the potential to enable the organisation to deliver on its key priorities.

High **relevance** indicates that key stakeholders see a very clear business case for creating a coaching culture – the links between coaching, mentoring and the organisation's top priorities are strong and direct. Low **relevance** suggests that it's not clear how coaching or mentoring could support the organisation in fulfilling its purpose and achieving objectives.

As illustrated in Table 3.1, we followed the logic of the balanced scorecard[1] to identify the areas of focus for relevance, as well as high relevance indicators.

Table 3.1 Coaching culture relevance indicators

Organisational Performance Area	High Relevance Indicators
Financial	It is important that individuals and teams at most levels contribute to identifying best ways of meeting financial performance expectations, such as revenue growth, profitability, operating costs, asset utilisation, etc.
	Individual and team level of performance has a direct impact on financial results.
	Financial results are directly or indirectly influenced by organisation's ability to identify and develop talent.
	Organisation's top line depends to a great extent on employees' resourcefulness, creativity and engagement.
Internal Business Processes	Internal business processes need to evolve to best serve the needs of the business.
	It's important that individuals and teams at most levels contribute to identifying ways of advancing and improving work processes.
	It is necessary to receive honest and constructive user feedback on the usefulness and effectiveness of internal business processes.
	The effective implementation of business processes largely depends on their users.
Customer (Internal and External)	It's important that individuals and teams at most levels contribute to identifying the best ways of delivering timely, accurate and high-quality services.
	It is critical for people at all levels to engage with their internal or external customers to identify and understand their needs and expectations.

---

[1] The balanced scorecard is a strategic planning and management system to align business activities to the vision and strategy of the organisation, improve internal and external communications, and monitor organisation performance against strategic goals. It was originated by Dr Robert Kaplan (Harvard Business School) and Dr David Norton as a performance measurement framework that added strategic non-financial performance measures to traditional financial metrics to give managers and executives a more 'balanced' view of organisational performance.

	Individual or team performance has direct or indirect impact on customer satisfaction.
	It is necessary to identify and develop talent to support high quality of products and level of customer service.
Learning and Growth	Ability to change and improve is of utmost importance for the success of the organisation.
	High level of leadership skills is one of the key conditions to succeed.
	Talent identification and development are key drivers of success.
	Knowledge constitutes a valuable intangible asset for creating and sustaining competitive advantages.

The more indicators there are, the greater the likelihood of starting a coaching culture initiative with good prospects of success. Since we are talking about perceptions here, a common difficulty is the lack of consensus on whether a coaching culture is strategically relevant for the organisation. It is not unusual to have as many individuals who consider developing a coaching culture highly relevant as those who strongly oppose that view. And while this situation is not ideal, it is not a deal-breaker. What a lot of organisations do to overcome this hurdle is pilot their key coaching initiatives in those parts of the organisation where coaching is already perceived to be relevant and important. Demonstrating tangible benefits of creating a coaching culture has proven to be a valuable tool in shifting perceptions of the more sceptical stakeholders.

An example of this is a manufacturing company which struggled to get senior leadership buy-in and support to introduce coaching to the organisation. What HR decided to do was to demonstrate the value of coaching by launching a pilot programme in a strategically critical department, the head of which was a firm believer in coaching. The programme was aimed at enhancing work practices in the department through using coaching skills on-the-job. A survey was run before and after the programme and key metrics were identified to measure the impact on business. After the first six months of implementation, the results were tangible enough for other department heads to start inquiring about the possibility of running the programme for their department as well. The decisive shift in perceptions around the usefulness of coaching came when the CEO of the company started working with an executive coach.

Another example comes from a professional services firm, where a senior manager asked for coaching while their superior was not only unsure if the person needed coaching, but also whether coaching worked. After talking to the person responsible for coaching in the firm, the senior manager's superior reluctantly agreed to sign off the coaching engagement. As the coaching relationship progressed, the results and impact of coaching started becoming so visible that the senior manager's superior eventually admitted that 'there is something to coaching' and . . . he asked for a coach himself!

SUPPORTIVE CLIMATE

Various studies indicate that the organisational context – and, in particular, the level of supportiveness perceived by employees – influences the dynamics and outcomes of a coaching culture, from how often learning conversations take place to how effective they are (Berke et al 2008; Hunt and Weintraub 2007).

To use the coaching culture tree metaphor from Chapter 1, a highly **supportive climate** for a coaching culture means that the seed falls on fertile soil and organisational climate supports its growth. In organisational terms, the necessary groundwork has been done, the critical enablers of a coaching culture are in place and the current context can support most coaching and mentoring initiatives.

A low **supportive climate**, on the other hand, means that any efforts to create a coaching culture will have minuscule chances to succeed, until at least the majority of **supportive climate** dimensions are sufficiently addressed.

We have identified four dimensions which, when sufficiently developed, constitute what we call a **supportive climate**. These dimensions are:

- encouragement for taking initiative
- trust and ability to have honest conversations
- diversity and constructive challenge
- learning and growth orientation.

Figure 3.1 Supportive climate dimensions

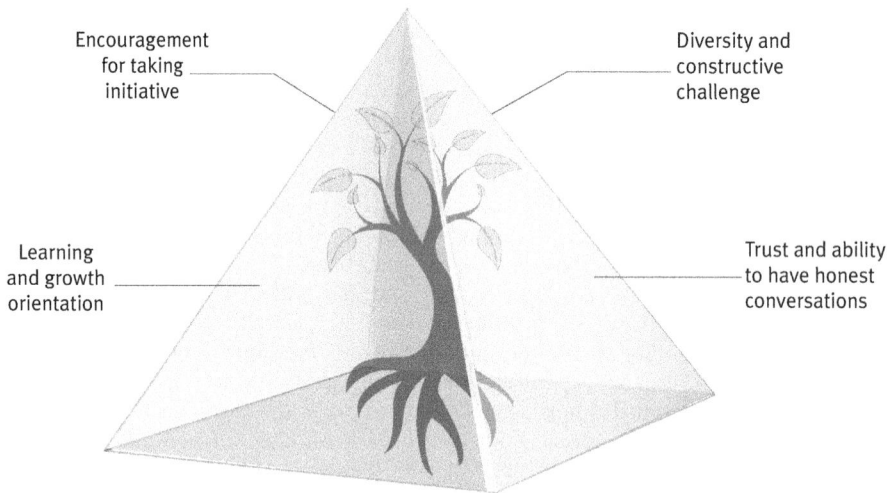

ENCOURAGEMENT FOR TAKING INITIATIVE

Organisations with a high level of **supportive climate** for a coaching culture encourage people to experiment, take initiative and see mistakes and failures as an excellent opportunity to learn and grow. In the last few years, failure has been seen as a step towards success, especially in Silicon Valley. Richard Sheridan, CEO and co-founder of Menlo Innovations, attributes the company's extraordinary success to one of its guiding principles of 'making mistakes faster'. Pixar co-founder Ed Catmull, in his book *Creativity, Inc.*, suggests that we should start seeing the cost of mistakes as an investment in the future (Catmull and Wallace 2014).

This radical approach to taking risks and making mistakes will not be appropriate (or necessary) for all organisations wanting to build a coaching culture. However, our research and observations indicate that it will be impossible to grow a coaching culture in a fear-based, risk-averse environment, where people are blamed and penalised for taking initiative.

Therefore, a minimum requirement is creating a 'safe space', where people can experiment and make mistakes in a relatively low-risk, controlled environment. Work teams and projects can offer an excellent opportunity to create this kind of 'safespace'.

Kara Penn and Anjali Sastry of MIT have done very interesting work around how to ensure that every failure is maximally useful. In their book *Fail Better* (Sastry and Penn 2014), they present a three-step process to use mistakes and failures as stepping stones towards positive outcomes.

TRUST AND ABILITY TO HAVE HONEST CONVERSATIONS

Numerous studies have confirmed the benefit of trust in organisations (Bader and Liljenstrand 2003; Reina and Reina 2007; Lyman 2003, 2012; Interaction Associates, 2009). Their findings indicate that high-trust organisations have greater profitability, attraction and retention of talent, and higher employee satisfaction.

Interestingly, the 2009 study by Interaction Associates found that high-trust organisations had leaders who coach rather than just manage and have many people participating in decision-making.

More than 20 years of studying trust in organisations led Amy Lyman, co-founder of the Great Place to Work Institute, to identify three characteristics of trust: credibility, respect and fair treatment (Lyman 2003, 2012).

In organisations with high levels of trust, employees see others (particularly the management) as credible, meaning what they say and speaking the truth. They also have confidence that the actions of others will remain consistent with their words and that they are ethical in their business practices.

High-trust organisations ensure that employees experience respect, which is demonstrated by employers' support of their employees' professional growth and the consideration of employees' ideas in decision-making processes.

Employees in high-trust organisations – regardless of their position – believe they are treated fairly. Finally, they have confidence in their leader's vision of the future (Lyman 2012).

In an organisation lacking trust, conversations tend to be guarded, with people saying what they suspect others want to hear, rather than what they truly think. It's also harder to admit to weaknesses.

In her book *Lean In: Women, Work, and the Will to Lead*, Sheryl Sandberg, the COO of Facebook, writes: 'People constantly back away from honesty to protect themselves and others. This reticence causes and perpetuates all kinds of problems: uncomfortable issues that never get addressed, resentment that builds, unfit managers who get promoted rather than fired and on and on. Often these situations don't improve because no one tells anyone what is really happening' (Sandberg 2013).

While coaching and mentoring may provide one of the few opportunities for honest conversation (with oneself and with someone else), the habit of conversational caution can be hard to break and therefore may be carried over into coaching and mentoring sessions.

DIVERSITY AND CONSTRUCTIVE CHALLENGE

In her paper on managing diversity, conflict and productivity, Karen A. Jehn said: 'There are many benefits of diversity. Social interaction among diverse perspectives can lead to deep conceptual restructuring and new insights. However, increased productivity, creativity, and enhanced morale depend not only on the presence of diverse viewpoints and perspectives about the task, but also upon the effective management of the conflict that arises due to these forms of diversity, as well as the smooth implementation of the new and improved ideas' (Jehn 1998).

This is aligned with our own experiences. We noticed that a diversity-friendly culture encourages people to perceive differences as positive opportunities, rather than threats. An important element here is the prevailing view on how acceptable constructive challenge (or even conflict) is, as it influences both the learner's willingness to question what they are told and their ability to challenge themselves.

In organisations which lack this dimension of supportive climate, internal coaches, mentors or managers using coaching skills tend to favour developmental conversations with people who they see as like themselves. This instinct may be reflected in the quality of coaching and mentoring conversations and limit potential opportunities for growth.

GROWTH AND LEARNING ORIENTATION

Growth and learning orientation is about the organisation's commitment to continuous learning and growth, both on the individual and collective level. It is reflected in practices such as:

- **Development and career planning**. This relates to how an organisation aligns the aspirations of individuals with the opportunities potentially open to them.
- **Accountability for learning and development**. In a positive developmental climate, people take responsibility for their own development, as well as the development of others.
- **Learning and development strategy**. How supportive of learning and development is the business strategy? Is it narrow and inflexible, or systemic and dynamic? Where do coaching and mentoring fit in and how serious are the organisation's leaders about creating a coaching and mentoring culture?
- **Resources**. The past and present investment in creating the underpinning for coaching and mentoring, for example, training, online support and promotion of coaching and mentoring by enterprise leaders.

Table 3.2 illustrates coaching culture supportive climate dimensions and their key indicators.

Table 3.2 Supportive climate dimensions and key indicators

Supportive Climate Dimensions	Key Indicators
Encouragement for taking initiative	Making mistakes and learning from them is generally viewed positively.
	Making suggestions for new or different ways of doing things is encouraged.
	More responsibility is given freely to people, provided that they are on top of their basic job and suggest new things they would like to work on.
	People feel supported in experimenting and innovating.
	When delegating, managers give people sufficient space and authority to carry the tasks through to completion.
	Generally, people are considered to be capable to perform well when given a chance and the right support.
	Management gives a clear and compelling direction while allowing people to define their own way of getting things done.
Trust and ability to have honest conversations	It's generally okay to say what you think.
	It's generally safe to admit weaknesses.
	There is a culture of giving and receiving honest feedback.
	What people say is congruent with what they do.
	People feel respected and valued.
	People at all levels perceive that they are treated fairly.
	People have confidence in their leader's vision for the future.
Diversity and constructive challenge	In general, there is a culture of valuing diversity.
	Managers often seek different opinions and perspectives when making decisions.
	Teams are created in a way that ensures sufficient diversity in terms of experience, personality and other factors that stimulate creativity.

	People often question what they are told and use their critical skills to evaluate the situation on their own.
	People constructively challenge the status quo.
	On most occasions, people can leverage the inevitable tension and pressure created by dissenting views in order to drive more creative outcomes.
	Team members handle style and preference differences with awareness and flexibility.
Learning and growth orientation	Managers who don't develop their teams are less likely to get promoted.
	Responsibility for personal and career development is usually shared between the individual, the organisation, their manager and their colleagues.
	Managers are trained in holding developmental conversations.
	People are generally encouraged to take time out for self-development.
	Training and development budgets are protected, even when money is tight.
	Coaching is seen mainly as a developmental opportunity rather than as a remedial process.
	People generally see coaching and mentoring as both relevant and valuable for them personally.

TO INVEST OR NOT TO INVEST?

Figure 3.2 shows a diagram which is the result of combining coaching culture **relevance** with **supportive climate**. The purpose of analysing these two factors in combination is to estimate the expected returns on investment in a coaching culture, as well as a possible course of action.

Figure 3.2 Expected returns matrix

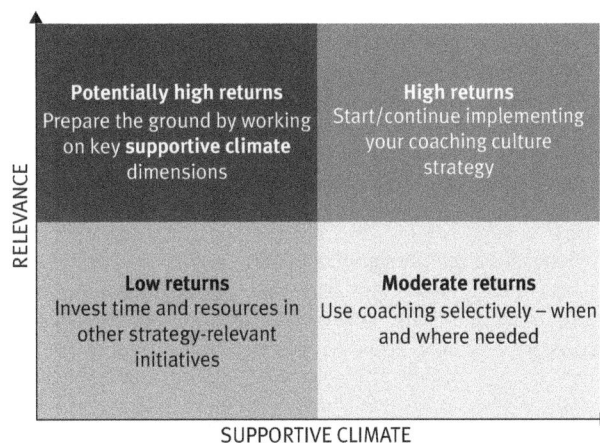

AREA OF LOW RETURNS (LOW PERCEIVED RELEVANCE, LOW SUPPORTIVE CLIMATE)

In this area, both the perceived **relevance** and **supportive climate** for a coaching culture are low. Lack of a compelling business case for coaching combined with a non-supportive environment makes the efforts to create a coaching culture seem like they are doomed to fail. Broadly, there are two possible courses of action in this case:

- investing time and resources in other strategy-relevant initiatives
- undertaking a huge, if not potentially futile, task of identifying and demonstrating a compelling business case for a coaching culture, shifting key stakeholders' perceptions regarding **relevance** for developing a coaching culture and building up the **supportive climate** for a coaching culture.

The second option can be very time-and energy-consuming and the expected return on investment will probably be pretty low. And while we are not advocating against it, we believe that there are possibly many other, better ways of using resources to achieve positive results in an organisation.

AREA OF MODERATE RETURNS (LOW PERCEIVED RELEVANCE, HIGH SUPPORTIVE CLIMATE)

When the organisational context seems to be potentially supportive of coaching and mentoring but developing or strengthening a coaching culture across the organisation is not yet perceived as imperative for the business, we are in the area of moderate returns. This means that, if used selectively and in a focused way, coaching and mentoring can still produce positive results for individuals and, indirectly, for the organisation. An example would be offering executive coaching to a selected group of leaders or individuals transitioning into a new, more challenging role, or introducing a coaching team process to a selected team. These selective initiatives can serve as success stories that might shift perceptions regarding the usefulness of coaching in other parts of the organisation. This, in turn, can help the organisation to shift to the area of high returns with time.

AREA OF POTENTIALLY HIGH RETURNS (HIGH PERCEIVED RELEVANCE, LOW SUPPORTIVE CLIMATE)

In this case, it is clear that developing a coaching culture would make a big positive impact on the organisation's ability to deliver results. However, the **supportive climate** is still not there. There are probably a few significant constraints in the organisational context that can potentially hinder the effectiveness of coaching and mentoring initiatives. What we would recommend here is focusing on removing these constraints first, and improving the **supportive climate** (or at least working on them in parallel with the coaching initiatives). Again, when the constraints are removed or minimised, the organisation will be ready to move to the area of high returns.

AREA OF HIGH RETURNS (HIGH PERCEIVED RELEVANCE, HIGH SUPPORTIVE CLIMATE)

This is the area where there are no significant inhibitors to coaching culture growth. The business need for coaching is crystal-clear and the organisational context is highly supportive. In this case, the right course of action is to focus on developing and implementing a robust coaching strategy. We will talk about how to do this in the following chapters.

WHICH AREA ARE YOU IN RIGHT NOW?

In order to establish which quadrant an organisation (or a part of it) currently falls into, it is necessary to assess both **relevance** and **supportive climate**.

This assessment is not a solitary exercise and cannot possibly rely on anyone's individual perceptions or estimations. It is necessary to get opinions of key stakeholders as we are aiming to understand their perceptions regarding both factors.

An important point to make here is that while taking a holistic view and analysing the **relevance** and **supportive climate** for a coaching culture at the organisational level can be useful, the same approach can be used for smaller parts of an organisation, such as subsidiaries, departments or even smaller teams within a department.

GETTING INITIAL SUPPORT FROM KEY INFLUENCERS

Anyone who tries to bring about change in an organisation quickly realises that their ability to succeed will largely depend on the amount of commitment and active support coming from the key influencers in the organisation.

There is a wide range of factors that make key influencers' role pivotal in creating or strengthening a coaching culture, from their decision-making power and control over resource allocation to the attention that is paid to their views by others.

Anything that a key influencer says and, more importantly, does has significant visibility and is often perceived as a clear message of what is truly valued and important in the organisation.

For example, it is hard to imagine an organisation reaching the embedded, or even strategic, stage of a coaching culture while the CEO and their team follow the 'command and control' model of leadership, failing to recognise the strategic importance of developing a coaching culture within the organisation or lacking belief in the effectiveness of coaching.

The same is true on a smaller scale as well: it would be utterly unrealistic to expect widespread coaching behaviours in a team whose leader doesn't believe in coaching herself.

So how do you bring the key people on board? There are probably as many possible approaches as there are organisations. However, three key elements have consistently come up in the stories about how coaching culture efforts gained top-level support:

- clear business need
- starting small
- positive experiences with coaching.

CLEAR BUSINESS NEED

Articulating and communicating a clear business need for developing a coaching culture is linked to the **relevance** of a coaching culture discussed earlier in this chapter. It is about demonstrating how the business will benefit from coaching and mentoring initiatives.

There is nothing more compelling for a CEO, a senior executive, a manager or a team leader than a clear answer to the questions, such as: 'What's in it for our business/division/department/team?' or 'How specifically will investing in developing a coaching culture enable us to reach our key objectives?'

Based on our research around what tends to work, we have developed a series of questions that can help in articulating a business need for a coaching culture. They are included in Exhibit 3.1, which illustrates an example of articulating a business need for a coaching culture in a hospitality business.

Exhibit 3.1 Example of articulating a business need for a coaching culture in a hospitality business

Questions	Answers from an organisation in hospitality business
What are the key business priorities of the organisation/division/department/team?	The key priority for our business is to create an exceptional experience for our guests while maintaining operational excellence and cost optimisation.

What will need to happen for the organisation/division/department/team to be able to achieve these objectives?	We need to be able to engage *all* our employees in finding the best way to improve operational effectiveness, reduce unnecessary costs and take responsibility for creating an outstanding experience for our guests. This can only be done with a bottom–up approach.
What are the skills, principles, attitudes, beliefs and mindsets that people will need to develop and display in order to support the required change?	Our team members will need to see themselves as those who are responsible for creating an outstanding experience for our guests at the front line. They will have to become more proactive and leverage their familiarity with daily operations to find solutions to operational challenges. They will have to support less experienced colleagues and bring them up to speed, so that everyone is equally well prepared to serve our guests in the best possible way. Our team leaders will have to be more effective in engaging all the team members in finding these solutions and taking responsibility for guest experience. They will need to develop the skills required to help people learn how to find their own solutions, challenge the status-quo and think for themselves. They will need to start seeing themselves as people-developers and enablers rather than agents of success.
How will developing a coaching and mentoring culture support the organisation/division/department/team in developing the necessary skills, attitudes, beliefs and mindsets?	A coaching culture is a culture which encourages people to question assumptions and keep an open mind in order to explore solutions to problems and challenges. It's a culture where people's potential is being tapped into and where everyone is being adequately challenged and supported to achieve extraordinary results. Coaching creates a thinking space where people can come up with their own solutions and suggestions for improving operational effectiveness, cost optimisation and guest experience.

There is a danger of approaching this line of questioning in a linear way and treating it as a tick-box exercise. In order to be effective, the process of articulating and communicating the business need for a coaching culture requires an ongoing exchange of opinions amongst the key stakeholders – a dialogue rather than dictat.

STARTING SMALL

Launching a new initiative has always been a hit or miss situation for most companies. A study by Towers Watson (2013) indicates that as few as 25% of change initiatives succeed. It's not surprising, therefore, that top management is rarely willing to commit to a significant investment in creating a coaching culture from the start.

Instead of pushing hard for large-scale and far-reaching coaching initiatives, effective organisations tend to focus on the 'low-hanging fruit' first. A lot of companies we interviewed for the book or worked with started growing their coaching culture organically. This often involved incorporating a couple of hours of coaching training in their management development programmes, and then gradually increasing that time, followed by integrating diagnostic tools and offering coaching sessions by professional coaches.

If managed well, this approach can be effective in taking an organisation from the nascent to tactical stage of coaching culture development. It builds the necessary understanding of coaching and its benefits at the grass-root level.

It also helps to identify those individuals who have a natural talent for developing others and to highlight those parts of the organisation where coaching works and brings tangible results. Identifying, supporting and documenting various success stories related to coaching and mentoring can be a powerful tool in the advocacy for coaching culture and achieving top management support for further coaching and mentoring initiatives.

Also, this slow, incremental increase in activities aimed at developing a coaching culture tends to build a firm foundation for larger-scale initiatives later on.

POSITIVE EXPERIENCE

We found that in terms of trying to get executive buy-in, no amount of statistics or evidence of coaching effectiveness can achieve results as powerful as providing people with an opportunity to experience the impact of coaching for themselves.

A study carried out by the Center for Leadership Development and Research at Stanford Graduate School of Business (2013) found that only one-third of CEOs receive coaching or outside counselling, although nearly all of them want it. This study makes it evident that senior executives are more open than ever to engaging in supportive relationships, such as coaching and mentoring.

In view of these findings, it is not surprising that one particular story consistently showed up in a lot of interviews for this book: an executive – very often a CEO – is offered coaching, takes the opportunity and finds the experience so powerful that he or she becomes a sponsor of coaching in their organisation.

However, as usual, there is a flipside to it: we also heard stories of coaching relationships that were not very successful and created major reputation damage for coaching. This highlights the importance of ensuring the quality of coaching that takes place in an organisation. We cover this subject in detail in Part 3 of the book.

THE ABCs OF COACHING CULTURE PLANNING AND IMPLEMENTATION

Building a strong and sustainable coaching culture requires a compelling vision, strategic thinking and a significant amount of effort and dedication to follow through (or adapt, as deemed necessary).

Peter Hawkins (2012) warns against the dangers of coaching culture strategy being 'just another policy document among hundreds of others in the organisation'. We agree with his view that coaching strategy needs to be firmly rooted in the organisational context, developed in a collaborative way with the purpose of supporting the overall learning and development strategy and organisational performance objectives.

So what is a coaching culture strategy?

Our view is that it is an integrated and planned approach to:

- building organisational competence to coach internally
- integrating the coaching approach, mindset and skills into day-to-day business activities and interactions with internal and external stakeholders
- using external coaching and mentoring resources with high efficacy
- achieving value for money from both internally and externally resourced coaching.

Documenting the steps successful organisations tend to follow in designing coaching culture strategy, we have outlined a process, depicted in Figure 3.3.

A — ASPIRATIONS

The first step of the process is about creating the vision of a coaching culture and how it will support organisational purpose, mission, vision and key objectives. It is about answering questions such as: 'What will a coaching culture do for us?' 'What does success look like?' and 'What will be different when we reach the desired stage of coaching culture development?'

Figure 3.3 The ABC-DE of coaching culture planning and interpretation

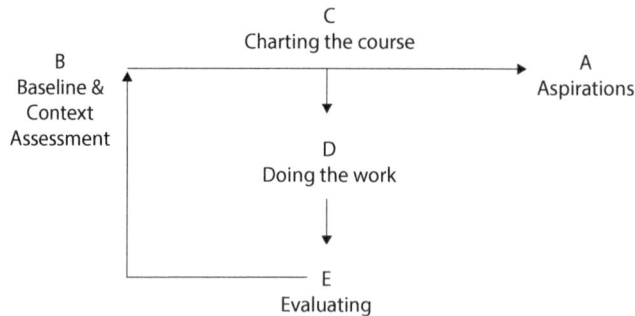

B — BASELINE AND CONTEXT ASSESSMENT

The second step involves taking a systemic view: looking at current coaching and mentoring practices, as well as other HR processes and examining how they could be linked to coaching. Contextual analysis is important to understand the current culture and how congruent a coaching culture is going to be with the current one.

C — CHARTING THE COURSE

The third step involves drafting a coaching culture strategy in a way that is aligned with the wider organisational strategy and that serves the wider people development and organisational performance objectives. It is about identifying key objectives, milestones and actions that need to be taken towards the desired direction. This stage results in a plan which, at the minimum, includes roles, actions and timelines.

It would be easy to stop here and say that the strategy creation process is finished as soon as the resulting document is printed and signed. However, studies and experience show that coaching strategy creation is not a one-off event, but a dynamic and ongoing process. It requires continuous adaptation to suit the changing conditions and requirements of the business and the individuals within it. As Hawkins says: 'The strategy, like a good map, informs the journey at each stage, but strategy is a map of the territory, which, at best, is only half known. As the journey proceeds, the map has to be changed and redrawn' (Hawkins 2012).

Knowing that the process wouldn't be complete if we ended here, we added a D and an E to our ABC model.

D — DOING THE WORK

This is the implementation stage of a coaching culture strategy. It is also the stage where most strategic planning efforts fail. Literature quotes a number of possible causes of failure in the implementation stage. As suggested in the white paper 'Dynamic strategy implementation: delivering on your strategic ambition', published by Deloitte University (2013), these causes of failure can be captured by the following headlines: translating strategy, adapting strategy and sustaining strategy.

We found that a crucial element that the implementation stage requires is a built-in learning mechanism that allows the organisation to understand what goes well and what doesn't go well. Without that mechanism, it is virtually impossible to be successful in a task as complex as culture transformation.

E – EVALUATION

The evaluation step is crucial, as it creates a vital feedback loop, allowing for course corrections and adaptation of coaching strategy. Successful companies tend to pilot important interventions first, identifying key drivers and barriers to coaching early on in the process. They regularly evaluate the effectiveness of their coaching initiatives. They also identify what Jerry Sternin called 'positive deviance', or 'bright spots'[2] – observable exceptions that produce results above the norm – and they learn from them, adjusting coaching strategy so that it includes the practices identified as highly successful.

The next chapters in this part of the book will go into more depth around each of the steps of the process.

WHO SHOULD BE INVOLVED IN THE COACHING CULTURE PLANNING PROCESS?

Our experience shows that, in many organisations, creating a coaching culture strategy remains strictly in the domain of HR. However, having recognised that instilling or strengthening a coaching culture only makes sense if it serves wider organisational objectives, it is clear that people outside of HR need to be involved in coaching culture planning as well.

So who specifically should be involved in coaching culture planning? The consensus is that it should be all stakeholders: the HR team, senior management sponsors, managers and professionals from within the organisation, and external advisors, if appropriate. There are many different ways of engaging these stakeholders in this process and we will refer to these varying approaches in the next chapters.

STORIES FROM THE FIELD

THE KEY STRATEGIC NEED FOR DEVELOPING A COACHING CULTURE IN SAVE THE CHILDREN

When asked about the key strategic need for developing a coaching culture, Shola Awolesi said: 'Our organisation has a very ambitious vision. We want to make a significant contribution to creating a world in which every child attains the right to survival, protection, development and participation. To achieve this, we need all hands on deck; everyone has to be able to contribute to the maximum of their capacity and to continuously develop their capabilities so that they can make an even bigger impact.

'Our work often involves interventions in crisis situations such as floods, famines, earthquakes and armed conflict and it can be very intense – emotionally and physically. People working under such conditions need a safe space, where they can reflect, recharge and regroup, and coaching provides such a space.

[2] Positive deviance is based on the observation that in every community there are certain individuals or groups whose uncommon behaviours and strategies enable them to find better solutions to problems than their peers, while having access to the same resources and facing similar or worse challenges.

'Since we've started using our network of volunteer executive coaches, we realised that coaching is an important enabler towards realising our vision and we are now looking at many different ways of growing a coaching culture within our organisation.'

CULTIVATING A COACHING LEADERSHIP CULTURE IN SCANIA

Contributed by Po Lindvall, MSc, PhD Candidate and EMCC-accredited Master Practitioner coach and mentor

The story below illustrates how Scania, driven by a clear business need, decided to invest in developing a coaching leadership culture.

Scania – the root of change

The change process initiated at Scania in 2000 was a response to low productivity and high costs. Interestingly, instead of pushing people to reach higher objectives or drastically cutting costs, Scania decided to focus on improving work processes.

The turning point in the change process can be best illustrated by what one of Scania's leaders commented on: 'We realised that instead of telling people what to do, we should listen more and ask for ideas – after all, the assemblers have all the experience and knowledge necessary to improve their work. . .'.

This signified a major mindset shift in Scania. The new way of thinking got full support and commitment from the top management and was the reason for a coaching-oriented dialogue becoming a way to communicate through the chassis plant (Lindvall 2005).

The involvement of co-workers in continuous improvements was inspired by 'the Toyota way' and subsequently modified to fit the Swedish culture. For example, the development of 'Lean' has originated from within, instead of being pushed top–down by experts. People were asked for their opinions and solutions for production and product improvements. As one of the employees commented: 'Today we own not just our problems but our solutions, in contrast to what it was like before, when nobody listened to what we had to say.'

An old Swedish tradition has come alive at Scania. 'When we adapted "The Toyota Way", we combined it with an old Swedish study circle methodology. It's a very good method to get people involved.' Interestingly, Toyota in Japan found it difficult to get their people to work well in the highly hierarchical system of their organisation, as the young generation demanded more participation. Consequently, Toyota turned to Scania to learn 'the Scania Way' (Pröckl, Ny Teknik 2009).

Creation of a coaching leadership culture

The coaching style of leadership has developed over time at Scania and is considered to be central to creating a continuous improvement or 'Lean' culture. Scania does share this learning with other 'Lean' leaders, such as Professor Daniel T. Jones (2009):

'I used to think that physical assets – product designs, facilities and equipment, IT systems, supply chains and distribution channels – are the biggest constraints to progress with Lean. But not so. In truth the biggest constraints in most businesses are the mental models and decision-making structures governing the behaviour of managers.'

The research at Scania showed that the change in leadership behaviours from a 'telling how to do something, to asking what we can do' presents a more effective decision-making model and has been central to the success achieved.

The results of a coaching leadership culture

Analysing the interviews and observations conducted on the assembly line indicated a clear correlation between employee satisfaction and the changes in leadership, participation in problem-solving and continuous improvements.

These changes also led to an increase in productivity, with a simultaneous decrease in sick leave and employee turnover. It is important to mention that the productivity increase was also due to implementing 'Lean' and having productivity experts present on the line for some years. Still, the improved leadership behaviours leading to daily dialogue and learning were identified as the most important contributor to the perceived improvements. The organisational metrics from 2001 and 2011 presented in Exhibit 3.2 show the level of impact that the changes in leadership and culture had.

Exhibit 3.2 Improvements achieved in Scania

	2000	2001	2011
Productivity	37 vehicles/day (800 workforce)	43 vehicles/day (800 workforce)	80 vehicles/day (1100 workforce)
Sick leave	9%	4.5%	3.3%
Employee turnover	35%	6%	4%

These results indicate that improvements in well-being and productivity are both strong and sustainable (maintained over time).

SUMMARY

In this chapter, we identified a number of preliminary conditions that need to be fulfilled for coaching culture development efforts to have a chance to bear fruits. These conditions are the relevance of coaching to wider organisational objectives, a climate that is supportive of coaching, initial support from key influencers, a dynamic strategy and active involvement of a variety of stakeholders in strategy creation.

Developing a coaching culture is not a panacea for all organisational ills. Moreover, it tends to require long-term commitment, which demands time, energy and valuable resources. Given the size of the investment, it is important to know that returns are going to be worth it.

?

FIELDWORK

Based on coaching culture **relevance** and **supportive climate** indicators, evaluate the **relevance** and **supportive climate** in your organisation or in an organisation that you are familiar with.

- Which quadrant of the Expected Returns Matrix (Figure 3.2) is the organisation in at the moment?
- Is it a good place to be to start or continue working on developing a coaching culture?
- If not, what actions could you take?

CHAPTER 4

Knowing Where You Want To Get To

'Would you tell me, please, which way I ought to go from here?
That depends a good deal on where you want to get to.
I don't much care where –
Then it doesn't matter which way you go.'
Lewis Carroll, Alice in Wonderland

OVERVIEW

In this chapter, we talk about 'knowing where you want to get to' – having a coaching culture vision and being clear about what success looks like. We define what a coaching culture vision is and examine why it is important to have one. We also look at what makes a coaching culture vision effective, who should be involved in its creation and how to achieve a shared vision that will have the power to mobilise the whole organisation.

In Chapter 3 we highlighted the importance of clear relevance of coaching to the organisation's ability to achieve its key strategic objectives. It is evident that for coaching initiatives to succeed, a coaching culture needs to be seen as a 'must' with a business imperative that is clear to key stakeholders. Most, if not all, organisations that have been successful in cultivating a coaching culture reflect on and identify that compelling 'why' for coaching early on in the process.

Interestingly, the term 'coaching culture' is hardly ever used in most organisations as they first introduce coaching. In the initial stages of coaching culture development, coaching is usually seen as a tool that can support other development initiatives, such as leadership development or succession planning, but there is little or no commitment to develop a coaching culture internally. It is usually not until it becomes evident that embedding coaching into everyday work would be beneficial that organisations start considering developing a coaching culture.

At that time (which typically coincides with reaching the strategic stage of coaching culture development), coaching sponsors and managers start considering developing some form of coaching culture vision.

WHAT IS A COACHING CULTURE VISION AND WHY IS IT IMPORTANT?

A coaching culture vision gives an organisation a vivid picture of what the future will look like when coaching culture achieves the embedded stage. It focuses on the direction without being too prescriptive about the specific route to take.

The purpose of a coaching culture vision is to energise and motivate people so that they are willing to set out on the journey and persevere in the face of difficulties experienced on the way. A coaching culture vision tells organisational stakeholders why they should let go of their current way of interacting with others and doing business and creates an appealing picture of the future, where coaching principles and practice play a crucial role. The better people understand the direction they are headed in, the easier it will be for them to buy into and focus on the strategic initiatives that support a coaching culture.

The importance of having a clear change vision has been stressed for decades by change management experts (Kanter et al 1992; Kotter 1995; Luecke 2003), who identify numerous benefits of articulating a powerful vision, such as:

- creative tension, which fuels culture change efforts and results from the desire to bridge the gap between the ideal and the current culture
- direction and purpose that enable the creation of an appropriate strategy
- alignment in setting and achieving objectives
- informing decisions and helping to solve dilemmas when navigating the change process

In spite of the wide consensus on the benefits of having a vision, we find that it is not uncommon for a coaching culture vision to be either non-existent or ambiguous and varied, with different versions and points of view being expressed by different people in the organisation.

Even when a coaching culture vision is an item on the organisation's people agenda, the invitation is usually extended only to a small circle of individuals who are involved in or support various coaching initiatives. As a consequence, the coaching culture vision is often clear exclusively to that group of individuals.

One of us witnessed an extreme example of this in a workshop, in an organisation that identified developing a coaching culture as one of its strategic objectives. When a senior executive (and one of the most passionate coaching champions in the organisation) expressed her frustration at the lack of shared coaching culture vision, her comment was met with intense disagreement on the part of HR. According to HR, the vision was there and it was very clear, the main challenge for the organisation being coaching culture strategy implementation.

Such disparity in perceptions can be a major limiting factor in an organisation's efforts to cultivate a coaching culture.

WHAT MAKES A COACHING CULTURE VISION EFFECTIVE?

Based on dozens of conversations which focused on identifying what works and what does not work when developing and communicating a coaching culture vision, we have been able to determine its key desired characteristics. It turns out that an effective coaching culture vision tends to be aligned, shared, clear and succinct, energising and evolving.

Table 4.1 Characteristics of an effective coaching culture vision

Characteristics	Description
Aligned	A coaching culture is not an end in itself – and a coaching culture vision needs to be aligned with the larger goals of the organisation. It helps when people involved in coaching culture vision creation have a good understanding of the organisation's mission, vision and strategic objectives.
Shared	For the maximum buy-in and support in the implementation of coaching culture strategy, it helps to involve a variety of stakeholders (not just the 'usual suspects', including HR and coaching sponsor) in ongoing dialogues regarding their expectations from the culture change. An effective coaching culture vision is a synthesis of conversations held with people across the organisation over a certain period of time. A shared coaching culture vision is one which people can fully understand and identify with.

Clear and succinct	In implementing a cultural change there is no room for ambiguity over the desired outcome. It is helpful to identify the main aspects of coaching culture, such as its visible manifestations, guiding principles, mindsets and beliefs. It is also important to be able to express that vision in a succinct way in the form of the vision statement. As John Kotter famously said in his HBR article 'Leading Change': 'If you can't communicate the vision to someone in five minutes or less and get a reaction that signifies both understanding and interest, you are not done' (Kotter 1995).
Energising	An effective coaching culture vision has emotional resonance, generates ongoing dialogue and gives a strong directional force to the organisation. It describes a future state that is aspirational while being achievable and realistic.
Evolving	As people engage with various modes of coaching and mentoring, adopt coaching principles and shift their mindsets, they will learn more about themselves and their organisation. New possibilities will emerge and the vision will evolve and change.

CREATING AN EFFECTIVE COACHING CULTURE VISION

While most organisations spend a lot of energy and time on creating the wider organisation's mission and vision, it is not always the case with coaching culture. In the vast majority of organisations that have a coaching culture vision, it was created and articulated by one of the senior leaders or a group of individuals, mostly consisting of HR, the executive sponsor and a handful of other stakeholders.

A popular format for defining the coaching culture vision is a workshop, where key stakeholders engage in a discussion and brainstorming on what will be different when the organisation achieves the desired stage of coaching culture.

Based on our observations of what successful organisations do, as well as the existing culture transformation literature, it is clear that investing in a careful design of a participative visioning process will pay significant dividends later on.

Figure 4.1 presents a suggested coaching culture visioning process.

Figure 4.1 Coaching culture visioning process

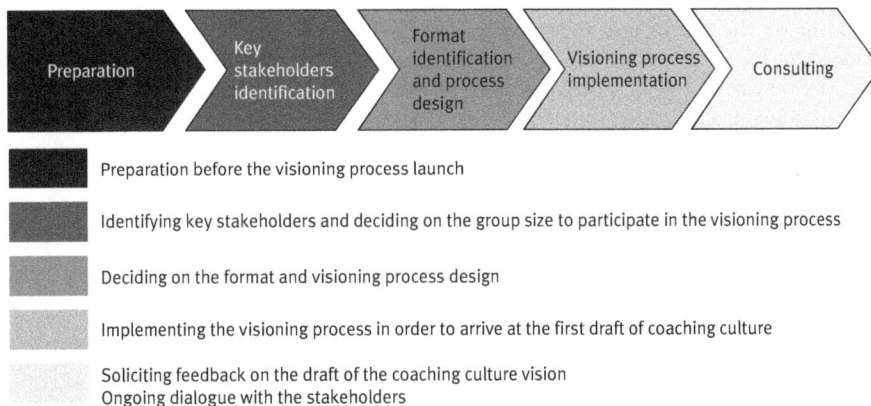

Preparation → Key stakeholders identification → Format identification and process design → Visioning process implementation → Consulting

Preparation before the visioning process launch

Identifying key stakeholders and deciding on the group size to participate in the visioning process

Deciding on the format and visioning process design

Implementing the visioning process in order to arrive at the first draft of coaching culture

Soliciting feedback on the draft of the coaching culture vision
Ongoing dialogue with the stakeholders

Preparation before visioning process launch

The person or the group of people driving the visioning process reflect on key issues to gain more clarity. Useful questions to reflect on are:

- Why do we want to create a coaching culture vision? What purpose will it serve? How will it be used?
- What do we hope to accomplish in the process?
- How can visioning improve existing coaching initiatives?

Identifying key stakeholders and deciding on the group size to participate in the visioning process

As in each stage of the coaching culture strategy process, identifying and successfully engaging key stakeholders will be one of the critical success factors. When thinking of who to invite to the table, it will be helpful to reflect on the following questions:

- Who are the most committed executive sponsors of coaching within the organisation?
- Who are the strongest, most respected voices in the organisation?
- Who is likely to be driving some of the future coaching initiatives?
- Who will be required to change the way they operate at work in order for the organisation to successfully embed a coaching approach and philosophy?
- Whose buy-in will be necessary for coaching culture efforts to be successful?
- What are the pros and the cons of having the 'whole system' vs 'cross-organisational committee' participating in the process?
- How many people is it realistic to involve in the process?

The 'whole system' approach focuses on ensuring that a significant number of the key stakeholders of coaching culture are present in the room and that the different voices of a 'whole system' are contributing. It stresses the value of diversity and encourages inviting large groups of people.

The 'cross-organisational committee' approach limits participation in the coaching culture visioning process only to a few representatives of key stakeholder groups.

Deciding on the format and visioning process design

Depending on an organisation's inclination towards 'cross-organisational committee' or the 'whole system' approach, as well as its desired level of co-creation and engagement, there is a wide spectrum of possible formats available, from a one-off workshop with a limited number of participants to a series of workshops and presentations involving a small or a large number of participants.

For example, Future Search (Weisbord and Janoff 1995), Real Time Strategic Change (Jacobs 1994), Visioning Conferences (Axelrod 1992) or Open Space Technology (Owen 1993) are just a few of the available tools to enable engaging large groups of people in the visioning process.

The flow and structure of the visioning process will largely depend on the chosen format. In one-off workshops with a limited number of participants, it is common to have a clear agenda and a facilitator, whereas large group events, such as Open Space, often use a blank wall in place of an agenda and rely on workshop participants to self-organise in discussion groups.

An important consideration in the process design can be the fact that not everyone works well in a group setting. In her book *Quiet: The Power of Introverts in a World That*

Can't Stop Talking, Susan Cain advocates taking a different approach to enable introverts to make a valuable contribution in the world that has been designed for extroverts (Cain 2012). Inviting people to reflect on their personal vision for a coaching culture before they engage in discussing it with others can be beneficial, especially for introverts. A series of questions (see examples in this chapter's 'Fieldwork' section) can guide individuals in their reflection and allow them to come prepared for the group discussion in the workshop.

VISIONING PROCESS IMPLEMENTATION

Implementing the visioning process to arrive at the first draft of a coaching culture vision

Irrespective of the shape and form the coaching culture visioning process takes, a capable coordinator and facilitator are always a valuable asset. The visioning process requires someone who is skilled in drawing people in, asking powerful questions and creating a safe environment where people feel comfortable to express themselves and share their aspirations. It is also important to ensure that any outputs are carefully documented for future reference.

As a minimum, the outcomes of the visioning process should be a general coaching culture vision statement. Additionally, it is useful to have a more detailed description, following the three levels of our coaching culture model.

Visible manifestations of coaching culture

- What processes and structures will we have in place?
- What specific skills will people develop?
- How will people behave and interact with others?

Core principles

- What unwritten rules that enable a coaching approach in the workplace will people live by?
- How will these principles be safeguarded and by whom?
- What will be our coaching philosophy?

Beliefs and mindsets

- What will be people's beliefs about abilities, growth and potential?
- What will be people's attitude towards performance?
- What will be the most common assumptions people make?

CONSULTING

Soliciting feedback and input on the draft coaching culture vision from the rest of the organisation and ongoing dialogue with the stakeholders

Ideally, the coaching culture vision should resonate with the whole organisation. A good way to check that is to consult with the rest of the organisation. Quite a few organisations we worked with decided to create their vision statement in a cross-organisational committee format and then to test the statement with various groups of employees within the organisation. An example that we describe in more detail in the 'Stories from the field' section of this chapter is EY.

When testing the vision with the rest of the organisation, it is useful to read the coaching culture vision statement to the respondent group (or present it on a slide) and then to ask a series of questions, such as:

- How did the vision statement make you feel?
- Which keywords can you recall? What do they signify?
- Can you identify with that vision? If the answer is 'no', what would have to change for you to be able to identify with it?

- How will you feel when we achieve this vision?
- Do you feel compelled to support the efforts to achieve that vision?

STORIES FROM THE FIELD

The process for an effective coaching culture vision creation which we outlined in this chapter can result in radically different and yet equally successful approaches. In some cases, the vision for coaching is initially drafted by an executive sponsor and it becomes a starting point for an ongoing dialogue about the desired future of coaching within the organisation. In other cases, as in EY, the vision is created by a group of people who then proceeded to share it with the rest of the organisation to gain buy-in and engagement.

What is common in all the successful cases that we have seen is that the vision, irrespective of whether initially drafted by an individual or a group of people, is eventually shared and owned by a significant number of stakeholders.

DEVELOPING A COACHING CULTURE VISION IN EY[1]

EY's Vision 2020 is their business strategy to help them become the leading global professional services firm. Investing in the development of EY people is fundamental to achieving this. EY's promise to its people is: 'Whenever you join, however long you stay, the exceptional EY experience lasts a lifetime.'

This promise is achieved, in part, through EY's vision to develop a coaching culture. The investment in coaching was agreed upon across the firm as a critical pillar in the EYU global career development framework. Some examples of how different parts of EY are delivering coaching to achieve this vision are provided throughout this book, specifically for the Americas and the UK and Ireland (UK&I), who are particularly advanced in their coaching practices.

How EY in the UK and Ireland developed its coaching culture vision and brought the senior leadership team on board

To develop a vision for what this coaching culture could feel like in EY UK&I, Nicki Hickson, Director of Coaching at EY UK&I, worked with a cross-section of senior managers in the business to brainstorm potential benefits and results when EY UK&I achieved their coaching culture goals.

The outcomes of that brainstorming were tested with the leadership team for all regions outside of London. The leadership team was asked to imagine what it would feel like if the story being told was a reality. The leadership team found this to be particularly powerful, given the focus on behaviours and the level of detail, enabling them to fully step into the experience and imagine what it would feel like to achieve the vision. The result of that experience was that all the members of the leadership team committed to being coached themselves. They also gave the go-ahead for the team to select a small number of new partners to be supported through their transition into the partnership through coaching. EY UK&I's internal coaching practice has grown from there.

Below is the EY UK&I coaching culture vision, as it was originally presented to the EY UK&I leadership team.

---

[1] Previously known as Ernst & Young.

The EY UK&I coaching vision

- We are at the end of fiscal year XY and the celebrations have just begun as our results show that we have reached our target revenues. We are also known as the fastest to market and the fastest growing of the Big 4. As we reflect on how we achieved this, it's clear that coaching has played a key role.
- We exist to realise the potential of our people, ourselves and our clients and we don't just talk about it anymore, we actually do it. The coaching culture that has evolved over the last few years ensures that all people are able to and want to have coaching conversations.
- There is now a genuine, long-lasting and sustainable programme for coaching from joining to leaving. Coaching is for everyone at all stages of their careers and seniority.
- In fact, EY UK&I is seen as a case study by coaching experts.
- The EY UK&I leadership team demonstrates coaching skills, as do all business leaders.
- A tipping point was when the partners transformed their approach to coaching as a way of being with people and clients, as opposed to optional intervention. They are true advocates of transformational coaching.
- All partners develop people and business (it's not just a skill; it's also a value that people hold).
- But this is not just about partners; ALL staff see coaching as a must-do.
- Coaching is a part of our employment contract; people expect to coach and be coached. They recognise that they don't only get monetary benefits as they move through the firm but that they accelerate in their personal development quicker than their peers at other firms.
- Coaching occurs downwards, sideways, is starting to happen upwards and this is happening cross-service line and with our clients.
- Coaching is embedded in our people process. People are recognised and rewarded for coaching and it is fully understood that progression through the firm relies on people's ability to coach and be coached as much as other metrics.
- In fact, coaching conversations occur at all times, from formal performance meetings to general meetings to coffee machine chats – every contact with someone else is recognised as a potential coaching moment. These opportunities are not lost anymore.
- We haven't lost our ability to be directive but we have much better judgement of when to use a directive style and when not to.
- Our people use their enhanced questioning and listening skills to benefit the people around them, including staff, clients and the wider community. Our people have become advocates of the EY coaching culture and improved retention levels and people scores reflect this.
- Our clients have noticed the change: they comment that the EY people they interact with listen to what they say and are not afraid to ask challenging questions. They see EY people as a sounding board to discuss issues they face and then help to solve them. And what they all want to know is how we manage to develop such talented people so quickly. This is regularly reflected in client care feedback plus there is increased client retention as a result of the enhanced relationships created.
- Preparation for all meetings is improved. Consultation has always been an EY strength but previously mainly on technical issues; we now consult and give or receive coaching in advance of client meetings and sales meetings and not just about content but behaviours.
- But this wasn't the result of a fanfare launch; it was a real commitment to a long-lasting, sustainable programme, and not a fad or an initiative. The EY UK&I

leadership team took a deep breath and was prepared to commit to this over a long period and not take a short-term view. They held their nerve throughout, even when initially the benefit was not clear, and should be applauded for doing so. The established coaching culture fundamentally underpins how we realise the potential of our people, ourselves and our clients.

SUMMARY

Investing in developing a coaching culture vision can pay significant dividends along the way. A good coaching culture vision is fully aligned with the wider organisational vision and objectives and shared by the majority of stakeholders. It is also clear and succinct, energising and flexible enough to evolve with the changing needs of the business and increasing the organisation's maturity. Organisations that create a coaching culture vision corresponding to most of these characteristics tend to benefit from higher levels of buy-in and easier coaching strategy implementation.

Coming up with a compelling coaching culture vision requires employing a well-thought-through visioning process which needs to be tailored to an organisation's needs. Company culture, available resources and wider organisational context are all factors to take into consideration when deciding on which path to follow in developing a coaching culture vision.

?

FIELDWORK

Reflection

Reflect on your organisation or an organisation that you are familiar with:

- Who are the main stakeholders you would involve in developing the coaching culture vision? Why?
- Which format of visioning seems to be most appropriate for the organisation? Why?

Individual visioning exercise: 'If we had a coaching culture . . .'

Cast your mind into the future and imagine that you have achieved success in developing a coaching culture in your organisation. On entering your workplace, talking to people and observing their behaviours, you notice that things are visibly different, indicating that coaching is deeply embedded within your organisational systems.

Describe what is different by answering all or some of the following questions:

- What does the office look like? Are there any artefacts that indicate a coaching culture? If yes, what are they?
- What is the level of energy that you perceive? How would you describe it?
- How are people feeling?
- What are people thinking?
- What makes you feel most proud?
- What are the key mindsets, beliefs and principles that drive people's behaviour?
- How do people behave when faced with challenges? What support do they get?
- What are the skills that people have mastered? In which contexts are these skills used and how?

CHAPTER 5

What's Your Starting Point and How Will You Measure Progress?

'Face the facts of being what you are, for that is what changes what you are.'
Soren Kirkegaard

OVERVIEW

In this chapter, we discuss the importance of establishing a baseline for coaching culture creation as well as having clear means of measuring progress. We begin the chapter by answering the question: 'Why is it so critical to know your starting point when striving to create a coaching culture?' We then explore which pieces of the puzzle are necessary for a sufficient picture of that starting point, and how this picture will inform decisions when charting the course towards a coaching culture vision. We also provide a number of useful tools to measure coaching effectiveness and culture transformation progress.

WHY PERFORM BASELINE AND CONTEXT ASSESSMENT?

As described in Chapter 4, 'knowing where you want to get to' is key in setting the direction for a coaching culture. However, having a compelling vision alone is not sufficient to create a coaching culture strategy. Before any actions are identified, agreed on and implemented, it is necessary to have a critical look at the current reality, something that we refer to as baseline and context assessment.

What emerges from juxtaposing current reality with the vision for a coaching culture is a 'gap': it becomes clearer what systems, practices, skills and behaviours are still not there and need to be developed over time. A general observation we made is that all too often coaching culture strategies are created with a strong focus on that 'gap' and the resulting 'deficiencies', rather than on the existing strengths and the potential that can be tapped into. Good baseline and context assessment focuses both on what is and what is not there and leads to a well-balanced strategic plan to build new strengths by capitalising on the existing ones.

The purpose of baseline and context assessment for a coaching culture is threefold:

- taking a snapshot of the wider cultural context
- establishing the starting point against which progress can be measured
- recognising the potential drivers and barriers of the desired culture transformation.

TAKING A SNAPSHOT OF THE WIDER CULTURAL CONTEXT

Legge has used a metaphor of 'riding a wave' to explain transforming culture: 'The best the surf-rider can do is to understand the pattern of currents and winds that shape and direct the waves. He/she may then use them to stay afloat and steer in the desired path. But this is not the same as changing the basic rhythms of the ocean' (Legge 1995, p207).

Just as understanding patterns of currents and winds is critical for a surfer, taking a snapshot of the wider cultural context is a necessary preparation for coaching culture strategists who want to keep their coaching initiatives afloat and steer them in the direction of their vision.

Obviously, culture is a vastly complex, multi-dimensional phenomenon; it is often not consistent throughout an organisation and can include a number of sub-cultures. To capture all these nuances, it can be helpful to use one of the many available culture assessment tools or to conduct focus groups.

Following the snapshot (or the series of snapshots) of the wider cultural context comes data analysis that aims at identifying patterns, common themes as well as positive and negative deviances that can be observed within the system.

Such data analysis gives invaluable insights into which 'waves' to ride and which to avoid in your efforts to strengthen a coaching culture within your organisation.

VARIOUS LEVELS OF MEASUREMENT

Establishing the starting point is about identifying where the individuals, teams and the organisation as a whole are currently in relation to coaching. It serves as a point of reference, against which progress will be measured in the future.

There are measurement systems operating at three levels that can be used for the purpose of identifying the starting point and measuring progress:

- macro
- meso
- micro.

At the macro-level, organisations can measure coaching culture overall and assess how much progress is being made. At the meso-level, organisations can evaluate the effectiveness of certain coaching initiatives, identify which ones are particularly effective and which need to be modified, improved or dropped. At the micro-level, individual line managers, and internal and external coaches can obtain feedback on their coaching skills and behaviours.

It is possible to use a combination of all three levels of measurement in order to perform a coaching culture audit. The results of such an audit provide a reliable baseline against which coaching culture progress can be monitored at each stage of strategy implementation. Rigorous measurement of progress allows an organisation to course-correct when needed and demonstrate tangible evidence of improvement.

RECOGNISING POTENTIAL DRIVERS AND BARRIERS

A snapshot of the wider cultural context, as well as establishing the starting point, usually sheds some light on what might be the potential drivers and barriers towards the desired culture change. Identifying both barriers and drivers tends to be a valuable preparation for the coaching culture strategy session(s). Table 5.1 gives a few typical examples of drivers and barriers towards creating a coaching culture.

Table 5.1 Examples of drivers and barriers towards creating a coaching culture

Drivers	Barriers
Coaching is well integrated with other HR systems, such as talent and performance management.	Coaching is not integrated with other HR systems.
There are strong coaching champions among senior executives.	Senior executives haven't bought into coaching.

There is a well-established and high-quality pool of internal and external coaches.	Well-qualified internal or external coaches are not readily available.
Coaching is considered as something desirable, or even as a reward.	Coaching is seen as a remedial activity to correct poor performance.
There is a good understanding of what coaching is and how it works.	People are not clear on what coaching is or how it works.
There are resources available to develop coaching skills among internal coaches and managers and leaders.	Resources are scarce or unknown.
People are willing to try new ways of working and relating with others.	People are set in their ways of working and operating in the work environment.
There is a climate of trust and people generally feel that they can have open conversations.	People mistrust each other or the management.
People understand the potential benefits of coaching.	People are not clear on the benefits of coaching.
People are encouraged to take initiative.	Taking initiative is limited and leadership style is highly controlling.
Diversity and constructive challenge are valued.	People put unanimity and harmony above innovation or excellence.
There is a widely held expectation that people will continuously grow and develop.	Growth and development are not perceived to be a top priority.

COACHING CULTURE AUDIT

A good coaching culture audit provides an organisation with a snapshot of the wider cultural context, a clear starting point for the culture change and identification of potential drivers and barriers towards the desired change. It is an investment worth making and it will pay dividends along the way.

We suggest the following steps to perform an effective coaching culture audit:

- putting together the audit project team
- audit implementation
- data analysis, report and recommendations.

PUTTING TOGETHER THE AUDIT PROJECT TEAM

Performing a coaching culture audit can prove to be a complex and demanding task and usually requires a dedicated project team to design and implement it, analyse the data and make recommendations that fit the existing culture and build on strengths. Testa and Sipe (2013) suggest a combination of executives from various areas of the organisation paired with an organisational development researcher, who would guide the efforts, minimise bias and ensure that the generated results are valid.

While having an organisational development consultant work with an organisation on the coaching culture audit can be of great value, it is important that the internal project team is well suited to the task as well. A critical factor to consider is diversity – inviting members representing different parts of the organisation and different tenures can be key. This, as Testa and Sipe note, will allow for multiple viewpoints and prevent the emergence of groupthink (Testa and Sipe 2013). Moreover, audit project team members should meet the following criteria:

- be familiar with coaching and your organisation's coaching culture vision
- have a good understanding of organisation's wider mission, vision and strategic objectives
- be perceived as trustworthy by their colleagues and have respect for the confidentiality of the auditing process
- have good organisational skills.

AUDIT PREPARATION AND DESIGN

An extensive amount of data is normally needed to understand the coaching culture and coaching behaviours. In the coaching culture audit preparation phase, the audit team needs to discuss and agree on issues such as:

- what levels we want our measurement to operate at (macro, meso, micro)
- what will be the right mix of auditing tools
- how to customise the surveys and other tools and what specific questions to ask
- who should be approached to take part and how many people should be involved in the research
- what specific times and locations will be appropriate.

Getting the right mix of tools

To get the best out of your audit, you first need to determine the right combination of tools. A coaching culture audit can consist of a number of elements, such as:

- a culture diagnostic tool
- a sample of individual assessments by coachees on themselves, their team leaders/ coaches and their teams
- a sample of individual assessments by team leaders on their own coaching performance
- a cross-section (horizontal and vertical) questionnaire relating to organisational issues
- a series of focus group semi-structured interviews
- one-to-one interviews with top management
- an impact or ROI study of one or more coaching initiatives currently taking place in the organisation.

We share a number of tools that can be used in a coaching culture audit in the 'Tools and templates' section of this chapter (Exhibits 5.1–5.7).

Data from the above diagnostics, questionnaires, interviews and studies can be valuable in establishing:

- the wider culture context in which coaching will need to grow
- what kind of coaching takes place on day-to-day basis
- how confident people feel about the coaching process
- how embedded (if at all) the basic coaching behaviours are
- how coaching initiatives impact the business, bottom line or what is their return on investment
- what the perceived drivers and obstacles towards the coaching culture vision are.

The same tools can be used subsequently to assess progress towards a coaching culture.

Demographics

An initial decision is how widely to audit. Issuing questionnaires to everyone in the organisation would establish the big picture and help identify local 'hot spots' of good and bad practice. However, a whole-company exercise is likely to be relatively expensive and time-consuming to analyse. It is important to strike the right balance between scope and expedience.

Picking the right people and deciding on the appropriate size of respondent and participant group can be a daunting task. A useful rule of thumb for surveys is:

- 5–10% of the employees in general
- 20–50% of the top 100
- 50% of the HR team
- 50% of trade union representatives, if any.

The number of focus groups and employees involved will greatly depend on the size of your organisation and the organisational structure.

There are many different approaches to select participants for focus groups. Some organisations use the demographic categories (length of service in the organisation, department, etc), while others run focus groups for departments or groups where 'hot spots' have been identified. There are also organisations which engage each directorate/department in the process.

When deciding on the composition of each focus group, it's important to ask the question: 'Are there any factors that could inhibit a discussion in this group?' For example, when a group is made up of employees of very different grade or authority levels, lower-ranking employees may not feel comfortable enough to express their views. The same problem might occur in groups where employees are incompatible with one another for other reasons.

Key points to keep in mind when picking participants of focus groups:

- The optimum size is 8–12 participants.
- People should feel comfortable together.
- Managers and their team members should not be in the same group.

AUDIT IMPLEMENTATION

Our recommendation would be to use a range of methods focusing on a variety of areas in the coaching culture audit and ensuring that the data comes from multiples sources. Implementing diagnostics, surveys, focus groups and interviews or impact and ROI studies can be a complex task, requiring excellent organisational skills. The role of the project manager and the project team is to ensure that things run smoothly and are done in an efficient and effective manner.

While focus groups and interviews can be a very useful source of information on current coaching culture, especially if combined with survey results, they require the most skill and time. We offer an example of a template for a focus group that describes its process and requirements in Exhibit 5.1.

In addition, we would like to stress the importance of having a skilled facilitator or interviewer. A particularly important skill of those who conduct focus groups and interviews is the ability to explore and inquire in a non-judgemental and non-threatening manner.

DATA ANALYSIS, REPORT AND RECOMMENDATIONS

The last step of the audit is analysing and interpreting the collected data, crafting a report and making recommendations for the possible next steps. As the report and recommendations will provide the basis for coaching culture strategy and plan, they need to be both detailed and forceful. An example of a table of contents of a coaching culture audit is presented in Exhibit 5.7.

While data analysis might seem like quite a straightforward process, there is a significant possibility of bias; therefore, care should be taken in how the data is being handled and interpreted by the audit team. Again, collaborating with a professional organisational development consultant or researcher can be of great help here.

To ensure reliable and objective results, it is advisable to follow these guidelines:

- Look for data and themes on all three levels of our coaching culture model: visible manifestations, core principles, as well as beliefs and mindsets.
- Both positive and negative observations should be used to seek patterns and themes. What you want to identify is not just what does not work, but also what already does!
- Only something that emerges from multiple sources of data can be considered a theme or a pattern. Conclusions should not be drawn based on a single occurrence or observation.
- Observations and data should be discussed in a non-judgemental manner. None of the audit team members should feel inhibited to point out what they have observed during the data analysis process.

TOOLS AND TEMPLATES

In this section, you will find a number of coaching culture audit tools and templates. While they can be used in their original version, we suggest customising them to the needs of your organisation.

Exhibit 5.1 Template for a structured interview/focus group

Focus group duration	120 minutes
Size of groups	8–12 people
Group composition	Coherent groups – ideally relatively homogenous in terms of where they work and their hierarchical level
Preparation	Prepare people for the focus group with a short description in writing about what the session aims to achieve and introduce the facilitation team.
	Prepare a slide or slides with coaching culture survey(s) data to present to and discuss with the participants.
Logistics	Book a reasonably private room.
	Arrange chairs in a circle, with no tables, so that people can have eye contact with everyone and interact.
	Have flip-charts and markers available.
	Allow at least half an hour between focus groups to make a first review of the session notes and any background on the group to come.
Facilitation	Two facilitators, one acting as a moderator of the discussion and the other one as a note-taker. Both facilitators should be prepared to perform either role, in case it becomes necessary to switch roles at some point.
Opening/ introduction (5 minutes)	Open the session with a restatement of why they are there. Explain that the session has three parts. In the first, you will explore with them a number of general themes. In the second, they are going to coach the organisation, using each other as proxies. Finally, you will ask them to discuss the implications of some specific results from the surveys.
Group discussion (45 minutes)	Have there been occasions recently when you would have appreciated some 'just-in-time' skills input, constructive challenge or someone to talk something through with?
	Would coaching have been an appropriate way to provide this?

	Did you receive sufficient coaching when you needed it?
	What did your team leader do to ensure you got the coaching you needed? What could/should s/he have done?
	What did you do to ensure you got the coaching you needed? What could/should you have done?
	What do you think are the main barriers to coaching in your workplace?
	How would you overcome those barriers, if you had the authority to do so?
Group discussion (20 minutes)	Put up your organisation's definition and/or vision of coaching culture on a flip chart (see Chapter 1, Table 1.2 for various definitions).
	Based on this definition/vision, to what extent do you think that this organisation has a coaching culture?
Coaching the organisation (20 minutes)	In this session, split the group into twos or threes. In each subgroup, one or more of the participants is going to represent the organisation. The others will coach them through the question:
	What do we need most to develop a coaching culture?
Review of the survey data and root-cause analysis (30 minutes)	Talk the group through the main points of coaching culture survey data. Ask them to give their opinions about what lies behind the score for each item. Use the technique of the 'why tree' to get to the root cause of the issues.
	If there are a lot of issues to explore, it might be a good idea to split participants into smaller groups, which will focus on two or three issues.
Closing	Close the session promptly on 120 minutes and thank the group for their participation and inputs.
	Let participants know what the next steps are going to be, for example:
	• how results will be summarised, interpreted and reported • what other specific actions will be taken • the timescales for reporting and subsequent action.

Exhibit 5.2 One-to-one interview with top management

Purpose of the interviews	Engaging top management in the coaching culture dialogue and gaining their understanding/commitment
	Demonstrating to other employees that top managers are taking coaching culture seriously
	Identifying the difference in perspective between top management and the rest of the organisation
	Setting the scene for subsequent feedback to top management
	Providing greater insights into issues relating to coaching within the context of strategic priorities
Demographics	Aim to do at least four or five interviews at the very top and eight to ten at the next two layers down.
Preparation & logistics	Send an invitation accompanied by an email informing of the reasons for the interview and how it fits into the larger picture.
	Stages of coaching culture development assessment questionnaire to be completed by the executives before the interview.
	Book a reasonably private room.

	Allow at least 15 minutes between interviews to make a first review of notes.
Interview duration	60 minutes
Format	A semi-structured interview built around the questions below. The more the interview feels like a coaching session in its own right, the more it is likely to promote the concept of the coaching culture.
Suggested questions	Can you describe the reasons that made you rate the organisation as you did on the four stages of coaching culture development?
	What's your personal vision of what a coaching culture would look like?
	Why do you think this organisation needs to achieve a coaching culture? What's the pay-off?
	What are the risks in doing so (a) assuming you succeed, or (b) assuming you run into problems?
	What stage of coaching culture development should this organisation be aiming for over the next 12 months? Thirty-six months? How realistic is that?
	Where does this sit in the top team's list of priorities? In your personal list of priorities?
	How good a role model for coaching behaviours are you?
	Do you think a coaching style could improve decision-making and strategy implementation? How?
	How important would some quick wins be? Where do you think these should best be looked for?
	What is your reaction to [result from surveys]?
	Have you gathered feedback on your coaching style from your direct reports? How do you feel about that? What are you going to do differently? How will you make sure that happens?

Exhibit 5.3 Assessing the quality of the coaching relationship

We give two ways of scoring these questionnaires, and both will be useful for different purposes. They will need a different calculation to be made for Column C, so decide which approach you will use first, and then do the relevant calculation in Column C.

Option 1

Multiply A times B and put the score for each item in Column C. Coach and coachee pairs can compare overall scores, which is a synthesis of quality and centrality of the relationship. Next, and more usefully, compare column scores in A (a measure of quality of the relationship) and in B (which is an indicator of the centrality of the relationship for both parties). This is a useful way of starting a conversation about the nature of the relationship and it can also highlight particular issues that are of concern to each of the parties.

Option 2

Subtract the score in B from the score in A for each item. This gives a rough measure of satisfaction – where no difference means highly satisfied (whether this is where 'I don't get much of this and it's not important' or 'I get lots of this and it is important'). Negative scores indicate that the respondent is getting less of the factor than they would wish; positive scores may mean that they are getting too much. In any event, this way of analysing the scores provides a useful starting point for dialogue about how the relationship might best be developed against each of the dimensions. A good place to start would be with statements where the importance is 4 or 5 and the 'How true?' score is 2 or less.

Questions	A. How true is each statement? 'Very true' = 5 and 'Not true' = 1	B. How important is this factor to you? 'Very' = 5 and 'Not at all' = 1	C. A × B or (see text) A – B
1. We are relaxed and able to speak openly.			
2. We have a high degree of respect for each other.			
3. We are both learning from the coaching relationship.			
4. We have clear learning goals from the coaching process.			
5. I value the opportunity to obtain a different perspective.			
6. We are able to confront and discuss difficult issues openly.			
7. I am confident in initiating coaching discussions.			
8. I am able to reflect during the coaching sessions.			
9. Our discussions are creative and reflective.			
10. We trust each other.			
11. We are both well prepared for planned coaching sessions.			
12. We review the coaching relationship regularly and discuss how to improve it.			
13. We are able to discuss relationships with colleagues in confidence.			
14. We both attach high priority to coaching sessions.			
15. I enjoy and look forward to coaching sessions.			
16. The coaching sessions have made a substantial, positive difference to the coachee's performance.			
Total scores			

Exhibit 5.4 Assessing the team leader as coach

The methods discussed in Exhibit 5.3 may also be used with this one.
However, the focus here is the team rather than a pair. Managers can get team members to fill out the questionnaire openly (or if that is seen as too confrontational, anonymously) and the range of responses can be presented on a chart. This can be useful for coachees as well as coaches, in that it often highlights different responses to the same stimulus. It reminds them that no single approach will work equally well for all.

Questions	A. How true is each statement? 'Very true' = 5, 'Not true' = 1	B. How important is this factor to you? 'Very' = 5, 'Not at all' = 1	C. A × B or (see text) A – B
1. My line manager will make time for coaching discussions, even when busy with other priorities.			
2. My line manager is a good role model for being coached (being a coachee).			
3. My line manager is a good role model for personal development in general.			
4. I have a very clear idea of what is required of me in my job, and how my performance will be measured.			
5. I feel my line manager is pleased when I ask for coaching.			
6. I have a very clear understanding of the areas on which I most need to concentrate to improve my performance.			
7. If my line manager agrees a time for a coaching session, s/he always sticks to it.			
8. I receive a lot of ad hoc, short-duration coaching help from my line manager.			
9. S/he is good at listening and empathising with the issues I face.			
10. S/he provides clear and useful feedback whenever I need it.			
11. S/he always knows when to help me work things out for myself and when to steer me in the right direction.			
12. S/he is very good at referring me on to other sources of expertise when needed.			
13. S/he helps me sort out priorities			
14. I receive willing coaching from my line manager as frequently as I need it.			
15. I feel motivated by my line manager's belief in what I can accomplish.			
Total scores			

Exhibit 5.5 Coaching culture visible manifestations questionnaire

This questionnaire can be administered to anyone in the organisation. Its purpose is to capture people's perceptions about some of the most explicit visible manifestations of coaching culture.	
Questions	A. How true is each statement? 'Very true' = 5, 'Not true' = 1
1. I receive coaching when I need it.	
2. My line manager is an effective coach.	
3. I understand my responsibilities as a coachee.	
4. Top management is committed to coaching.	
5. I am encouraged and supported in developing my skills as a coach.	
6. I am encouraged and supported in developing my role as a coachee.	
7. Managers who do not coach and/or mentor are less likely to be promoted than those who do.	
8. Top management are positive role models for coaching behaviours.	
9. Taking time for coaching and mentoring is regarded as a high-priority activity.	
10. We use coaching approaches in a wide range of situations.	
11. Coaching is continuous, rather than spasmodic.	
12. It's okay to ask your boss to coach you.	
13. People here expect to share knowledge with colleagues.	
14. People here welcome and respond positively to feedback.	
15. Managers here are generally very good at delegating and empowering.	
16. Coaching is more about achieving potential than remedying weaknesses.	
17. People here expect feedback on their performance as coaches.	
18. It's clear to me why the organisation wants to promote coaching as a way of working.	
Total scores	

Exhibit 5.6 Development stages of coaching culture

At a more complex level, the leadership team may wish to evaluate progress towards the coaching culture on the basis of the four development stages of coaching culture presented in Chapter 1.			
A Nascent	B Tactical	C Strategic	D Embedded
1A Coaching happens without reference to strategy and process	1B Coaching is referred to in strategy documents	1C Managers are measured on the effects of their coaching	1D Key organisation performance measures include coaching outputs

2A Coaching is used to correct poor performers	2B Coaching is used to contribute to performance of all	2C Coaching is used as the main driver of performance	2D Coaching is the way of performance-managing individuals, teams and the organisation
3A A coach is seen as 'nice to have'	3B Coaching is compatible with core business drivers	3C Core business drivers are articulated and coaching is the means of delivering them	3D The more urgent/important/mission-critical a project, the more coaching is used
4A Coaching is a specialist activity separate from normal managing	4B Coaching is used by bosses one-to-one to improve performance	4C Coaching is widely used as a way of working in teams and projects	4D Coaching is used in all settings from shop floor to boardroom
5A People are coached only if their boss is keen on it	5B Coachees are coached as part of performance management processes	5C From induction to retirement, people expect to be coached	5D Staff seek coaching internally and from customers/suppliers/outside benchmarks
6A Staff accept it if their bosses can't or won't coach	6B Staff frequently ask for coaching	6C The right to be coached is accepted throughout the organisation	6D Coachees will coach their coaches in coaching if they need it
7A Learning to be coached comes from being lucky to have a coaching boss	7B Training of coachees has as much attention as coach training	7C The coachees' drive to learn and perform stimulates coaching	7D Coaching is seen as one of many alliances to be managed by coachees
8A External coaches used as the stage before outplacement	8B External coaches widely available to support a range of development issues	8C External coaches support supervision/development of senior managers as coaches	8D External coaches work with internal leaders to steer coachee-led development agenda
9A Managers do a range of coach training or none at all	9B Coach training is widely available	9C Different coach training offerings are integrated	9D Coach training pervades development opportunities and agenda
10A Coaching is a private concern, not noticed or commented upon	10B Coaches get feedback from staff on whether they coach	10C Coaches get ongoing feedback from coachees on how they coach	10D All managers get 360-degree feedback on how they coach
11A Once trained, coaches are left to their own devices.	11B Coaches get follow-up support from tutors after training.	11C Coaches get feedback between and after training workshops from peers, coachees and tutors.	11D Coaches have on-going supervision of their practice from peers and tutors.
12A The organisation does not recognise or certificate coaches.	12B Coaches are recognised for their contribution to the performance of others.	12C Coaches have opportunities to deepen their learning through certification.	12D Accreditation widely used as part of CPD of coaches.

13A Knowledge is used as a source of power.	13B Knowledge-sharing is common, from experienced staff to new colleagues.	13C Knowledge-sharing is used, recognised and valued.	13D Knowledge-sharing upward, downward and between peers is a way of life.
14A Having a coach is seen as a fashion accessory.	14B Coaching helps to improve performance.	14C High-performing team members coach one another.	14D Coaching is widely used to develop a high-performing organisation.
15A Top team members who are coached don't talk about it.	15B Top team members talk about their coaching.	15C Top team talk about challenges in their coaching/being coached.	15D Top team seek and use feedback on their coaching.
16A Coaches encourage coachees to take responsibility.	16B Coaching is led as an HR/ development project.	16C Line people take significant leadership of the move to coaching.	16D Dedicated line staff are committed to developing coaching.
17A Coaches focus on plugging skills gaps as seen by the coach.	17B Coaching begins from development goals of coachees.	17C Coaching is fuelled by learners' dreams or aspirations.	17D Coaching integrates individual dreams and shared organisational vision.
18A Coaching starts from individual needs.	18B Coaching involves shared learning and dialogue.	18C Networks of coaches develop together, using co-coaching.	18D Learning agendas and aspirations are widely shared throughout the organisation.
19A There are several different initiatives on coaching that are not connected.	19B Coaching initiatives have their own life and are linked to each other.	19C Coaching is used to develop an enquiring stance towards organisation agendas.	19D Autonomy and co-operation equally valued in widespread coaching between divisions/functions.
20A Coaches are often blunt and abrasive.	20B Coaches are often candid and forthright.	20C Mutual dialogue about tough issues – coach and coachee open to learning.	20D Organisation blind spots and weaknesses addressed in coaching relationships.
21A Coaching is an HR/development initiative.	21B Senior group endorse the move to coaching.	21C Senior group demonstrate the use of coaching in achieving goals.	21D Senior group integrate development of organisation with use of coaching style.
22A Some individuals are enthusiastic about being a coach.	22B Line managers lead coaching initiatives in their own areas.	22C Line managers take responsibility for coaching throughout the organisation.	22D Coaching is used to manage projects and in a wide range of meetings.
23A Coaches are conscious of the need for culture change.	23B Coaches use coaching to advocate culture change.	23C Coaches make the link between management style, coaching and culture.	23D Coaches live the link between management style, coaching and culture.

| 24A Coaches encourage coachees to take responsibility. | 24B Coaches provide or create opportunities for coachees to perform. | 24C Coachees and coaches actively manage mutual support & challenge between them. | 24D Coachees take responsibility for their own performance accountably and in a no-blame way. |

Exhibit 5.7 Audit report table of contents

Section	Content	Description	Suggested length
1	Audit objectives	Explain the main objectives of the audit	1/2 page
2	Process	Outline how audit was carried out, who took part in it, what combination of tools was used and how results were analysed	1/2 page
3	Audit results headlines	Outline the key results of surveys, interviews and focus groups that were carried out as part of the audit	Maximum 10 pages
4	Conclusions	State the main conclusions of the audit	Maximum 1 page
5	Recommendations	Make recommendations based on the audit conclusions	1/2 page
6	Appendix 1	Statistical data in tabular form	As appropriate
7	Appendix 2	Qualitative data – illustrative quotes	As appropriate

TAKING STOCK – MEASURING PROGRESS TOWARDS A COACHING CULTURE IN A DIVISION OF A MAJOR AUSTRALIAN FINANCIAL INSTITUTION

Contributed by Julie-Anne Tooth PhD and Hilary Armstrong PhD, Sydney, Australia[1]

In February 2013, a division of a major Australian financial institution decided to benchmark their progress towards the development of a coaching culture and, therefore, demonstrate an integrated coaching approach. The division's executive management had previously identified that enhancing the coaching capability of people leaders was a key strategic priority, enabling leaders to assist their people to realise their potential and deliver strong and sustained business performance.

A significant investment in coaching skills development had been undertaken in the business, with approximately 500 people leaders completing training in a standardised framework of coaching skills. A number of different coaching frameworks had also been embedded in other sales and relationship management training programmes. Across the institution, there had also been a sizable investment in the development of an internal 'Coaching Academy', consisting of trained internal coaches

STORIES FROM THE FIELD

---

[1] At the time this survey was completed both authors were contracted to the IECL

and resources, and the utilisation of external coaches as well as a range of other coaching initiatives.

To benchmark progress and to determine the necessary elements of their coaching culture strategy going forward (including areas for improvement and future investment), the division deployed an online Coaching Readiness Survey (CRS) via email to 1,200 people leaders in the business, achieving a response rate of 62 per cent.

The instrument

The Coaching Readiness Survey (CRS) survey instrument was designed in two parts. Part A was developed by adapting the 24 items contained in the Clutterbuck and Megginson (2005) questionnaire, which assesses the following question: 'To what extent is the organisation as a whole moving to integrate coaching into its deep processes of performance and renewal?' An additional eight questions were added to the survey in Part B. These were designed to benchmark and assess people leaders' coaching capability in terms of competence, confidence and application. Sections for free-text responses were included and, while the survey was confidential, selected biographical data was collected to assist with interpretation and analysis.

Results and analysis

In Part A, people leaders were invited to rate their experience of coaching across the division on a rating scale of 1 to 4 (where 1 was the lowest and 4 was the highest level). The overall mean score for the division across the 24 items was 2.39, demonstrating that, as rated by people leaders in the organisation, they had reached Stage 2 (tactical) and were moving towards Stage 3 (strategic) on a four-point progressive scale (Clutterbuck and Megginson 2005).[2] Overall, this represented approximately 60 per cent progress towards a coaching culture. The need to focus on consistency and integration was consistently evident in the responses from people leaders, suggesting that there was still much diversity in coaching approaches and application across the division. Overall progress towards a coaching culture was summarised by one people leader as follows: 'Coaching is a journey we are on in this division. We are making good progress; however, we are not where we need to be yet. There is still inconsistency in delivery and quality.'

The lowest-rated question in the survey responses (mean score 1.81) indicated that coaching in the division was viewed by people leaders as more process-driven than organic. This was not surprising as, until this survey, the division had focused on the introduction of system- and process-based elements including training, tools and processes to guide people leaders in using a coaching approach.

The results for people leader coaching capability in Part B were consistently high and provided evidence (albeit self-reported) for the value of the investments made by the division in coaching skills training. For example, the majority of people leaders agreed or strongly agreed that they:

- were competent in using a coaching approach in their work (79 per cent)
- conducted regular coaching sessions with their team members (77 per cent)
- utilised a coaching approach with others (77 per cent)
- had improved their coaching skills (83 per cent)
- were confident in their coaching ability (79 per cent).

---

[2] The four stages include: (1) nascent – deemed in this study as 25 per cent progress; (2) tactical – 50 per cent; (3) strategic – 75 per cent; and (4) embedded – 100 per cent.

Recommendations

Clutterbuck and Megginson (2005) outline that a move from Stage 2 (tactical) to Stage 3 (strategic), as in the case of this division, requires a focus on tying a myriad of activities together and making them whole. Recommendations following the survey analysis, therefore, focused on the need for an integration of the approaches used across the business, recognising the potential for other things going on in the business to cut across the values and behaviours associated with coaching. For example, people leaders reported that the processes, which focused on the need for them to document coaching conversations, had actually become a barrier to more informal coaching occurring.

While the development of a coaching culture in a systematic way is valued for ensuring consistency and coherence (Clutterbuck and Megginson 2005), the challenge for the division in its stage of progress was to ensure that the processes that had been implemented did not become obstacles to realising the intent of coaching, that is, the generation of learning through the co-creation of the coaching relationship and the dialogical aspects of the coaching conversation (Armstrong 2012; Tooth 2014).

MEASURING THE IMPACT OF COACHING IN EY

The story below illustrates how EY measures the impact of coaching in both the Americas and UK&I, and how the results of that measurement contribute to strengthening the business case for coaching within the organisation, consequently leading to further enhancement of a coaching culture within the firm.

In the early days of the formation of the EY UK&I internal coaching team it was crucial to focus the limited resource available in a way that would maximise return. It was agreed that this focus should be on providing transition coaching to new partners since this is a major step in an individual's career and one where the existing support in the UK&I was inconsistent, and this also aligned to priority populations globally in terms of who should receive formal coaching. The hypothesis, verified by the finance team, was that new partners take, on average, 18 months to make a return on investment. The aim of the coaching intervention was to reduce this to 12 months or less by providing specific support to this important group.

EY UK&I started this programme in July 2009 and measured individual partner performance (revenue) for two cohorts of partners (2009 and 2010) who had received coaching support and compared it with the July 2008 cohort, who did not benefit from this additional formal support. The number of partners in each cohort was 13 (2008), 23 (2009) and 12 (2010). EY UK&I specifically focused on partners who were promoted internally, rather than external hires, for this initial study as there was less variance in their background and experience.

The new partners were offered six sessions of coaching during the first six to nine months in the role. This coaching was provided by internal coaches. In addition to the quantitative feedback below, coaches also received strong qualitative feedback.

The data shows the average performance for each cohort at the same quarterly stage of maturity post-admission. It shows the performance of the 2008 control group to be much flatter. Although the absolute level of net engagement revenue (NER) starts higher in the 2008 group, we do not see the clear performance improvement that we do in the latter two groups. In addition, the 2009 and 2010 cohort were outperforming the 2008 group within nine months of admission to the partnership. Sales pipeline and sales performance growth figures for the same cohorts show a similar trend.

This data serves to support how transition coaching has improved the performance of the partners to the significant benefit of the firm.

Exhibit 5.8 Benefits of transition coaching for new EY partners measured by net engagement revenue

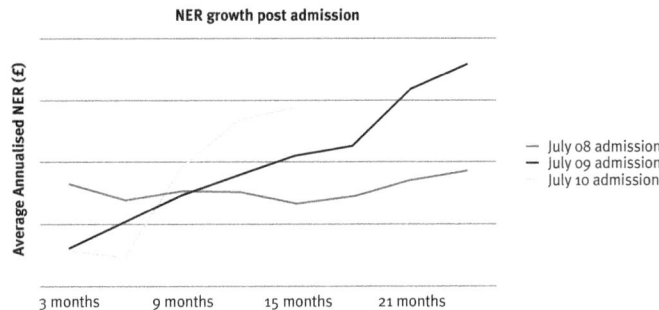

NER growth post admission

Average Annualised NER (£)

— July 08 admission
— July 09 admission
　 July 10 admission

3 months　9 months　15 months　21 months

Following this programme, the dedicated Coaching Centre within EY UK&I was launched in July 2011 and is described in a later section.

Similar benefits of transition coaching have been seen in EY Americas. After five years of coaching over 3,000 leaders in transition, EY Americas has seen a clear shift in their ability to:

- reach their goals at a faster and more engaging pace
- articulate their values and their personal brand
- build and lead highest-performing teams
- align personal and professional goals
- build relationships
- have greater success in the market.

Both EY UK&I and EY Americas track their coaching assignments through a tool called 'CoachNet', which allows them to survey all clients at the conclusion of the coaching engagement. In EY Americas, results to date show that out of 215 respondents, 81 per cent reported that coaching had a game-changing/important impact on them and 79 per cent reported their coach has been instrumental in helping them take their leadership or engagement to the next level.

SUMMARY

When setting out on the journey towards creating a coaching culture, it is not enough to know the direction in which you want to go – you also need to know your starting point. A careful examination of current reality linked to coaching can prove invaluable not just in designing a coaching culture strategy and plan, but also in measuring progress towards the desired outcome. There are a number of approaches and tools available that an organisation can use to perform baseline and context assessment. Designing a fit-for-purpose coaching culture audit is a good time investment: it will pay dividends in valuable insights and in effective progress measurement tools, thus increasing the possibility of the coaching culture strategy being successfully implemented and followed through.

FIELDWORK

?

Reflect on the following questions:

- If you were to put together a coaching culture audit team in your organisation (or one that you are familiar with), who would be on it? Why?
- Which tools would be most appropriate to use in a coaching culture audit in your organisation?
- Which stakeholder groups would you consider important to involve in the coaching culture audit? Why?

CHAPTER 6

Charting the Course

'If you built castles in the air, your work need not be lost; this is where they should be. Now put the foundations under them.'
Henry David Thoreau

OVERVIEW

In this chapter we talk about charting the course towards a coaching culture and identifying specific actions that will enable progress in the desired direction. We start off with four broad areas of a coaching and mentoring strategy and proceed to give details on each of them. We then outline a process to follow in order to gain the commitment of key stakeholders and create a robust plan that is well suited to the needs of your organisation, its culture, and the business in which it operates.

The importance of having a detailed, multi-perspective and integrated approach, in which change is supported in both the short and long term, cannot be overestimated when planning to build and sustain a coaching culture. Even the best-intentioned initiatives are unlikely to have much impact if they are done in a random, uncoordinated manner or without considering the systems involved and the forces at play.

The main themes of Chapters 4 and 5 – identifying a coaching culture vision (A – aspirations) and establishing the starting point (B – baseline and context assessment) are a necessary preparation for this stage of the ABC-DE model (see Figure 6.1). The findings and documentation from the A and B stages will offer invaluable input for the stage we are discussing here, namely charting the course. Armed with this information, the coaching strategy team will be able to work with both general and specific foci to create a plan enabling the organisation to get to the desired level of a coaching culture.

CRITICAL COMPONENTS OF A SUCCESSFUL COACHING CULTURE STRATEGY

We will not pretend that we have found the right way to go about creating a coaching culture in an organisation. However, while analysing material gathered through interviews with hundreds of HR professionals responsible for coaching and mentoring, we noticed that successful organisations tend to focus on four main areas when strategising to cultivate a coaching and mentoring culture:

- **accessibility and relevance:** creating or increasing access to an appropriate and relevant coaching or mentoring modality
- **support and reinforcement:** building and sustaining the momentum for coaching and mentoring in the organisation
- **integration:** making coaching part of the way 'we do business around here'
- **measurement:** evaluating progress and effectiveness of coaching.

In this part we outline these areas, as well as their constituting components. Some of these components were first mentioned in the article 'What Every HR Director Should Know about Coaching and Mentoring Strategy' (Clutterbuck and Merrick 2014).

Figure 6.1 Charting the course in the context of the ABC-DE model of coaching culture planning and implementation

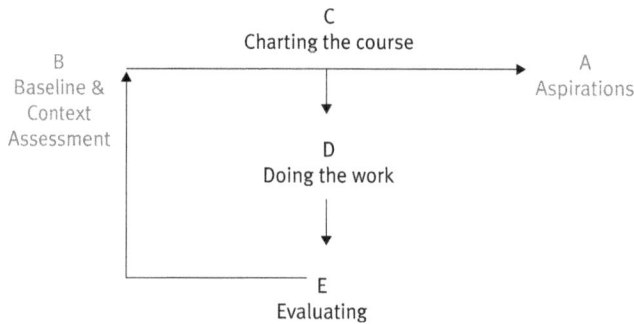

Figure 6.2 Main areas of coaching and mentoring culture strategy

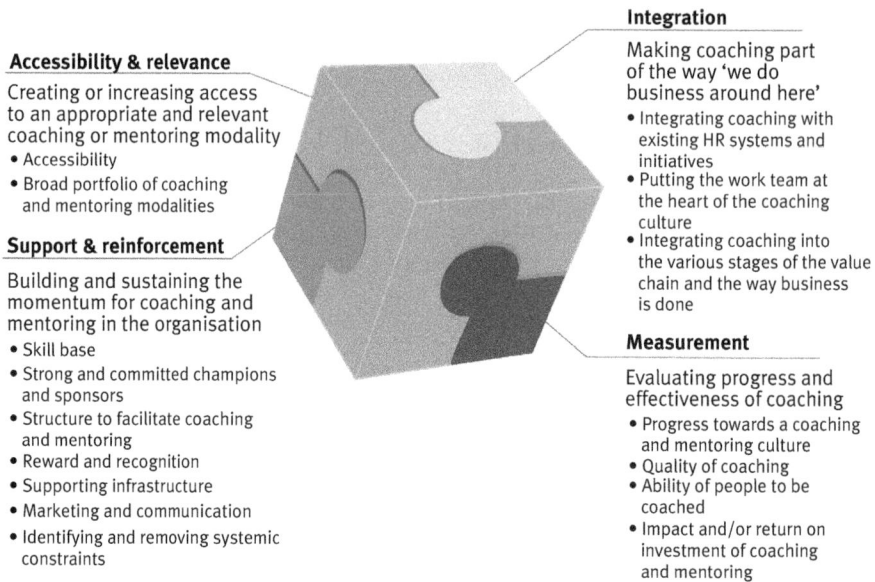

Integration

Making coaching part of the way 'we do business around here'

- Integrating coaching with existing HR systems and initiatives
- Putting the work team at the heart of the coaching culture
- Integrating coaching into the various stages of the value chain and the way business is done

Accessibility & relevance

Creating or increasing access to an appropriate and relevant coaching or mentoring modality

- Accessibility
- Broad portfolio of coaching and mentoring modalities

Support & reinforcement

Building and sustaining the momentum for coaching and mentoring in the organisation

- Skill base
- Strong and committed champions and sponsors
- Structure to facilitate coaching and mentoring
- Reward and recognition
- Supporting infrastructure
- Marketing and communication
- Identifying and removing systemic constraints

Measurement

Evaluating progress and effectiveness of coaching

- Progress towards a coaching and mentoring culture
- Quality of coaching
- Ability of people to be coached
- Impact and/or return on investment of coaching and mentoring

ACCESSIBILITY AND RELEVANCE

Creating or increasing access to an appropriate and relevant coaching or mentoring modality

Accessibility

For coaching culture to take root and grow, coaching cannot be an exclusive offering reserved for the selected few. An important part of coaching and mentoring strategy is finding ways to make coaching available to more people, at various stages of their professional career.

This is linked to the next component – ensuring that there is a broad portfolio of coaching and mentoring formats and applications that can meet people's current needs.

A broad portfolio of coaching and mentoring formats and applications

There is a danger in using a limited portfolio of coaching formats and applications. It was perfectly captured by Maslow, who said that if the only tool that we have is a hammer, it can be tempting to treat everything as if it were a nail (Maslow 1966).

Rigid approaches based on a single coaching or mentoring model usually defeat the purpose of introducing them. Trying to force them to work in a context where they are not well suited can breed cynicism, if not outright resentment, among the recipients of coaching. For example, the popular GROW model is of limited use outside of skills and basic performance coaching. Solutions-focused coaching only works when people are looking for solutions to fixable problems, but is inappropriate when there is a need for reflection and deeper insight. Our research shows that, as coaches become more experienced, they develop more flexible, person-centred approaches.

For coaching culture to work in an organisation, coaches need to develop a portfolio of models which can be adapted to the complexities of the situations which organisations and people encounter.

Moreover, it is very helpful to have different coaching and mentoring modes that people can turn to, such as:

- externally resourced professional coaching/mentoring
- internally resourced professional coaching
- coaching by line managers or within work teams
- group coaching
- team coaching (someone external to the team coaching them collectively)
- developmental mentoring
- sponsorship
- maternity mentoring and maternity coaching.

This list could be further extended with items that serve a specific purpose, such as career coaching, ethical mentoring, diversity mentoring as well as different modes of delivery, for example, face-to-face, virtual, email and so on.

We will cover some of the above modes in more detail in Chapters 7 to 10.

SUPPORT AND REINFORCEMENT

Building and sustaining the momentum for coaching and mentoring in the organisation

Anyone who was involved in any kind of change, whether of a personal or organisational nature, knows that the initial excitement and enthusiasm can quickly fade away if not sufficiently sustained or reinforced. There are a number of components that can be included in a coaching and mentoring strategy to serve that purpose:

- skills base
- strong and committed champions and sponsors
- structure to facilitate coaching and mentoring
- reward and recognition
- supporting infrastructure
- marketing and communication
- identifying and removing systemic constraints.

Skills base

Perhaps the most fundamental of all components of a coaching culture strategy is building a skills base for coaching. As already noted in *Making Coaching Work* (Clutterbuck and Megginson 2005), in order to cultivate a coaching culture, everyone in the organisation will need appropriate skills to either:

- self-coach
- coach others
- be coached
- help promote coaching in the organisation
- adopt a coaching approach in a variety of situations and with a number of stakeholders.

Identifying the best way to create that skills base is one of the most important components of a coaching culture strategy.

Strong and committed champions and sponsors

Cultivating coaching culture requires a strong network of champions and sponsors, both within HR and the business.

Our experience of working with international organisations tells us that without that network:

- There is a wide variation of understanding about the nature and utility of coaching and mentoring across the HR and business community. It's not uncommon, for example, for people in different regions to have opposite definitions of coaching and mentoring.
- Particularly in HR business partner structures, time-pressed HR professionals don't have space or energy to become proficient champions of coaching and mentoring.
- Wherever purchasing of externally resourced coaching and mentoring services has been handed over to a purchasing department, there has been a substantial (and sometimes disastrous) slump in the quality of provision and relationships with external providers.

By contrast, some companies have been able to support gradual culture transformation by focusing on the role of senior line managers and HR professionals as champions of coaching and mentoring. They have devoted resources to educating business leaders and HR for various levels of involvement, but at a minimum with the skills and knowledge to help the business decide when coaching or mentoring will be helpful in resolving business issues ranging from retention of key staff to performance improvement for individuals.

Structure to facilitate coaching and mentoring

When a lot of coaching initiatives and modalities are being implemented in an organisation, establishing a structure which enables their facilitation becomes a must.

The role of head of coaching and mentoring is relatively recent but strategically important within HR functions of large organisations. There is a movement towards establishing professional qualifications in the role.

Additionally, it is becoming increasingly clear that it takes more than one individual to effectively facilitate coaching and mentoring within a large organisation. A lot of organisations have formed a coaching steering group, which includes various stakeholders, usually representing the whole organisational system. This steering group, in varying degrees and depending on individual roles, is usually involved in all the stages of our ABC-DE model, from coaching culture vision creation to evaluating progress.

Reward and recognition

It is true to say – even if slightly oversimplified – that culture can only be transformed when the new behaviours are perceived to (a) produce desired results and (b) be socially acceptable. An important element in creating that perception is reward and recognition.

More and more organisations realise that for recognition and reward to support the growth of a coaching culture, it needs to go beyond rewarding people for holding formal coaching conversations. As a result, organisations start looking at a variety of behaviours that are considered to be visible manifestations of a coaching culture.

We give examples of some of these behaviours in Chapter 1. However, it is important to remember that each organisation needs to define these behaviours itself, as they will depend on its vision and aspirations for a coaching culture.

A useful exercise, therefore, would be to identify:

- Which are the behaviours that you consider to be visible manifestations of your desired coaching culture?
- How can you ensure that these behaviours are sufficiently reinforced, recognised and rewarded by individuals, managers and the organisation as a whole?

Supporting infrastructure

Organisations that have been relatively successful in pursuing a coaching and mentoring culture tend to have a variety of different forms of continuous support. These might include:

- professional supervision – usually group supervision, intended as a source of regular skills development, as a safety check and as a means of identifying themes that need to be addressed
- a database of further reading and practical guidance usually held on the HR intranet. This can be supplemented by video demonstrations of coaching and mentoring good practice
- peer support groups, often in the form of action learning sets, or networks, which promote continuous learning in the coaching/mentoring role
- a progression path for those coaches and mentors who want to gain qualifications beyond the basic levels
- 'on demand' training and further education, via webinars and other electronic media
- coach development centres, to promote continuous skills development
- an online community of interest in coaching and mentoring, involving HR, line managers and invited external experts
- publications on how to maximise benefits of coaching and the dos and don'ts of being a 'coachee'.

Marketing and communication

As with any organisational change, cultivating a coaching culture requires a robust and well-targeted marketing and communication campaign. While putting a coaching culture strategy together, it is worthwhile identifying the main objectives of your communication efforts, key messages, target audiences and the most appropriate means of transmitting these messages.

There is a wide array of available tools that can be used for this purpose, including:

- messages on the intranet
- leaflets and newsletters
- conferences
- emails and other forms of direct communication such as desk drops

- meetings
- informal communication.

We present the subject of marketing and communication in more depth in Chapter 12.

Identifying and removing systemic constraints

An important element of an effective strategy is creating a mechanism capable of identifying and removing systemic constraints in developing a coaching culture.

Getting regular feedback and identifying the most important limiting factors that stand in the way of people adopting a coaching approach or using coaching skills on the job can make a huge difference to the effectiveness of the coaching culture strategy.

A few examples of possible constraints could be:

- lack of skills and confidence in using or engaging in coaching
- lack of executive buy-in and support
- perceived lack of time to coach
- employee (coachee) excessive workload
- blame culture
- lack of private space to coach in
- systems and processes that don't support (or even hinder) the growth of a coaching culture
- senior management does not model the desired behaviours
- lack of reward or recognition for personal and professional development and other behaviours considered to be visible manifestations of a coaching culture.

A good illustration of identifying and removing systemic constraints comes from a professional services firm, which prepared for introducing its first mentoring programme by conducting a survey to assess how supportive the organisational culture would be. One of the biggest impediments was that staff were required to log every ten minutes of time so that it could be billed back to the appropriate client. However, there was no provision for assigning personal development time, so people felt they would be penalised for any working time spent on mentoring, or any other form of personal development. The leadership team recognised that it needed not only to give people an allowance of personal development time, but to create an expectation that this time would be used for either mentoring or some other form of formal learning in connection with job roles.

INTEGRATION

Making coaching part of the way 'we do business around here'

The embedded stage of coaching culture development (see Chapter 1) is the 'holy grail' of coaching in organisations. When this stage is reached, people at all levels use the skills of learning dialogue on an everyday basis and regularly engage in coaching with stakeholders inside and outside of the organisation.

If an organisation has an aspiration to attain the strategic and eventually embedded stages of coaching culture development, its strategy needs to contain components that integrate coaching with existing systems and weave a coaching approach into the fabric of everyday business dealings.

The most common elements of strategy that organisations employ to achieve this are:

- integrating coaching with existing HR systems and initiatives
- putting the work team at the heart of the coaching culture
- integrating coaching into the various stages of the value chain and the way business is done.

Integrating coaching with existing HR strategies, systems and initiatives

When putting together a coaching culture strategy, it is important to look at the existing HR strategy, systems and initiatives. There is no doubt that coaching should be aligned with the wider HR strategy. Moreover, looking at what is already there will allow the coaching approach, skills and mindset to be embedded into many existing HR systems, processes and initiatives, such as:

- recruitment
- onboarding
- talent and performance management
- succession planning
- learning and development
- exit management or outplacement.

Some organisations also attempt to link their coaching and mentoring strategy to corporate social responsibility objectives. For example, they promote cascade mentoring (where junior people mentored from above are expected to mentor someone in the wider community after six months – a very direct and immediate way of paying back). Other companies have opened out their training in coaching and mentoring to employees of charities.

Putting the work team at the heart of the coaching culture

Experiments in organisations including Asda (Walmart), University College London and PwC indicate that much can be achieved by building a coaching culture within the team. Integral to doing so are:

- educating everyone in the team about the value of coaching and how to coach and be coached
- getting everyone to take responsibility for both their own learning and the collective learning of the team
- giving the learning process sufficient time – coaching is a mindset, not an activity, and mindsets take months to acquire
- building comfort with coaching processes and behaviours by applying them consensually to real, tough decisions and challenges that the team faces.

When enough work teams establish a coaching culture, it creates the impetus for wider cultural change across the organisation.

An interesting observation that we have made is that some organisations decided to go about cultivating what is essentially a coaching culture within work teams without making a clear and direct reference to coaching. The most frequently quoted reason for doing so is what can be called 'coaching fatigue', caused by various coaching initiatives that had been undertaken in the organisation in the past.

We will talk more about creating a coaching culture within work teams in Chapter 8.

Integrating coaching into the various stages of the value chain and the way business is done

While creating a coaching culture strategy, you might want to look at how to integrate a coaching approach and philosophy into the way business is done in your organisation.

In *Making Coaching Work*, we identified the various stages of the organisation's value chain and business processes where a coaching approach could be useful. The view that we expressed back then can be summarised in the following statement: 'It is difficult to imagine any significant business process that cannot benefit from the application of coaching principles and opportunities for managed reflection' (Clutterbuck and Megginson 2005).

Not much has changed in the past ten years, apart from the fact that we see more and more organisations making conscious efforts to integrate a coaching approach into everyday business practices and processes, from team meetings to business development activities. In many instances, this integration is done in a discreet, seamless way; the word coaching is rarely used and the main focus is on enhancing work practices to achieve better results.

A good example of this is how the majority of professional services firms successfully weave a coaching approach into the process of business development. Some of their formal business development guidelines cover subjects not unlike the ones that would be discussed in a coaching training: how to build relationships based on trust, how to continually assess client needs and perceptions, agree on desired outcomes, focus the discussion on client needs, ask powerful questions, seek out feedback and so on.

MEASUREMENT

Evaluating progress and effectiveness of coaching

A good coaching culture strategy includes various ways of measuring progress. Some of the most common measurements include:

- progress towards a coaching and mentoring culture
- quality of coaching (both internally and externally delivered)
- ability of people to be coached
- impact and/or return on investment of coaching and mentoring (both internally and externally resourced).

The validity of these measures is gradually improving, giving HR the data it needs to demonstrate the effectiveness of coaching and mentoring interventions. In our experience, HR teams who introduce robust measurement, both as a formative process whilst the coaching and mentoring interventions are taking place and then as a final summative process, create a highly credible business case for more investment in coaching and mentoring.

The role of the coaching and mentoring steering committee is to integrate some or all of the above components into a coherent strategy. We will now talk about how this can be achieved.

COACHING CULTURE STRATEGY WORKSHOP AND BEYOND

Provided that the required preparation has been done and the coaching culture vision and coaching culture audit produced the desired results, it is not uncommon to create the first draft of the coaching culture strategy in a workshop, especially if it is then followed up by a series of shorter progress meetings. Figure 6.3 outlines a process for an effective coaching culture strategy workshop.

SET OBJECTIVES AND IDENTIFY EXPECTATIONS

One of the key success factors of any effective strategy workshop is being clear about the desired outcomes. Clear objectives inform decisions that you have to take before the workshop, such as:

- Who should participate?
- What will be the best meeting structure and flow?
- Which decision-making tools should we use?
- What pre-reading (if any) needs to be sent out?
- Who is the best person to facilitate the workshop?

IDENTIFY KEY PARTICIPANTS

Coming up with an implementable plan to change a system as complex as organisational culture requires the involvement of various stakeholders. People who participate in the workshop will have a big influence on strategy implementation and, ideally, should represent all those parts of the organisation that will be affected by or can contribute to the change. As Adam Kahane says in his book *Transformative Scenario Planning* (Kahane 2012): 'The team should be a microcosm or fractal of the whole system.' At a minimum, we would suggest involving:

- those who will monitor plan implementation (for example the coaching culture steering committee, the HR team or the sponsors of coaching)
- representative(s) of those who will be implementing the plan (HR team members, managers, coaches)
- representative(s) of those who will be affected by the plan implementation (managers, team members, coaches)
- others who can contribute to the plan development (for example specialist advisers – internal or external – as needed).

Figure 6.3 Effective coaching culture strategy workshop access

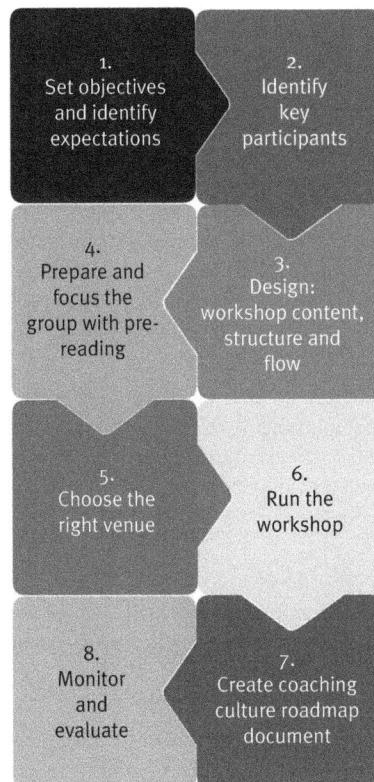

As far as the individual characteristics of key participants are concerned, we can only echo Kahane in saying that you are looking for people who are insightful, influential, committed, energetic, action-oriented and willing to speak openly about the discussed issues.

Just like any similar event, a coaching culture strategy workshop requires a significant amount of preparation. While there is no 'one size fits all' approach, it is clear that in terms of content, there are certain themes worth covering.

Mission, vision and current business and people strategy

An organisation's mission, vision and current business strategy, including human capital strategy, are critical in setting the context for the workshop and creating an alignment of coaching culture strategy with the wider organisational goals.

It is possible to either have a quick refresher on these at the beginning of the workshop or to have them presented on flipcharts around the room, so that they are readily available for reference.

Vision of coaching culture

Vision of coaching culture will have been discussed and created before the workshop. A refresher might be needed, or, if not all strategy workshop participants took part in vision creation, a short discussion might be needed to engage everyone and get their ideas and contributions.

A visual reminder, just as in the case of the mission, vision and current business objectives, can be helpful.

Baseline and context assessment findings and their possible implications

The findings of the baseline and context assessment stage need to be shared with the group. Depending on the scope of the coaching culture audit that was performed, these findings might include information on what is already in place in terms of coaching, the level of skills in various demographics or which development stage of coaching culture the organisation is perceived to be in at the moment. Context information might include a snapshot of current culture and its implications for coaching.

The purpose of sharing this information is to help the group establish the starting point as well as have a common understanding of the current context and its implications.

Extent of the desired change

Coaching culture vision usually implies a relatively distant future. In order to obtain focus for the workshop and establish timeframes, the group will need to discuss and agree on the extent of the desired change in short to mid-term. The most frequent coaching strategy planning period encompasses three years.

Priorities

There may be a lot of ideas and ambitious plans to achieve within the designated period. If that is the case, it will be necessary to identify key priorities and focus on those.

Possible coaching culture strategy components

Not all workshop participants will be fully aware of the options available to achieve the desired coaching culture priorities, or of the possible components of coaching culture strategy. It might be helpful to review the critical components of coaching culture strategy in a 'shop window' so that participants can get a sense of which ones might be most appropriate to place high on their agenda.

Agreed actions and action plan

Actions and action plan or, at least, their first draft, need to be discussed during the coaching strategy workshop. The most critical elements to be agreed on are the key actions to be taken to achieve the objectives, the timelines and the actions' owners. If there is insufficient time to develop a detailed action plan, action owners can create an action plan with their working group as a follow-up to the workshop.

How these themes get arranged into a specific agenda will depend on a number of factors, such as workshop objectives, the number of participants and the available time.

Exhibit 6.1 presents a sample agenda of a coaching culture strategy workshop.

Exhibit 6.1 Sample agenda of a coaching culture strategy workshop

Coaching culture strategy workshop Agenda		
Day 1		
Time	**Session**	**Description**
8:30–9:00	Coffee on arrival	Coffee, registration, informal greeting, introductions at tables
9:00–9:30	Welcome, project overview, workshop objectives and agenda	Welcome, overview of 'coaching culture' project, objectives of the workshop and overview of workshop process Introduce 'group memory' (a method where a volunteer documents important outputs of each session on a flipchart)
9:30–10:30	Gallery walk and discussion	Gallery walk – viewing and discussing the relevance of coaching and mentoring to organisation's mission, vision and strategic objectives Coaching culture vision – thoughts and reflections
10:30–10:45	Coffee break	
10:45–12:15	Coaching culture audit findings	Coaching culture audit findings Questions and initial reactions SWOT analysis of coaching culture in four sub-groups, presentation and comments
12:15–13:00	Components of coaching culture strategy	Possible components of coaching culture strategy Q&A
13:00–14:00	Lunch break	
14:00–15.30	Goals and objectives	Goal grid: what do we already have that will help us achieve our coaching culture vision? What don't we have yet that would help us achieve our vision? What is missing that actually helps us to achieve our vision? What is there that is an obstacle to achieving our coaching culture vision?
15:30–15:45	Coffee break	
15:45–16:30	Prioritisation	Group discussion and multi-voting to decide which goals will be a priority for the next three years

		Goals placed on 'path to success' according to where their achievement is expected and how high their priority is
16:30–17:00	Review and wrap-up	Review of workshop outputs so far and wrap-up
Day 2		
9:00–9:15	Review and preview	Review of Day 1 and preview of Day 2
9:15–10:45	Identifying actions	Identifying innovative, practical actions that can be taken to achieve the goals identified yesterday
		Individual brainstorming follows
		Sub-group work to create clusters of ideas
		Naming idea clusters
		Impact of identifying ideas on achieving the desired goals
		Confirming the consensus of the whole group
10:45–11:00	Coffee break	
11:00–12:00	Actions prioritisation	Criteria for evaluating actions identified and agreed
		Actions evaluated against the criteria and prioritised
12:00–13:30	Action planning	Action owners and supporting teams are identified
		Action owners and supporting teams create a high-level action plan for their actions, including resources, budgets, timelines and communication

A note on workshop design and facilitation: if you don't have a lot of experience in designing and facilitating similar workshops, it is worth seeking the advice or help of someone who does.

PREPARE AND FOCUS THE GROUP WITH PRE-READING

It can be useful to provide reading before the workshop. Preparation pre-reading can include:

- the organisation's vision, mission and main strategic objectives
- the coaching culture vision document
- coaching culture audit results.

The above reading can give workshop participants a valuable opportunity to familiarise themselves with the materials and reflect on key issues, something that tends to speed up the process during the workshop.

CHOOSE THE RIGHT VENUE

Obvious as it may sound, we have seen too many workshops being delivered in venues that were completely unsuitable for the task.

Think about the logistics and practical details of your workshop when you choose the venue. Some of the questions that you might want to answer before making the choice are:

- Will everyone be able to reach the venue easily?
- Does the venue provide all the necessary equipment, such a flipcharts, projector, sound-system, break-out rooms and so forth?

- What catering facilities will you need? Does the venue provide that?
- Is there sufficient privacy?

RUN THE WORKSHOP

If the right participants accept the invitation to participate in the workshop, you will be faced with a room full of really busy people. It is safe to assume that for most of them there will be nothing more frustrating than participating in an unproductive and disengaging meeting which doesn't capitalise on their potential contributions and fails to produce satisfying outcomes. The workshop, therefore, needs to be facilitated in a way that is engaging and encourages everyone to participate, think creatively and offer their input (diverging), but also to prioritise and take important decisions (converging).

Workshop style

We suggest facilitating the workshop in a way that reflects a coaching style and approach. There are many ways of achieving this, for example:

- Have people agree on the desired outcomes of the workshop and contract with each other regarding the way they want to work together. A few helpful ground rules are:
  - When thinking by some of the members of the group races ahead of others, they have a responsibility to pause and help the others catch up.
  - Intellectual/rational responses may be enriched by parallel emotional responses, and vice versa – a solution is only complete when both perspectives have been considered.
  - It's acceptable to say that you have 'tuned out' of the discussion briefly to follow another train of thought, and to ask for a recap every 10 minutes or so (everyone tunes out in this way, but we don't like to admit it!).
  - Good questions are captured and recorded. The summary of decisions at the end of the meeting should be accompanied by a list of good questions because (a) they are likely to need revisiting at some point, and (b) they provide insights into the thinking behind the decisions (Exhibit 6.3 gives a few examples of such questions).
- Participants take turns to facilitate the group in a coaching style (provided that facilitations skills are strong in the group).
- Split people into twos or threes at the beginning of each topic discussion to identify (a) the critical questions that should be asked about this issue, (b) their individual and collective concerns, and (c) their individual and collective aspirations.
- Have short sessions throughout the day for quiet reflection.
- Adapt de Bono's hats metaphor (De Bono 1985). Each participant takes responsibility for one or more of the following roles: asking naïve/insightful questions, making sure everyone is fully engaged in the process of dialogue, capturing decisions and good questions, reality checking, focusing the discussion (that is, managing the balance between convergent and divergent thinking), ensuring logical rigour, and ensuring emotional rigour (for example, that emotional aspects are given appropriate space).

Workshop outputs

It is important to document all the outputs of the coaching strategy workshop. There are a number of possible methods for doing this, from noting all the important conclusions on a flipchart to assigning someone to take minutes. Outputs of the strategy workshop will constitute an important part of the strategy document.

CREATE A COACHING CULTURE ROADMAP

In essence, a coaching culture roadmap document should refer to all the stages of the ABC-DE model of coaching planning and implementation and show how coaching will help the organisation fulfil its mission and achieve important organisational objectives.

Exhibit 6.2 shows an example of a coaching culture strategy document contents page.

Exhibit 6.2 Example of a coaching culture strategy document contents page

Coaching culture strategy document Table of contents
Executive summary Definition of coaching and coaching culture Business case for a coaching culture What success looks like – vision of a coaching culture in our organisation Key findings of coaching culture audit – the foundations to build on, the gaps we need to close Three-year coaching culture strategy plan Evaluating progress – measures and tools Communication plan

Exhibit 6.3 Examples of questions from coaching culture workshop strategy

1. Who owns this strategy?
2. What are the organisational drivers for a coaching strategy?
3. What outcomes does the organisation require, by when:
   (a) performance outcomes (individual, team, organisation)
   (b) reputational and compliance outcomes (eg diversity, employer branding)
   (c) enabling outcomes (skills, mindset, behaviours)?
4. What are the priority issues and audiences that need to be addressed?
5. What coaching/mentoring interventions will be most effective at addressing these issues and needs (in a cost-effective way)?
6. What is the minimum level of capability and impact we can accept in each of these interventions?
7. What has already been done, which can be built upon?
8. What barriers will need to be overcome, and how?
9. What resources will we have to invest and when?
10. What support structures will we need?
11. What funding will be required for these resources and support structures?
12. Who are the key players (sponsors, champions, budget-holders etc.)?
13. What risks are there in this strategy (risks of succeeding as well as risks of failing)?
14. How will we engage people, whose support and participation will be needed?
15. How will we measure progress?

MONITOR AND EVALUATE

The focus of this stage is the D and E of our ABC-DE model: doing the work and evaluation. The coaching culture steering committee is usually responsible for monitoring the implementation of coaching culture strategy and for evaluating progress. One of its tasks is making sure that there is a learning mechanism built into the implementation process so that the organisation continuously reflects on what works and what doesn't and adjusts accordingly. We described an example of such a process in the 'Stories from the field' section in Chapter 2, when we talked about how Deloitte facilitates organisational learning from individual and team coaching. Progress towards a coaching culture is usually evaluated in order to:

- encourage ongoing improvement
- provide evidence of the impact of coaching and mentoring
- create a sound basis for decision-making and planning.

Monitoring and evaluation should be an ongoing process of learning, embedding and continual improvement and development.

A SNAPSHOT OF CURRENT PRACTICE – CRITICAL COMPONENTS OF COACHING CULTURE STRATEGY IN SELECTED ORGANISATIONS

In this section, we present examples of how some of the organisations we are familiar with incorporate the elements of the strategy described in this chapter in their efforts to cultivate a coaching culture.

Accessibility and relevance – professional services firm

Organisations that have a high degree of accessibility and relevance of coaching identified key target groups for coaching and mentoring, based on the organisation's strategy and needs. An example of different coaching modalities in a professional services firm is shown in Exhibit 6.4.

Exhibit 6.4 Coaching and mentoring modalities in a professional services firm

Modality	Target group	Objective
Transition executive coaching	Newly promoted partners	To facilitate a quick and successful transition to the new role
Career coaching	Young, talented professionals who have been with the firm for two to three years	To support young professionals choose the line of service that is best suited to their needs, ambitions and talents
Mentoring	Everyone in the firm	To allow everyone to have meaningful career and development conversations with people who are familiar with the firm's culture and strategy
Maternity mentoring	Mothers preparing to return to the workplace after maternity leave	To support returning mothers to successfully transition back into the workplace
Family and career	For all levels of managers	To enable individuals in high-pressure jobs to balance work and personal life
High-performing teams	For teams working on demanding long-term projects	To facilitate team performance, enhance synergies and leverage team dynamics

| Line manager coaching | For all team members | To support individuals in growing and learning on the job |
| Peer coaching (via action learning sets) | For senior managers | To support exchange of experiences and facilitate learning from real-life work challenges |

Support and reinforcement – a consumer goods company

In order to efficiently deliver coaching and mentoring, a global consumer goods company focused on setting up and maintaining a strong external and internal pool of coaches, as well as developing coaching and mentoring skills among all of its employees.

The coaching curriculum of this organisation includes modules for employees at all levels, including team members with no managerial responsibilities. The company intranet contains a variety of useful tools people can use to improve their coaching skills.

To further professionalise the company's coaching offering, the emphasis is on internal coaches and mentors obtaining qualifications and accreditation by one of the coaching bodies. The company also invested a lot in creating and facilitating a network of coaches and mentors to ensure consistency and quality of coaching, as well as alignment with the wider organisational goals.

Additionally, a network for managers interested in leading with a coaching style has recently been launched. The network provides its members with an opportunity to keep up to date with the recent developments in coaching and offers a forum for discussion and exchange of experiences. Many of the network members are informal coaching and mentoring champions, regularly advocating for coaching. This has been mentioned as an important factor in encouraging coaching and is believed to contribute greatly to strengthening a coaching culture.

The organisation regularly issues newsletters or organises webinars on coaching. An annual conference for all coaches and mentors has taken place for a few years now.

Integration – a global hospitality company

A hospitality company started focusing on integrating coaching into the way business was done because of the urgent need to maintain its competitive edge by focusing on operational excellence and creating an outstanding experience for its guests.

Coaching has been included in the organisation's competency model and is being evaluated both in the performance appraisal and the global employee survey, with the aim of creating clear expectations. The results are closely monitored and followed up to ensure that coaching is used consistently.

All team members have been trained in coaching skills designed to be used in regularly held team meetings. The purpose of these meetings is to elicit bottom–up ideas for improvements and to resolve the operational challenges the hotels are facing on a daily basis.

Measurement – a financial institution

As part of a wider business strategy, a financial institution had explicitly set a goal of developing a coaching culture. A team was formed and the organisation collaborated with a consultancy in order to draft and implement a robust strategy. Part of the strategy was evaluating the coaching culture development stage, the quality of coaching (by external and internal coaches, as well as coaching by line managers), readiness for coaching of its whole employee population, as well as the return on investment of some of the most recent coaching engagements. The organisation adopted the four stages of coaching culture tool (Clutterbuck and Megginson 2005) and a number of other measurement tools to perform the audit.

The findings served as a baseline against which the bank's progress can be measured in the future. They also offered a number of valuable insights into the priority areas to focus on in order to move to the next stages of coaching culture development.

SUMMARY

As with every change initiative, a good strategic plan can be key to achieving success in cultivating coaching culture. After establishing a vision of coaching culture and assessing its baseline, the strategic plan provides actions that will close the gap between the two. The four main areas that organisations often look at when putting their coaching culture strategy together are: accessibility and relevance of coaching and mentoring, support and reinforcement, integration and measurement. These four areas have a number of components that need to be carefully chosen and put together into a cohesive plan. It is possible to draft this plan in a workshop, provided that the necessary preparation has been done beforehand.

?

FIELDWORK

Think of your organisation (or one that you are familiar with) and answer the following questions:

- If you were to organise a coaching culture strategy workshop for the organisation, who would you invite? Why?
- Who should own the coaching culture strategy?
- Based on the coaching culture vision, as well as the baseline assessment, which components of coaching culture strategy should the organisation be focusing on in the next three years? Why?
- What resources will you need?
- What are the risks of this strategy (risks of succeeding as well as risks of failing)?

PART THREE

LAYING THE FOUNDATIONS

CHAPTER 7

Making Effective Use of External Coaches

'The meeting of two personalities is like the contact of two chemical substances: if there is any reaction, both are transformed.'
C.G. Jung

OVERVIEW

This chapter covers a number of important aspects of the use of external coaches, such as its potential benefits and drawbacks, the importance of creating alignment with organisational priorities and objectives, ways of establishing and maintaining an appropriate pool of external coaches, managing and evaluating coaching engagements, measuring results, and leveraging individual coaching for organisational learning.

EVOLUTION OF EXTERNAL COACHING

In the early days of coaching in organisations, external executive coaches were called in an ad hoc manner, often to 'fix' executives' performance or behavioural problems. They often found themselves involved in remedial, one-off and stand-alone assignments (Coutu and Kauffman 2009; Feldman and Lankau 2005).

However, as organisations became more familiar with coaching, they quickly recognised that it is more beneficial when used as part of a wider HR strategy. Moreover, instead of 'fixing' people, coaching began focusing on accelerating the development and career progression of highly talented individuals who already excelled (Feldman and Lankau 2005; Peltier 2009; Peterson and Little 2008). As a result, coaching gradually freed itself from the stigma it carried for years of being an intervention addressed predominantly to those who need a 'tune-up' due to their performance or behavioural issues.

According to the Ridler Report (2013), working with a coach (particularly an external one) is now associated with being successful rather than an underperformer – a big change compared with the not so distant past.

This change, however, is not without consequences. The growing popularity of coaching leads to an increasing number of people requesting coaching. Without specific criteria, guidelines, matching process and effectiveness measurements, a lot of organisations end up spending huge amounts of money on coaching without having much influence on its quality, process or outcomes.

The sobering realisation that millions are spent annually on external coaching, often without a concrete plan on how to realise its full potential, leads a lot of organisations to re-evaluate the way they utilise it. What they discover through this process is that, indeed, the potential benefit of coaching turns out to be much larger than the sum of individual coaching engagements, especially if it is well aligned with the overall business and HR strategy.

BENEFITS AND DRAWBACKS OF USING EXTERNAL EXECUTIVE COACHES

The gradual evolution in the way external coaching is being used does not mean that it is on a decline. Various studies (the Ridler Report, the ICF Global Coaching Study, the ICF Organisational Coaching Study) indicate that organisations intend to maintain the use of external coaches at the same level as during the previous years, or even increase it – a testimony to the strong standing of externally resourced coaching.

And while the 2014 Building Coaching Culture Study by the ICF suggests that resourcing coaching externally is not as supportive of cultivating a coaching culture as other coaching modalities (for example internal coaching or managers using coaching skills), there are a number of factors that speak in its favour. It is generally believed that external coaches:

- enjoy higher credibility in some organisations and have a greater ease of working with senior leadership
- are independent and therefore beyond any suspicion of a personal agenda or involvement in internal politics
- inspire more trust among senior leaders to share confidential business and personal information, as well as their strengths, development areas and career goals
- are more committed to the coaching relationship, as this is their main job (as opposed to internal coaches, some of whom devote only a fraction of their time to coaching)
- tend to have more experience and better training in coaching (and, therefore, are a really good role-model of coaching, enabling leaders to develop their own coaching skills)
- are more likely to bring a perspective that is entirely different from that of their coaching clients (and consequently can be more effective in challenging their clients).

The main drawbacks of using external coaches, as expressed by organisations we interviewed, are:

- high cost
- lack of proper understanding of company culture
- inability to observe coaching clients 'in action' and giving them feedback based on this observation.

As a result of these perceived benefits and drawbacks, many organisations use external coaches mostly with senior executives and those management populations, where the need for high credibility, confidentiality, unbiased perspective and experience with senior leaders outweigh the high price tag usually attached to it.

KEY STEPS TO MAKING EFFECTIVE USE OF EXTERNAL COACHES

A coordinated, methodical approach to external coaching allows for better alignment with an organisation's priorities, more effective management and more accurate evaluation. Many of the organisations we came across during our research successfully reviewed and redesigned their approach to external coaching, often integrating and aligning it with their approach to internal coaching.

The process depicted in Figure 7.1 is a synthesis of their practices. It is worth noting here that although we focus on making effective use of external coaches in this chapter, many stages described in the process are equally relevant to managing an internal coaching pool.

Figure 7.1 Key steps to making effective use of external coaches

ALIGNMENT

The first thing to look at when setting out to systemise the use of coaches is to check if you have the fundamentals in place (or whether these fundamentals need to be updated or revised). We suggest a simple checklist consisting of three essential elements:

- purpose and scope of external coaching
- organisation-specific definition of coaching
- coaching policy and guidelines.

Purpose and scope of external coaching

Externally resourced coaching will most probably serve a different purpose than other coaching and mentoring modalities. Gaining clarity about what that purpose is for each modality, and what the most appropriate scope of external coaching should be, helped a lot of organisations to make a far better use of coaching. A few helpful questions that can guide reflection on the subject are:

- What are our organisation's current priorities and strategic objectives?
- How can externally resourced coaching support us in achieving these strategic objectives?
- Which populations will it serve best? Why? At which stage of their career?
- What specific outcomes do we expect from external coaching?
- What format (face-to-face, virtual, blended) and duration will be most appropriate for our organisation?

As the answers to these questions crystallise, it will be possible to move on to the next item on the checklist, and reflect on what is your organisation's definition of coaching.

Organisation-specific definition of coaching

Generic definitions, such as: 'Coaching is unlocking a person's potential to maximise their own performance' (Whitmore 2009, p10) or 'Coaching is the art of facilitating the performance, learning and development of another' (Downey 2003, p21) are often too broad and abstract to use with success in a business context.

A number of publications stress the importance of creating an organisation-specific definition of coaching (Hawkins 2012; Bresser 2010). Cultural fit, alignment with the overall strategy, expected outcomes – all these factors will play a role in how you define coaching in your organisation.

An example of an organisation-specific definition is the one used by PwC, which states that coaching is 'a relationship-based productive conversation in which people learn. It is an authentic dialogue that takes place both with our people and our clients.' This definition is more aligned with PwC's overall strategy, priorities and competency model than any of the generic ones could be. It also clearly expresses the firm's expectations of what is required from people – investing in building strong relationships that support an authentic dialogue, which in turn leads to mutual learning and positive outcomes.

A few questions that can be helpful in thinking about an organisation-specific definition of coaching could be:

- What are the key behaviours and outcomes we expect from our people?
- Which of these behaviours can be re-inforced by coaching?
- Which outcomes can be supported by coaching? How?
- How can these behaviours and outcomes be captured in a definition of coaching?
- How do we define the roles of all the parties involved: the coach, the coaching client, the organisation?

Coaching policy and guidelines

At this stage, it is worth considering creating (or revising) the coaching policy and guidelines. Any organisation that offers external coaching on a regular basis will find it useful to answer questions such as:

- Who is eligible to receive external coaching?
- What should be the specific criteria against which we assess requests for coaching?
- What should be the procedure for obtaining external coaching?
- How and where do we communicate that procedure?
- What should be the standard length of a coaching assignment? Do we allow extensions?
- Do we want to limit coaching engagements per coach? If yes, what is the upper limit?
- What are the main coaching engagement process steps (see Exhibit 7.5 for an example)?
- What are the additional resources that will help people in establishing an effective coaching relationship (for example coaching client 'guide to coaching')?

Exhibit 7.1 presents a sample coaching policy and guidelines content page.

Exhibit 7.1 Sample coaching policy and guidelines in a public organisation

Table of contents

- Our coaching philosophy – what is coaching and why we use it
- Our vision for coaching
- Coaching options
- Are you eligible for coaching?
- The role of the coach
- The role of the coaching client
- Confidentiality policy
- Coaching engagement standard duration
- Extensions policy
- Coaching approval policy
- Communication between coach and client
- Other activities in support of coaching

ESTABLISHING AND MAINTAINING AN APPROPRIATE POOL OF COACHES

After reviewing and updating the fundamentals – the purpose for coaching, organisation-specific definition of coaching, as well as policy and guidelines – it is time to look at how to establish and maintain an appropriate pool of external coaches. This is particularly important for organisations that use coaches on a regular basis as part of their wider learning and development agenda.

The key elements of establishing and maintaining an appropriate pool of coaches that emerged from our interviews and experience are presented in Figure 7.2.

Figure 7.2 Key elements in establishing and maintaining an appropriate pool of coaches

A.
Defining the
required
coach pool

C.
Coach
support &
development

B.
Coach
assessment
& selection

D.
Coach pool
marketing

Defining the required coach pool

Being clear about the kind of coaches you require will pay off in the future. In some organisations, a requirement for two (or more) levels of coaches, for different audiences, can emerge. Understanding that early on in the process helps prevent delivering confusing messages to both internal and external audiences.

Issues to consider when defining the desired coach pool include:

- level
- coaching purpose
- specialists vs generalists
- diversity
- psychological qualifications
- existing vs new coaches.

Level

Are you looking for the very best coaches available, to work with your most senior people? Or for competent coaches, who can work with middle and junior managers and professional staff?

While the basic criteria for selection will remain the same whatever the level of coach required, the detail of the questions asked and evaluating their responses may be very different. Top-level coaches can be expected to have more experience, more breadth, greater levels of self-awareness, reflectivity, and to be at a much higher level of socio-emotional maturity.

Coaching purpose

Hawkins and Smith (2006) define four levels of coaching complexity:

- skills
- performance
- developmental
- transformational.

The breadth of knowledge and level of general personal competence required increases significantly at each level.

Specialists versus generalists

There may be a need for some coaches, who have particular expertise, especially at the skills coaching level (for example, presentation skills) or who have particular experience in a sector or discipline (for example banking, or international sales).

Diversity

The coach pool is a reflection of the organisation itself. While you may not wish to engage in positive discrimination, an appropriate balance of racial/cultural origin, gender/sexual preference and discipline should be borne in mind.

Psychological qualifications

At this level of operation, all coaches should have at least a sound general understanding of coaching psychology or behavioural science. For some clients who wish to make deeper changes, the coach will need to be qualified in a relevant psychological discipline. It is worth noting that coaches who can do that kind of work also come in many varieties. A coach who bases their practice in cognitive behavioural theory will have a very different approach from one whose training emphasises positive psychology or Gestalt.

Existing versus new coaches

It is likely that you will have some coaches already working in the business. They may be well liked and have a positive reputation, but sadly that doesn't necessarily mean that they are effective coaches. Our experience in coach assessment and selection activities shows that there are many cases of well-entrenched coaches who are very good at networking within the company, but who prove to be severely incompetent if assessed by a professional.

Coach assessment and selection

Large organisations are often overwhelmed by the number of responses to a request for proposal (RFP) for executive coaching services. Frequently, there are hundreds of applications to sieve through and the selection process can be a daunting task.

That is the main reason some organisations hire consortiums of coaches or groups of small coaching consultancies. However, there is a growing trend away from the practice of hiring those ready-made pools of external coaches, for two main reasons:

- high variability in quality of the coaches provided
- inadequacy of supervision and continuous professional development in many providers.

Additionally, more and more organisations decide to invest in the selection and assessment process, being aware of the high probability that, if not chosen carefully, some of the coaches they hire will prove to be ineffective, or worse, will cause harm (Berglas 2002, pp86–92).

A typical selection and assessment process consists of the following stages:

- preparing an RFP for provision of executive coaching services
- initial evaluation of individual candidates – shortlisting
- evaluating shortlisted candidates
- follow up and report back to the coaches – feedback to help with their continuous professional development.

Preparing an RFP for provision of executive coaching services

Creating a good RFP for the provision of executive coaching services can save a lot of time and effort in the later stages of the selection process.

The aims of the RFP are to:

- encourage sufficient applications from high-quality coaches of different and diverse backgrounds
- ensure that coaches with insufficient experience, skill or understanding of their practice are weeded out at an early stage.

A typical RFP normally has three parts:

- information about the company and the expected role, qualifications and experience of executive coaches
- the application form
- contract details.

Potential coaches will need a reasonable amount of information about the organisation and the role of executive coaching within it in order to appropriately respond to the RFP. An example table of contents of an RFP for executive coaching services provision is given in Exhibit 7.2.

Exhibit 7.2 RFP for the provision of executive coaching services

Table of contents

- General background to the organisation
- Nature of business (what it does, who the customers are, etc)
- Number and location of employees
- Size (and, if appropriate, location) of the executive population
- Vision and values
- The organisation's people strategy
- The coaching strategy
- What it is looking for in terms of externally resourced executive coaches
- Description of the intended target audience
- Purpose of the selection and assessment process
- Schedule and process overview
- Details of the application process

Initial evaluation of individual candidates – shortlisting

Irrespective of whether the applicants are freelance coaches or belong to a large coaching organisation, an application for each of the coaches will be necessary for the initial shortlisting of individual coaches. Typically, some questions on the application should be aimed at simplifying the sifting process by weeding out poor candidates at an early stage. Immediate rejection is likely for applicants who:

- have little or no experience coaching
- have only just qualified/entered the profession
- have no evidence of appropriate supervision
- have little or no evidence of continuous professional development as a coach.

For those candidates with a satisfactory or good response, it is important to ensure a fair, consistent and transparent process. Ideally:

- Each scored applicant should be assessed by two or more assessors independently.
- These assessors should review together the first 10–20 applications, to ensure they are applying the criteria consistently.
- A coaching specialist should be available to review any applications that they are unsure of how to mark, or where there are more than two points in their total scores.
- Borderline cases should also be referred to the coaching specialist.

It is also important to ensure that the initial selection process does not exclude people who may be highly competent coaches, but who, for example, do not have high-level formal qualifications or who are niche coaches in an area of relevance to the organisation. So, for example, in considering applications, a candidate who has an advanced diploma in coaching but shows little evidence of CPD should not outscore someone who has a much lower level of initial accreditation but can demonstrate a high quantity and quality of continuous professional development through other means, such as multiple short courses.

If there is a high proportion of borderline candidates, you may wish to interview these by telephone to sort them further. The interview should concentrate on areas of lower scores, giving them an opportunity to rectify any omissions they may have made in their applications.

Evaluating quality and efficacy of coaching

It is particularly challenging to select and assess external coaches based on the quality and efficacy of coaching they provide. Measuring the quality of coaching is difficult for two main reasons:

- Executive clients may find the experience of being listened to rewarding in itself and over-rate the benefits they receive.
- Measuring outcomes against goals set at the beginning of the relationship only gives a partial picture. Many of the outcomes are unexpected and may take longer than the duration of the coaching relationship to become obvious.

However, our experience indicates that hiring external coaches solely according to their paper qualifications and references can be highly unsatisfactory.

Organisations that aim to check the quality and efficacy of coaching commonly use at least one of the following methods to evaluate the shortlisted coaches:

- psychological interview
- panel interview
- observed session and post-session reflection
- coach assessment centre.

Psychological interview

Some organisations use a semi-structured psychological interview, which explores the coach's personal and professional development and their awareness of psychological issues related to coaching. The interview is conducted by a chartered psychologist according to a specifically designed scheme of assessment.

Panel interview

The aim of the panel interview is to explore the candidate's depth and breadth of coaching expertise and their 'fit' with the organisation and the intended clients. The interview is usually led by a panel consisting of three to (maximum) five persons, responsible for different aspects of the interview. Interviews typically take 45 minutes and are followed by a discussion amongst the assessors, to agree on scorings.

Observed session and post-session reflection

The aim of the observed session is to see the coach in action. Do their behaviours and demonstrated skills match their rhetoric and theoretical knowledge?

A minimum of two observers is required to achieve optimum results. They will normally be outside the room, watching via a video, to avoid influencing the coach/coachee interaction. You may wish to offer dyads as an alternative to having the observers in the room.

Either way, we suggest that the observers greet the coach and coachee at the beginning and end of the session.

The intention of post-session reflection is to:

- assess the coach's level of self-awareness and reflectivity – a strong indicator of potential for continuous improvement in the role
- enable them to gain greater value from participating, through structured reflection.

Organisations usually allow individual coaches 24 hours to email their reflections. This can be extended to 48 hours in special circumstances, but the quality of recall deteriorates rapidly, so it is in their interest to respond in this period. Experience has shown that many coaches tend to focus on the mechanics of the session, rather than on what they did well or less well, or might have done differently, or what they learned. It might therefore be useful to emphasise that you are looking for real evidence of their ability to critique their own performance.

Sample instructions used in a public organisation are presented in Exhibit 7.3.

Exhibit 7.3 Sample post-session reflection instructions

Please reflect on the coaching session that you have undertaken today.
The assessment criteria for this element of the process are:

- self-awareness
- ability to articulate the client's perception
- extent of critical self-review
- flexibility
- ability to define strategies to progress the coaching process.

You may find the following questions helpful for your self-reflection:

- From the perspective of the client, how do you think the session went?
- If you had an opportunity to do the session over again, what would you do differently? What choices did you make working with this client?
- If you were to work with this client in a number of sessions, what strategy would you use to help the client to progress?

You do not need to spell out the client's issue. Please respect their confidentiality in your responses.

Please limit your response to 1,000 words and return it by attachment to [email address] by 12:00 tomorrow.

Follow up and report back to the coaches

The majority of applicants will not make it to the final pool. Nonetheless, it is important that they should feel the company has acted responsibly and fairly towards them. At the minimum, written feedback should be given to all candidates. It might prove useful to give special attention to:

- existing coaches who don't make it – at a minimum, a personalised addendum to the form letter and a follow-up telephone call
- coaches whose strong reputation in the market is not represented in the quality of their application – again, personalised feedback may be helpful in maintaining the company's good reputation.

For those coaches who were shortlisted and invited to the panel interview, psychological interview or observed session, feedback will have developmental character.

In the case of coaches who participated in an interview or observed coaching session, the feedback to the coach also needs to be captured while the observations are fresh. In the discussion, agree at least three positive and up to three negative observations you wish to provide. Issues to consider include:

- What is the evidence for this observation?
- Is this a general or specific observation?
- Will the coach be able to use this feedback to improve their coaching practice?

Coach assessment centre

An increasing number of organisations use a combination of all the above methods in a coach assessment centre.

Coach assessment centres can provide a pragmatic way of evaluating new executive coaches (before they are hired), as well as the existing ones. In most cases, they save far more than their cost, by weeding out ineffective coaches the business is currently using and helping to avoid hiring ineffective ones.

A well-designed, well-run assessment centre is an advertisement for the organisation in terms of its commitment to coaching quality and fairness in the selection of coaches. It has a positive impact on both internal and external audiences.

Coach support and development

In order to maximise the quality and efficacy of coaching and to align it with the organisation's strategy and top priorities, many organisations invest in supporting and developing the external pool of coaches.

The main elements of this support are:

- induction
- continued professional development and supervision
- coach pool marketing.

Induction

After coaches have been selected, it is important to have an induction process to ensure that coaches:

- familiarise themselves with the company and its HR strategy
- know of the relevant initiatives and tools that are being used by the organisation, such as psychometrics, 360-degree feedback, development programmes
- get the overview of policy, guidelines and coaching engagement process
- are informed of the support available, including supervision and continuous professional development sessions.

Continuing professional development

There are several very good reasons for investing in continuing coach development:

- to ensure the coaches understand enough about the organisation, its culture and its strategy to contextualise their coaching
- to provide a consistent quality of supervision
- to enable coaches to learn from each other. Some organisations mix internal and external coaches to maximise the learning potential, although there may in some circumstances be issues of confidentiality in this arrangement.

The format of the supervision or continuous professional development (CPD) sessions is negotiated between the coaches and the supervisor, with approval as necessary from the company. Sessions where the primary emphasis is on CPD may be up to 20 people. Sessions where the emphasis is on supervisior would usually be no more than ten people.

Exhibit 7.4 gives an example of a typical supervision-oriented session with a duration of four to six hours.

Exhibit 7.4 Typical supervision-oriented session

> **Part one: Review of information from the company** (eg results of an employee opinion survey, changes in key priorities, etc)
> **Part two: Group supervision**
> Each participant has an opportunity to present one or more issues for discussion.
> Two or more issues are selected.
> The participant presenting the issue chooses which method of group supervision they would find most helpful.
> The supervisor facilitates the discussion(s).
> The presenting participant summarises their learning.
> Other participants also summarise their learning.
> **Part three: Knowledge input and skills practice in an area of coaching chosen by the coach pool**

Coach pool marketing

A coaching pool is not helpful unless it is used: the greater the usage, the stronger the reputation of coaching within the organisation.

Issues to consider include:

- To what extent will you be able to insist that executives can only use coaches who have been included in the coach pool? (What sanctions will be available in case of breaches of this rule?)
- What media will you use to ensure that potential coaching clients are aware of the coach pool and the quality of its members? Options include:
  - articles in employee publications (print or web)
  - management briefings
  - letter from the CEO to all executives eligible for externally resourced coaching
  - inclusion of promotional material in all executive development events
  - using top management champions, who use coaches from the pool, to promote the value of properly assessed coaches.
- How will potential coaching clients access the pool? Common options are:
  - a website with coach details
  - printed publications with coach details
  - a central advisory resource in HR
  - all of the above.
- Will coaches be assigned by HR or selected by coachees themselves?

MANAGING COACHING ENGAGEMENTS

External coaching engagements require careful management if we want to maximise their effectiveness. It is clear that large organisations need a person or even a small team devoted to managing external and internal coaching engagements.

A typical coaching engagement process includes a number of stages (Exhibit 7.5 presents an example of externally resourced coaching engagement steps).

We would like to focus on two important stages of this process here:

- matching coaching clients with coaches
- three-way contracting.

Matching coaching clients with coaches

There is a wide consensus that a high-quality coaching relationship is an important factor for successful outcomes (for example Asay and Lambert 1999; Kampa-Kokesch and Anderson 2001; O'Broin and Palmer 2006; McKenna and Davis 2009). However, the subject of client–coach matching is still marginal in the literature on the subject.

A review of literature (Boyce et al 2010; Hollenbeck 2002; Homan Blanchard and Miller 2008; O'Broin and Palmer 2006) identified three key criteria:

Commonality

It has been recorded in literature that having things in common can help coach and coachee to build trust, openness and rapport. There are three key areas that can contribute to that feeling of commonality:

- demographics (age, gender, race, ethnicity)
- personal (interests, hobbies, religious affiliation or even sexual orientation)
- professional (credentials, professional training and professional experience).

Compatibility

Compatibility refers to the ability of coach and coaching client to establish rapport and trust and is often based on similarities in temperament and personality. However, it is important to mention here that although these similarities help initial bonding, they can be detrimental to the learning potential of the coaching relationship. A coach who is too similar to their client might not be able to offer a radically different perspective or challenge the client sufficiently enough.

Credibility

This criterion focuses on whether the coach has the necessary skills and credentials to meet their clients' needs. It is a reflection of clients' perception of their coach's credibility. The literature reports cases when the effectiveness of coaching was reduced because of the client's perception that their coach did not have sufficient experience or skills to assist them with their challenges (Sue-Chan and Latham 2004).

There are many different ways to match coaches with coaching clients.

Free selection

Coaching clients have access to the coaching pool and make their own choice, based on coaches' available bios and arranging a few phone or face-to-face interviews.

Limited selection

A common approach is for the HR or coaching manager to shortlist three coaches, based on coaching client needs and profile, and then allow the coaching client to make the final choice using face-to-face 'chemistry' meetings.

Centralised selection

In some cases, selection of an appropriate coach is made centrally, by the HR or coach manager. This approach is particularly common when coaching is part of a larger leadership development programme and there is a large number of coaching engagements that need to be initiated at once.

After a coaching engagement is under way, it might be worthwhile to check whether the match was indeed a good one. This can be done either by informally checking with the coaching client or a short survey administered to measure the coaching client's satisfaction with their coach.

Three-way contracting

The three-way contracting between coach, client and the client's line manager or coaching sponsor is relatively commonplace in coaching. Organisations that use it believe that it can provide a valuable opportunity to clarify and align agendas, establish the support needed from the line manager and sometimes even improve the direct report–line manager relationship.

The three-way meeting usually takes place after the first client–coach session. However, some organisations choose to have more than one, often to review progress and evaluate final outcomes of coaching.

The issues that are commonly addressed in the first three-way meeting are:

- defining the success of the coaching assignment
- discussing coaching client strengths and areas they wish to work on/develop
- support the client will need from their line manager
- way and time of reviewing the coaching engagement.

Although potentially beneficial, three-way meetings are not without risk, the most common ones being:

- the coaching client might feel uncomfortable discussing some of their goals with their line manager or coaching sponsor, especially if those goals concern managing upwards
- having agreed goals with the line manager or sponsor at the outset of the engagement can lead to a single-mindedness and excessive focus on performance, which vastly limits the developmental potential of coaching
- in multinational/global organisations, the boss may know very little about the work or ability of the coachee – so their contribution may be irrelevant or misleading.

Exhibit 7.5 Example of externally resourced coaching engagement steps

Application
Candidates for coaching are identified (either through referral or application to coaching manager)
Candidate's need is being evaluated to see if they qualify for coaching and what kind of coaching will be most appropriate
Coaching client completes the application for coaching, including coaching readiness questionnaire
Coaching client's sponsor reviews and signs off coaching application and submits it to the coaching manager
Coaching manager reviews and approves/rejects the application

Selection
Potential coaches for the client are identified
Client shortlists, interviews and selects the coach
Coaching manager notifies the selected coach and coach initiates the first meeting with the client

Coaching
Coach, client and their sponsor have their initial meeting
Coach and client complete the coaching agreement and send it to the coaching manager
Coach and client complete action plan and roadmap for coaching and send it to the coaching manager and sponsor
Coach and coaching client have ongoing coaching sessions

Evaluation
Coaching manager conducts mid-point check-in with the coaching client
Coach and coaching client complete final check-in and close of the engagement
Coaching evaluation is sent to the client within one day of coaching engagement completion
Follow-up evaluation is sent to the client and sponsor after three months from the engagement completion

EVALUATION AND MEASURING RESULTS

Most organisations make at least one attempt at evaluating coaching, and it is usually done when the engagement draws to a close.

In some cases, as in the process described in Exhibit 7.5, there are mid-point checks and follow-up evaluations used as well.

However, relying on the coaching client's perception of the quality and usefulness of coaching is often regarded as insufficient. In most organisations, there is intense pressure to measure the *effectiveness and efficacy* of coaching. Coaches and sponsors both feel driven to demonstrate a high return on investment (ROI). Unfortunately, most of the attempts to measure ROI are not methodologically robust and hence don't carry much credibility. In particular, they rely on self-report by clients and/or sponsors, who have vested interests in positive outcomes; and they lack evidence of cause and effect. The problem isn't helped by the fact that effective coaching typically changes the goals people are working on, so any initial SMART measures agreed can become rapidly obsolete. Sometimes achievement of initial goals may not be a positive outcome at all!

Then there's the issue of timescale. The simple, relatively shallow objectives tend to be achievable within the lifetime of the coaching intervention. But the deeper, more beneficial outcomes may not occur until much later. The most important outcome of coaching is often propensity – the creation of a capability for change that may only be exercised with future circumstances and opportunities.

Return on investment from coaching is extremely difficult to calculate with any degree of accuracy or credibility, for a number of reasons. Among them:

- Client feedback is not a reliable measure.
- Achievement of initial specific objectives may not be a valid measure, because goals evolve and change, and because the presented issue is typically only part of the value added by effective coaching.

So, if you are an HR director, head of L&D or coaching manager and your CEO wants to know what return the company is getting from investment in external executive coaching, what do you say?

External coaching ROI is a calculation of the ratio of inputs (external coaching fees) versus outputs. There are two main ways to start the ROI calculation. One is to assess broad organisational outcomes, based on centralised data, such as retention or engagement levels. Where appropriate, these can be reinforced by comparison with control groups, for example, employee engagement index in departments whose leaders worked with a coach versus those who have not been coached.

The other is to focus on the outcomes of specific external coaching engagements and to aggregate the data from multiple sources. At an individual level, the ratio of cost to benefit needs to take into account the following questions when coaching is recommended or initiated:

- In what specific ways does this person or their team need to improve their skills, behaviour or performance?
- What specifically will be the:
  - direct impact – immediate effect on the bottom line (for example, from increased sales, reduced rework)
  - indirect impact – for example, reduced customer complaints should lead to increased customer loyalty and/or higher income per transaction.
- What proportion of any resultant savings or increased income might we realistically attribute to a coaching intervention?

Once coaching has taken place, the questions become:

- In what specific ways did this person or team improve their skills, behaviour or performance (both expected and unexpected)?
- What direct impacts did occur?
- What proportion of any resultant savings or increased income can we realistically attribute to coaching?

In both the organisational and individual perspectives, it is important to establish how outcomes will be measured and how the ROI calculation will be made. Engaging stakeholders – coach, coachee, their line manager and perhaps peers and members of their team – in defining the basis for calculating ROI both tests the validity of the measure and helps to maintain the focus of the coaching. However, there is always a danger that coaching may become too focused and miss the opportunity to address wider and deeper issues, something that well-trained coaches should be fully aware of.

LEVERAGING INDIVIDUAL COACHING FOR ORGANISATION DEVELOPMENT

Up until recently, the sponsoring organisations benefited from individual coaching only indirectly, through the development and potential performance improvement of individual coaching clients. However, in their quest to maximise the benefits of individual coaching, companies start seeking trends and patterns emerging from individual coaching engagements and use them as valuable input for other organisation development initiatives. These trends and patterns can focus on issues such as coaching needs, challenges or systemic barriers encountered by coaching clients, commonly held beliefs and mindsets or main drivers and obstacles towards achieving organisational effectiveness.

Some organisations, such as Deloitte (see 'Stories from the field' in Chapter 2), use a structured process to leverage the work done in individual coaching. The process, always performed within the bounds of confidentiality, aims at increasing an organisation's ability to identify and address issues that impact organisational performance.

Collective findings from individual coaching engagements usually complement other sources of organisational learning, such as engagement or employee surveys, assessment or development centres or focus groups.

Exhibit 7.6 gives an example of leveraging individual coaching for the organisation development process used by an organisation in the private sector. It describes a short workshop-style session, where external and internal coaches are brought together to discuss issues and identify emerging trends. Our experience shows that these sessions are often combined with coaching supervision or CPD in the organisations that use them.

Exhibit 7.6 Process for leveraging individual coaching for organisation development process

Objectives

- Gain insight into the main challenges coaching clients bring into coaching.
- Identify main drivers and barriers towards organisational effectiveness (could be processes, structures, aspects of organisational culture, leadership style, mindsets and espoused beliefs, etc).
- Feed the insights back to the organisation.

Format

A short workshop-style session(s) (2–3 hours), where internal and external coaches meet to discuss issues, identify patterns, etc.

Tools and materials

- Post-its
- Flipcharts
- Handouts with questions

Methodology

Discussion

The following questions are discussed in small coach groups (4–5 coaches per group):

- What are the main issues/challenges/pain points/dilemmas that clients bring into the coaching conversations (for example difficulty in communication with the HQ, overpowering leadership style of their boss, their personal improvement as a leader, difficulty to balance work and life, etc)?
- What are clients' aspirations/goals, vision of success?
- What are the drivers of your clients' success (internal, such as beliefs and mindsets, and organisational, such as structures, processes, culture, etc)?
- What are barriers towards your clients' success (internal and organisational – as above)?

Themes identification

Answers are noted on Post-its and placed on a flipchart. Then coaches are split into four groups to identify the main themes. After looking at the themes, coaches ask one last question, which is:

- What is missing (what would we expect to see here and yet it is not present, e.g. focus on some of the organisational priorities, etc)?

Root-cause analysis

Coaches identify a few key themes around which they feel they might have insight as to the root causes. The method of root-cause tree and five whys can be used here. For example, if one of the themes on main issues is difficulty in communication with HQ, the process could look like this:

- Why is there a difficulty to communicate with HQ?
- Because of cultural differences. And lack of familiarity. And limited accessibility (now we have three branches).
- Then we take each branch and ask: 'why are cultural differences such a big issue?', 'why are people not familiar with each other?', 'why is there limited accessibility?'

... and so on until coaches identify what seems to be a root cause.
The outputs of this session are then communicated to HR.

STORIES FROM THE FIELD

SAVE THE CHILDREN: BUILDING THE FOUNDATIONS FOR COACHING CULTURE THROUGH LEVERAGING THE EXTERNAL COACHING NETWORK

This story is based on a series of interviews with the following individuals:

Shola Awolesi – Global Leadership Development Manager at Save the Children

Leonie Lonton – Director of People & Organisational Development at Save the Children

Gareth Owen OBE – Humanitarian Director at Save the Children

Mavis Owusu-Gyamfi – Director, Programme Policy and Quality at Save the Children

Jane Molloy – a Coach in the Coaching Network of Save the Children

Toby Lindsay – a Coach in the Coaching Network of Save the Children

Overview

The story of coaching in Save the Children (SC) is an illustration of leveraging a pool of external coaches to create the essential foundations for a coaching culture and to trigger an organic growth of coaching. It is also an example of a unique partnership between an organisation and its external coaching network, a partnership that, in the case of SC, is rooted in mutual respect and shared commitment to the values and mission of the organisation.

Creating and maintaining the coaching network

When asked about when the SC coaching network came into existence, Shola Awolesi recalls: 'Like many things in life, it was an accident, albeit a positive one. In 2009 Leonie Lonton, Director of People and Organisation at Save the Children, met with Jonathan Stanley, an external consultant, who offered some time on a probono basis to strengthen and improve our Leadership Development Programme (LDP). Jonathan suggested incorporating coaching into the programme. Leonie was a strong champion of that idea. With zero budget and a great desire to bring our leadership development to the next level, we had to get creative! Jonathan introduced us to the first volunteer coaches, who were willing to commit to 12-month probono coaching as part of our programme in 2009. And the rest, as they say, is history.'

In six years (from 2009, when SC first created its coaching network, to 2015), the pool of coaches grew from 25 to 100 volunteers. Each year, 48 senior leaders, such as country directors or regional directors, participate in a 12-month LDP. They are supported by a volunteer coach for the duration of the year-long programme; sometimes these coaching engagements are extended and go beyond the duration of the LDP.

Many leaders who benefited from coaching incorporated coaching skills into their leadership portfolio. Some of them became vocal champions for coaching, openly talking about the transformative nature of their experience. This buzz around coaching contributed to an increase in the demand for coaching and resulted in a new offering called 'developmental coaching', which is focused on managers moving into more senior roles or taking on more challenging projects. These coaching engagements are shorter and typically last up to six months.

The value and impact of coaching

When talking about the value of coaching, Shola Awolesi said: 'We have been incredibly fortunate to be able to tap into the amazing resource that our coaching network has provided over the years. It is not just the access we have to high-quality coaching; we have developed relationships that help us get better in what we do, on an individual and organisational level.'

Leonie Lonton adds: 'The pro bono network has been a piece of magic in the organisation. A fantastic win-win partnership in which Save the Children are able to draw on the support and expertise of highly talented coaches to support our leaders who are working in an ever more volatile and complex world with the most marginalised children and dealing with highly emotional situations and demands.'

All coaches who collaborate with SC do so on a probono basis. It has been estimated that the value of coaching that SC has received since 2009 is around £750,000.

'To give an idea of what this translates into, £380,000 could provide waste collection and disposal in camps in Syria to help reduce the spread of disease. £174,000 would fund a rapid response health team to deliver a mass vaccination campaign. £150,520 would ensure we have the medical supplies and equipment needed for an emergency health unit team to deliver primary health care services ready for immediate access in the event of an emergency. £50,000 could provide a month's supply of nutrient-rich peanut paste for more than 2,700 severely malnourished children. That is what £750,000 gives us.'

But the value of coaching for SC is perceived to be much greater than that. Shola Awolesi reflects: 'Although mostly anecdotal, the positive impact of coaching is undeniable. We consistently get feedback from people who report that coaching helped them raise more funds, get a promotion, lead their teams more effectively, achieve strategic goals.'

Leonie Lonton adds: 'Coaching fits well with our "whole person" approach and has proven to be a transformative experience for a number of our people ... not only for the individual leaders themselves but for their wider environment, especially as SC leaders start to explore using a coaching approach within their teams.'

Gareth Owens says: 'We work in a perpetual motion enterprise that is hostage to world events. The challenges we face are never-ending and the agenda is continuously hijacked by the most recent crisis – Nepal earthquake, Ebola outbreak, Myanmar flood, the war in Syria and so on. Anomaly is our norm. Working in such an environment can often feel terribly out of control. The genius of coaching is that it offers people a little bit of steadiness, a safe space where they can stop for a moment, reflect and regroup. This often leads to major shifts in how people perceive their reality and lead others and has a significant ripple effect in the organisation.'

Jane Malloy, one of the volunteer coaches, contributes by saying: 'On an individual level, coaching helps people develop confidence in their role and focus on what is of vital importance. That creates a virtuous circle, where the positive changes in the coachees bring even more positive changes in their teams, leading to improved teamwork, collaboration and eventually better performance.'

Toby Lindsay, another coach working with SC, says: 'All of my coaching clients valued the time and space that coaching gave them. They were able to map out various elements of their role and go beyond the immediacy of their daily job, which often has them functioning in a highly reactive mode to face a crisis or a humanitarian disaster. People became more aware of their leadership style and the impact it had on others. All my clients have also become more inclined to add a more facilitative and coaching style of leadership to their portfolio.'

For the department that Mavis Owusu-Gyamfi is leading, coaching turned out to help her managers step into their leadership role. Mavis says: 'I run a technical department and most of my managers are experts in their field. While the technical aspects of the job come naturally to most of my people, leading teams can be a challenge. Coaching helped my people develop the skills they need to make their teams more effective and bring about the desired change.'

A unique partnership

SC developed a unique partnership with the volunteer coaches. This partnership is underpinned by a philosophy of mutual benefit, something that Shola Awolesi feels very strongly about: 'We always aim at creating win–win relationships with our coaches. Our end of the bargain is pretty clear – we get high-quality coaching and access to our coaches' expertise on a probono basis. We are mindful that this is a two-way partnership and coaches need to benefit as well.'

SC is very intentional about making coaches feel valued. Unlike many organisations in the private sector, a lot of thought and planning goes into holding up their end of the bargain. For example, SC organises two formal annual gatherings, where coaches can exchange experiences with their peers, learn the latest news about the organisation and the impact of coaching, as well as meet senior executives. Those meetings are also used to get coaches' feedback on what works and what does not work and get their suggestions on how things can be improved to maximise the impact of coaching. SC puts a lot of effort into marketing the coaching network, both inside and outside the organisation, for example by participating in various conferences, contributing to publications and documenting people's testimonials.

The Learning and Development Team continuously educates people about coaching so that they come better prepared and can fully engage in the relationship. Coaches are asked for their feedback regarding how engaged coaching clients have been in the process. An initial three-way contracting is encouraged to demonstrate the organisation's commitment to coaching. Coach—coachee matching is done by focusing on mutual needs and interests; an equal amount of time is invested in understanding coaches' and coachees' needs, interests and preferences.

When asked about their experience, coaches collaborating with SC identified a multiplicity of benefits. The key themes arising from our conversations were:

- a sense of meaning and gratification that comes from supporting a cause close to their hearts
- ability to work with senior executives of an international organisation who face extreme challenges, such as:
  - managing incredibly complex operations, often with extremely scarce resources
  - withstanding tremendous amounts of pressure during disaster relief and emergency response
  - risking their own or their people's lives
- opportunity to hone their coaching skills
- being acknowledged for their contributions
- being consulted and involved in thinking about further developing coaching in the organisation
- belonging to a network of like-minded people
- a sense of being acknowledged and appreciated as a person
- opportunity to contribute to SC coaching and people development strategy.

Ensuring effective use of the coaching network

SC puts great emphasis on educating people in the organisation about coaching and its value. Shola Awolesi recalls: 'In the past we had instances where a coach would arrive for a coaching session to be informed that the manager had been called to respond to a humanitarian disaster. The reasons for not being there were justified but it didn't change the fact that it was a terrible waste of the coach's time and a lost opportunity for the individual and the organisation. We addressed this issue in a number of ways:

- highlighting the cost of coaching in terms of money and time
- incorporating a session about coaching on the Leadership Development Programme
- sharing testimonials and feedback from leaders that have worked with a coach
- developing briefing notes on roles, responsibilities and expectations.

Education was one of our biggest learnings on how to leverage coaching.'

Other factors that support effective use of the coaching network in SC include:

- clear purpose and scope of coaching
- alignment with people strategy
- clear policy and guidelines
- effective matching process
- coaching effectiveness evaluation (both formal and informal, at various stages of the engagement)
- feedback from the coaches and coachees
- keeping the coaching network alive through formal and informal meetings
- leveraging individual coaching for organisation learning
- vocal coaching champions.

While SC is now working on its coaching strategy, which includes embedding coaching into people's daily interactions, those next steps in creating a coaching culture would not be possible without the executive coaching offered by the network of volunteer coaches.

As Leonie Lonton stresses: 'Our network of coaches has been an amazing source of support and ideas as we have worked together to improve and embed our practice and to look at different ways of strengthening our coaching and mentoring support.

We have used an evolutionary approach and are nearly ready to say we have a coaching strategy. More importantly, we have a vision for how this partnership can continue to grow and evolve to make an impact not only within the Save the Children family but within the wider sector.'

MAKING EFFECTIVE USE OF EXTERNAL COACHES AT BOURNEMOUTH UNIVERSITY

Contributed by Dr Colleen Harding, Head of Organisational Development at Bournemouth University

Recruitment to the External Coaching Bank

Bournemouth University (BU) believes that staff development is crucial to the university in helping to meet its strategic and operational objectives and in adding value by raising individual and organisational performance levels.

The university has therefore invested in a range of staff development activities, including coaching. The purpose of the External Coaching Bank, established in 2012, is to:

- provide coaching for senior staff and other leaders and managers
- provide coaching on some of the university-wide staff development programmes
- increase the capacity for providing coaching opportunities internally, by developing a community of internal BU coaches who have experienced high-quality coaching.

Coaches were recruited via an invitation to tender. The two-stage tender process involved an application form where coaches needed to respond in detail to a series of questions. Shortlisted suppliers were then invited to attend an interview process comprising three stages:

- to discuss the context, the purpose of the Coaching Bank and the expectations of the supplier
- a panel interview at which they were asked questions about their coaching experience
- a practical assessment where they were asked to coach an individual member of staff, typical of a coaching client at the university.

Successful providers are placed on the Coaching Bank of approved suppliers under a framework contract for a defined period.

The operation of the External Coaching Bank at Bournemouth University

Coaching is provided as an embedded part of university development programmes.

The programmes themselves are set within the context of the university's strategy and are designed to support individuals working within a wider organisational context. Participants meet their coach for five or six individual coaching sessions over a six- to eight-month period. The coaching is designed to provide business-focused, individually centred development and support.

The organisational development team identify which coaches will be most appropriate to support which programmes. Participants are provided with a selection of coach profiles and invited to express their preference for a particular coach. While this is taken into consideration, coach and coachee availability often provides a pragmatic solution. Thus far this method of matching has been successful.

As the provision of coaching represents a significant investment in the development of individual staff, it is necessary to be able to identify ways to measure the efficacy and benefits of coaching, both for the individual and the organisation.

At the start of the coaching programme, a colleague from the Organisational Development Team meets with the coach and coachee to agree on evaluation principles. Coach and coachee are encouraged to utilise an adapted version of Phillips et al (2012) to prompt a discussion about what they are hoping to gain, what they would like to be different by the end of the coaching, where they are starting from, and preferences for how they like to learn and how they would like to work with the coach. This clarifies the expectations and boundaries and provides a baseline against which the coach, coachee and organisation can identify the impact of the coaching.

Learning from evaluation of coaching at Bournemouth University

The staff at Bournemouth University can access coaching by applying for a programme that has been designed to support individuals in delivering the university's strategy and they are 'sponsored' by their line manager. In theory, this should facilitate alignment between the individual's and the organisation's agenda for coaching.

While the content of individual coaching sessions remains confidential, coaches and coachees are asked to feed back on their experience and process of coaching for evaluation purposes. Informal feedback is sought several times during the process to ensure any arising issues are appropriately addressed. At the end of the coaching process, coaches and coachees are invited to give feedback via an anonymous online survey.

The most recent survey suggests that coaching has been highly beneficial, with over 80 per cent of respondents rating coaching as highly effective or effective, and expressing the willingness to recommend it to others.

In addition to any tangible or intangible benefits of coaching, BU seeks feedback on the coaching programme administration and on anything that it can learn from ongoing individual coaching assignments as an organisation.

As BU is now several years into the operation of the External Coaching Bank, it has also commissioned an independent consultant to conduct telephone evaluation with willing coaches and coachees to find out more about their experience of coaching at the university.

In spite of numerous efforts to create a 'clear line of sight' and strategic alignment, the external evaluation has identified cases of a disconnect between the benefits for the individual and the organisation. The benefits at a personal level were easier to articulate, while the connection to an explicit corporate agenda was less clear. This is leading BU to reconsider ways to effectively establish value and purpose at a personal level that link explicitly to a corporate agenda; this includes a more effective approach to ensuring 'readiness for coaching' and targeting coaching where it will be most effective.

A separate study (Harding 2013) has set out more clearly the ways in which coaching and mentoring at BU have supported staff during a period of significant organisational change and where coaching and mentoring, along with other support, have provided reciprocal benefits for the organisation and individual academics. It is likely that this was the case as the decision to provide coaching and mentoring support was grounded in a genuine intention to support individuals in a challenging and changing environment, rather than with the objective to make academics do what the organisation wanted them to do.

SUMMARY

Effective use of external coaching requires close alignment with the wider business and HR strategy; it is particularly important to be clear on how the organisation defines coaching and how it will help the achievement of business goals. A part of this alignment is identifying the specific purpose of external coaching and creating a policy that outlines when and how external coaching can be used.

To establish and maintain an appropriate pool of executive coaches, you will need clarity on what kind of coaches are needed, a robust process of coach assessment and selection, support and development offered to external coaches, as well as effective marketing of the coach pool.

The frequent pressure to demonstrate return on investment in coaching calls for evaluation and measurement of results. However, it is important to remember that some of the outcomes of coaching will not be measurable, or can even manifest much later, long after the coaching engagement is finalised.

Individual coaching can also be used as a source of information that can serve as crucial input for other organisation development initiatives.

?

FIELDWORK

Reflect on your organisation or an organisation that you are familiar with and answer the following questions:

- What are the needs that can be addressed with external coaching?
- Is the current pool of external coaches appropriate to meet those needs?
- How could the process of establishing and maintaining an appropriate pool of coaches be improved?
- Are external coaching engagements well managed? What are the potential areas for improvement?
- How does the organisation evaluate coaching and measure results? What can be done differently?
- Is the organisation using the learning from individual coaching engagements for organisation development? If not, how could this be achieved? If yes, would you make any improvements to the process?

CHAPTER 8

Developing Internal Capacity for Coaching

'If I learned anything ... it is the notion that we need to be working on all different parts of the system in order to successfully change the whole system.'
Peter M. Senge, *The Fifth Discipline: The Art & Practice of the Learning Organization*

OVERVIEW

In this chapter we talk about how developing an internal capacity for coaching can help develop a coaching culture within an organisation. We focus on three main modalities of internal coaching: manager as coach, coaching within work teams and professional internal coaching.

We share our findings around how these modalities are being used in various organisations and make suggestions as to how they can be leveraged to strengthen coaching culture.

While developing a well-functioning pool of external coaches can be hugely beneficial both for an organisation and individuals being coached, we have yet to hear of a case when it was sufficient to create a coaching culture. In fact, our research suggests that it is virtually impossible to move beyond the tactical stage of a coaching culture without developing internal capacity for coaching.

So what are the key elements of developing such a capacity?

A lot of organisations start from educating managers and employees on the value of coaching and helping them develop the skills, the mindset and the confidence to coach others. Larger organisations create pools of internal coaches, who coach either part- or full-time, depending on the business needs and their availability. Finally, some organisations take it a step further and look at integrating coaching into the various stages of their value chain and the way teams collaborate and achieve goals.

This chapter will take a closer look at the key elements of building internal coaching capacity and capability:

- manager as coach
- instilling a coaching culture in work teams
- internal semi-professional or professional coaching pool.

IS COACHING BY MANAGERS REALLY SO IMPORTANT?

In case you were wondering if coaching by managers might be getting more attention than it deserves, here are a few facts.

Around 2007, Google launched Project Oxygen, a large-scale, multi-year research project, the aim of which was to identify what successful Google managers do (Garvin et al 2013).

Google's people analytics team spent over a year collecting data from performance appraisals, employee surveys, nominations to top manager awards and other sources. Quantitative data was supplemented with qualitative information from interviews.

The findings of Google's research are quite revealing. The number one behaviour associated with being an effective manager was identified as 'being a good coach'. Furthermore, five out of eight key behaviours displayed by effective managers can be seen as directly linked to the coaching style of leadership. Apart from 'being a good coach', the remaining four behaviours, are:

- empowers their team and does not micromanage
- expresses interest in and concern for team members' success and personal well-being
- is a good communicator – listens and shares information
- helps with career development.

We mention Google's Project Oxygen not because its findings are particularly groundbreaking, but because they validate what has been known for decades – that managers should coach their team members if they want to have good results (Evered and Selman 1989; Goleman et al 2002).

If you are still not convinced, there is also the latest research published in ICF, *Building A Coaching Culture* (2014), and CIPD, *Learning and Development* (2015), to support the case. Both reports reveal that the adoption of coaching skills by managers has now become the norm in most organisations. Coaching is also considered one of the most effective development methods available at the moment. Furthermore, it is the number one development method expected to grow further in the coming years (CIPD 2015).

All this data suggests that managerial coaching can have an enormous contribution to the development of coaching culture in an organisation. This seems especially true if we consider that coaching by line managers can be used with a frequency significantly higher than any other development method available, as the managers using coaching skills tend to interact with their employees on a daily basis.

MANAGER ACTING AS A PROFESSIONAL COACH OR A MANAGER USING A COACHING STYLE?

Before examining how managers can contribute to developing a coaching culture in their organisations, we want to make an important distinction, between a manager acting as a professional coach and a manager using a coaching leadership style during the daily interactions with their team.

A manager acting as a professional coach takes off their 'manager' hat for the whole duration of the coaching conversation with their team member and replaces it with a 'professional coach' hat. All principles and norms of professional coaching apply and coaching has a largely developmental nature. This is a relatively rare form of managerial coaching and it poses a number of serious challenges, such as inequality of power (Bresser 2010; Whitmore 2009), confidentiality issues (Anderson et al 2009), and vested interest in the coaching relationship (Matthews 2010).

A manager using a coaching leadership style integrates the coaching approach into their daily management routine (Bresser 2010; Goleman et al 2002). Coaching is not perceived as something over and above their normal managerial duties but as an integral part of their role. This type of coaching doesn't require separating the roles of a coach and a manager and there is no need for signposting the transition between the styles by saying 'let me put my coach hat on'. Coaching style is used only when appropriate, in response to what is required by the situation and people involved.

Our main focus here will be on the latter form of coaching by managers. This is mainly because our experience, as well as research (CIPD 2008), consistently show that expecting a manager to be able to fulfil the role of a professional coach can be both unrealistic and undesirable.

WHAT IS A COACHING LEADERSHIP STYLE?

Paul Hersey and Kenneth Blanchard were among the first to describe coaching leadership style in the late 1960s (1969). In 2000, Daniel Goleman followed suit, documenting findings of Hay/McBer[1] research which found that coaching was one of the leadership styles that had a positive impact on organisational climate and consequently on bottom-line results.

Research by the CIPD, *Coaching at the Sharp End* (2008), identified two main characteristics of coaching style:

- **primary coaching characteristics,** such as development orientation, performance orientation, effective feedback processes, and successful planning and goal-setting
- **mature coaching characteristics**, such as using ideas from team members, powerful questioning, team-based problem-solving, and shared decision-making, all of which are linked to a more participative style of management.

Our own observations of managers who use a coaching style show that they:

- understand the wider organisational objectives and how they translate into their own individual objectives, as well as the objectives of their team
- create clarity on what is expected from their team members in terms of performance
- follow up on progress towards the agreed objectives
- observe performance and give feedback which facilitates performance improvement
- establish accountability
- convey strong belief in their team members' abilities to perform, learn and improve
- create space for learning and reflection
- encourage their team members to solve their own problems
- look for their team members' strengths and ways of leveraging these
- engage their people in identifying long- and short-term development goals and help them create a plan to reach these goals
- create development opportunities through delegation and stretching tasks
- give feedback in a way that builds self-awareness and facilitates growth
- express genuine interest in their people, ask powerful questions and listen deeply
- support their people in implementing their development plan by providing the necessary resources
- create accountability by following up on actions and development plan implementation
- involve their teams in decision-making and problem-solving.

SUPPORTING MANAGERS IN DEVELOPING AND USING A COACHING LEADERSHIP STYLE

There are a number of factors that tend to play an important role in helping managers adopt a coaching leadership style at work. These factors appear to be:

- making the link between coaching style and managerial and organisational effectiveness
- setting clear expectations
- adequate support in developing coaching skills

---

[1] Hay McBer carried out research based on a random sample of 3,871 executives, drawn from a database of 20,000. They identified six distinct leadership styles: coercive, authoritative, affiliative, participative, pace-setting and coaching

- removing systemic barriers
- rewarding the use of coaching style.

MAKING THE LINK BETWEEN COACHING AND MANAGERIAL AND ORGANISATIONAL EFFECTIVENESS

Mastery in coaching style starts with the right mindset. While for some managers a coaching mindset is largely innate, others struggle to adopt it.

Hunt and Weintraub (2007) describe that mindset as having 'an attitude of helpfulness; less need for control; empathy in dealing with others; openness to personal learning and receiving feedback; high standards; a desire to help others develop, a theory of employee development that is not predicated on "sink or swim approach"; and a belief that most people want to learn' (Hunt and Weintraub 2011).

Our observations of leaders in the workplace indicate that developing a coaching mindset hinges on the perception that developing others is a 'must-have', as opposed to a 'nice-to-have'. Unless the business case for a new leadership paradigm is crystal clear, managers used to the old leadership model of 'command and control' will struggle to see the point in approaching things differently. That leads us to the conclusion that any efforts to encourage or support managers in using coaching skills should be linked to business results and communicated as such.

As described by David Garvin and colleagues in their *Harvard Business Review* case study 'Google Project Oxygen: Do Managers Matter?' (2013), Google managers were only willing to experiment with coaching behaviours because the data uncovered by the Google analytics team clearly indicated that coaching leads to managerial effectiveness and better results.

As Olympia Mitsopoulou, the Managing Partner of Atom Wave, put it in one of our conversations: 'Encouraging and supporting managers to coach goes way beyond the development of coaching skills – it has to be a part of a larger effort aimed at management culture change. There is not much point in focusing on the skills if the top management is not committed to making a shift from a "command and control" to a more collaborative and participative leadership style. And there is only one good reason to make such a shift – to help the organisation fulfil its purpose and impact the bottom line in a positive way.'

SETTING CLEAR EXPECTATIONS

There are many different ways in which an organisation can set clear expectations regarding line manager coaching – from senior executive sponsorship, role-modelling and communication to including coaching in the organisation's competency framework and key performance expectations and objectives.

In most organisations, coaching is part of the performance management process. Some organisations ask their line managers to set both quantitative and qualitative goals regarding their role as a coach and the use of a coaching style. This could be anything ranging from a set number of coaching conversations per day to specific ways of enabling others to achieve their individual and team goals.

ADEQUATE SUPPORT IN DEVELOPING COACHING SKILLS

The coaching mindset can be powerful, but without the right coaching skills it delivers suboptimal results. If this seems common sense, you might be surprised to find that in spite of being the most common modality of coaching in organisations, managers who coach have the least amount of coach-specific training, with 51 per cent receiving less than 30 hours of formal coach training and 22 per cent receiving no training at all (ICF 2014).

Of course, the answer to the challenge of developing the necessary skills doesn't lie solely in how much training managers receive: training has to be effective and achieve its objectives.

Driven by curiosity about what seems to work, we asked various coaching skills training providers and internal L&D departments what makes good coaching training. The characteristics presented below are a synthesis of the answers we received, as well as our own experiences.

Tailor-made or customised for the specific needs of the organisation

Training should address the real-life challenges managers face and be tied to the key strategic objectives of the organisation to ensure relevance and usefulness. This speaks in favour of in-house training, as opposed to generic open-house programmes.

Providing some form of baseline

It is important to know what the starting point for each manager is, so that they can easily follow their progress by using the same tool at the end of the programme or a few months afterwards. Some organisations use only self-evaluation, but well-designed (non-generic) 360-degree feedback is considered more reliable.

Well integrated with other leadership development initiatives

Coaching skills training should be aligned with or integrated into the wider leadership development initiatives. Not only does this prevent overlaps or repetition, but it also reinforces both the skills and the messages conveyed in the programmes.

Practical

Good coach training should provide managers with the skills that enable them to integrate a coaching leadership style into their daily management activities. This often means equipping them with techniques, tools and models that can be used informally, in team meetings or in short casual conversations.

Modular and delivered over a period of time

Most of our respondents reported that short, one-off training is ineffective in supporting managers to use coaching skills on the job. Modular interventions, delivered over a period of time (at least three months), give managers an opportunity to implement the newly acquired skills on the job and report back on their progress, thus facilitating their learning, creating accountability and providing the necessary guidance. Some organisations have been using blended learning with good results, combining face-to-face modules with e-learning.

Accompanied by one-to-one coaching by a professional coach

An experience of being coached is considered to be a major accelerator in developing a coaching leadership style. Managers who have an opportunity to work with a coach on the implementation of their own coaching or leadership skills can benefit both from practical support and having a role model.

Providing additional opportunities for practice on job-related issues

Effective coach training programmes provide managers with an opportunity to practise the use of coaching skills to solve various job-related issues. This could take the form of peer-coaching, coaching clinics, or action learning sets.[2]

Having a well-developed evaluation process

It will not be possible to say if the programme was effective without a well-developed evaluation process. A coaching skills programme can be evaluated on a number of levels. Some organisations use evaluation that addresses only the initial levels of Kirkpatrick's Framework (up to the level of job behaviours), whereas some go all the way to level 4 or use Phillips' five-level ROI framework to calculate return on investment. We even came across organisations that added a level to Phillips' framework. The additional level focused on the sustainability of the results and is described in more detail in 'Developing solution-focused coaching and feedback skills in a Greek bank' in the 'Stories from the field' section of this chapter.

REMOVING SYSTEMIC BARRIERS

There are a number of serious challenges that managers face when trying to use coaching skills with their teams. Heads of HR or training and development often lament that millions invested in trying to support line managers in developing and implementing coaching skills on the job have had minimal effect. There are considerable practical barriers to effective line manager coaching. Many of them are of a systemic nature. A few examples of potential systemic barriers to coaching are:

- a highly competitive culture, where acts of personal heroics are valued more than collaboration
- reward systems and incentives based mostly on financial results; or on individual, rather than team, results
- a fast-moving business where taking action is perceived to be more important than occasional reflection
- where coaching is not part of formal or informal manager role description
- where there is a lack of psychological safety
- team dynamics that lock the manager and the team into a set of habitual dysfunctional behaviours.

We will talk about the possible implications of the last barrier in the next part of this chapter: 'Coaching within the work team'.

REWARDING THE USE OF COACHING STYLE

Although the issue of rewarding coaching is controversial, some organisations believe that it can support the cultivation of a coaching culture. The most common way of rewarding coaching is to do so indirectly, by making it one of the criteria that contribute to the

---

[2] 'Action learning is an approach to solving real problems that involves taking action and reflecting upon the results. The learning that results helps improve the problem-solving process as well as the solutions the team develops. The action learning process includes (1) a real problem that is important, critical, and usually complex, (2) a diverse problem-solving team or "set", (3) a process that promotes curiosity, inquiry, and reflection, (4) a requirement that talk be converted into action and, ultimately, a solution, and (5) a commitment to learning. In many, but not all, forms of action learning, a coach is included who is responsible for promoting and facilitating learning as well as encouraging the team to be self-managing.' Source: Wikipedia.

overall performance evaluation and, by inference or overtly, to career progression for the manager.

Other organisations decide to reward coaching directly, through awarding titles of 'coach of the year' accompanied by a tangible reward, such as a trip or a gift.

We agree with Peter Hawkins, who warns against rewarding coaching too early in the process, before coaching is seen and accepted as an integral part of the manager's role. The danger there is that it may lead to the perception that coaching is yet another 'tick box' exercise that needs to be performed to get the annual bonus (Hawkins 2012).

DEVELOPING SOLUTION-FOCUSED COACHING AND FEEDBACK SKILLS FOR MANAGERS IN A GREEK BANK

This story was contributed by Olympia Mitsopoulou, the Managing Partner of Atom Wave

In 2007, a Greek-owned bank employing more than 12,000 people and operating in seven countries turned to Atom Wave asking for support in equipping its Greek branch managers with the necessary skills to develop their teams.

At that point, most of the branch managers carried most of the burden associated with sales generation, restructuring non-performing loans, and ensuring that other key objectives were being met. The culture of 'personal heroics' was so prevalent across the branches that most of the team members had very little space for initiative. This led to a host of issues, the main ones being branch manager burn-out and team members' skills being underutilised.

The desired outcome of the programme was for all team members to contribute to the branch's sales and productivity.

Exhibit 8.1 Stages of the coaching and feedback development programme in a Greek bank

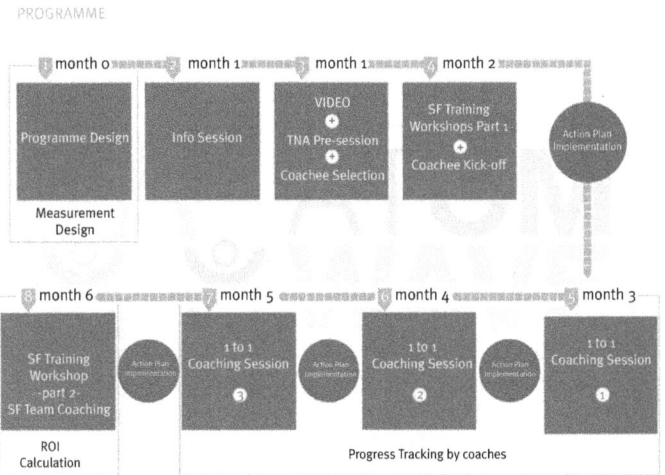

Based on the bank's brief, a solution-focused[3] (SF) coaching and feedback development programme was designed and delivered to a total of 16 groups and 270 branch managers.

The programme combined skills training and one-to-one coaching and had a duration of six months to provide support in incorporating the new solutions-focused way of managing people.

In addition, each participant was required to select a member of their team to focus and apply a development plan during the programme, so that progress can be more visible.

In essence, the programme was about shifting the management style from telling to asking. Participants learned how to ask their team solution-focused questions, how to identify their people resources and how to have solution-focused feedback conversations that are constructive and useful.

How did Atom Wave measure the intervention?

Below is a study focusing on one of the participating groups consisting of 14 branch managers with teams of between 5 and 10 people.

Atom Wave followed Phillips' methodology for measuring return on investment and added one more level of their own – sustainability.

Exhibit 8.2 The six levels of coaching and feedback development programme evaluation

THE SIX LEVELS OF EVALUATION

	Evaluation method
1. SATISFACTION	EVALUATION FORMS (SMILEY SHEETS)
2. LEARNING	BEFORE & AFTER VIDEO RECORDING SIMULATION
3. IMPLEMENTAION	FOLLOW-THROUGH OF ACTION PLAN DURING COACHING SESSIONS
4. BUSINESS IMPACT	DATA COLLECTION DURING COACHING SESSIONS
5. RETURN ON INVESTMENT	ROI CALCULATIONS OF SALES / TIME / PRODUCTIVITY / COST SAVINGS
6. SUSTAINABILITY	QUESTIONNARIES 12 MONTHS AFTER THE START OF THE PROGRAMME

What were the results?

Level 1: How did they like it?

All participants completed a survey at the end of the programme. Questions were about the level of satisfaction/reaction. As shown in Exhibit 8.3, reaction to the programme was positive.

---

[3] For more information on how solution-focused coaching works, go to: https://www.youtube.com/watch?v=JX2FnFUqLMo

Exhibit 8.3 Reaction to the coaching and feedback development programme

Level 1: Satisfaction results (Scale 1-10)

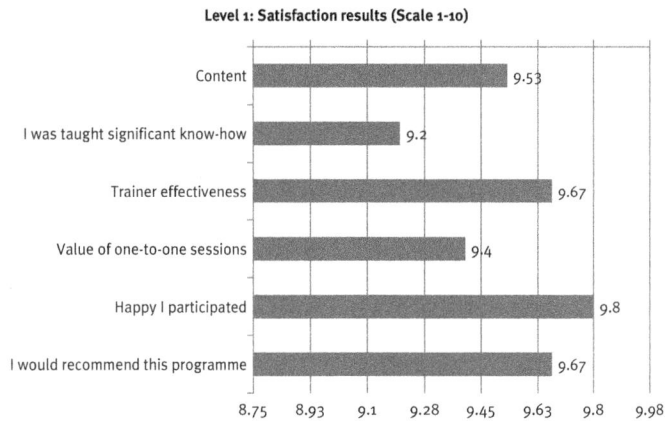

Content	9.53
I was taught significant know-how	9.2
Trainer effectiveness	9.67
Value of one-to-one sessions	9.4
Happy I participated	9.8
I would recommend this programme	9.67

(x-axis: 8.75 8.93 9.1 9.28 9.45 9.63 9.8 9.98)

Level 2: What did participants learn to do differently?

Learning data were mainly captured through the video recording of two coaching simulations at the start of the programme and at the end of the programme.

Exhibit 8.4 presents the BEFORE and AFTER results. Results indicate that all participants enhanced their skills.

Exhibit 8.4 Before and after results of the coaching and feedback development programme

LEVEL 2. LEARNING EVALUATION RESULTS:
COACHING & FEEDBACK SKILLS ASSESSMENT / (BASED ON DVD RECORDINGS)

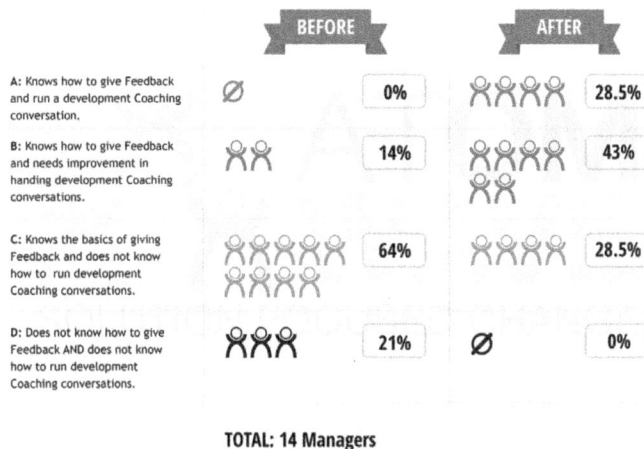

	BEFORE	AFTER
A: Knows how to give Feedback and run a development Coaching conversation.	0%	28.5%
B: Knows how to give Feedback and needs improvement in handing development Coaching conversations.	14%	43%
C: Knows the basics of giving Feedback and does not know how to run development Coaching conversations.	64%	28.5%
D: Does not know how to give Feedback AND does not know how to run development Coaching conversations.	21%	0%

TOTAL: 14 Managers

Level 3: How applicable was what the participants learned?

Atom Wave followed through the implementation of the new solution-focused ways of working during the three coaching sessions that took place in the six months following the first workshop.

During each of the sessions, programme coaches tracked progress and recorded results in each of the different development areas set by each participating manager.

Out of the 14 participating managers, all applied the new solution-focused techniques during the programme duration.

Level 4: What is the business impact of implementing this solution-focused coaching programme?

The 14 participating managers achieved a total of 50 objectives that had tangible and/or visible results. These results were in the following five categories:

- sales increase
- productivity increase
- better management skills
- attitude change
- communication and collaboration improvement.

Level 5: What is the ROI of the business impact of this SF intervention?

For the ROI calculations, time savings were calculated. These time savings were the result of improved delegation, increased productivity due to increased motivation, more efficient time use, less time for supervision because of better development, and more. They were all related to the adoption of a solution-focused way of coaching the team.

These time savings were calculated to amount to a total of 16.5 hours daily across the group of the 14 participants as a whole. These 16.5 hours multiplied by the €30 average man-hour cost corresponded to a saving of €495, which annualised to €125,235.

Based on the ROI formula:

$$ROI = \frac{\text{Programme Benefits} - \text{Programme Costs}}{\text{Programme Cost}} \times 100\% =$$

$$\frac{€125,235 - €58,334 \times 100\% = 115\%}{€58,334}$$

All the presented results were validated by the client.

Additionally, 9 out of the 14 participating managers reported significantly increased sales results of their team. However, because of the difficulty in establishing the monetary value of additional sales for a bank, these have not been included in this study.

Level 6: Sustainability

Wondering how many of the new skills would have remained with the participants, Atom Wave addressed a questionnaire to all programme participants six months after the programme's completion.

As shown in Exhibit 8.5, participants' answers rate the programme's contribution even higher than at the end of the programme, thus indicating that its effect sustained through time.

Exhibit 8.5 Sustainability of results

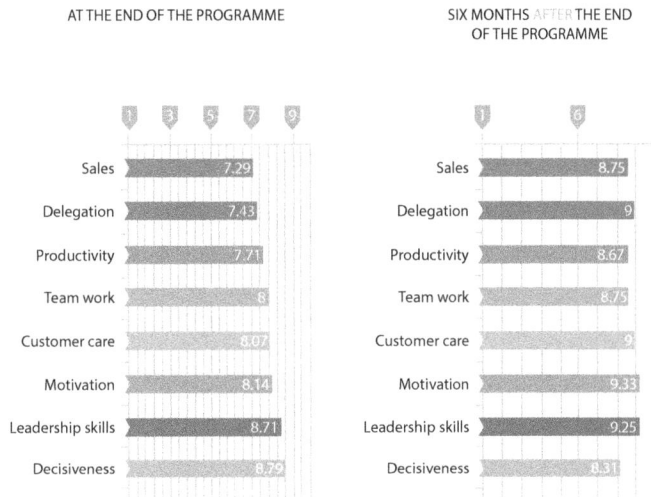

AT THE END OF THE PROGRAMME

Sales	7.29
Delegation	7.43
Productivity	7.71
Team work	8
Customer care	8.07
Motivation	8.14
Leadership skills	8.71
Decisiveness	8.79

SIX MONTHS AFTER THE END OF THE PROGRAMME

Sales	8.75
Delegation	9
Productivity	8.67
Team work	8.75
Customer care	9
Motivation	9.33
Leadership skills	9.25
Decisiveness	8.31

The programme was executed by a team of three Solution-Focused coach/trainers, Marialexia Margariti, Katy Charalambidou and Olympia Mitsopoulou, who also was the principal designer of the programme content and the measurement process described.

INSTILLING COACHING CULTURE WITHIN THE WORK TEAMS

One of the most significant and most common barriers hindering the success of managerial coaching relates to the existing team dynamics. This is because line managers and their teams form complex systems. Over time, they develop patterns and habits of working together, and these can be hard to break. Once a system is established, it will react to any change from within or without by attempting to revert back to the way things were before, even if those ways were dysfunctional. Given that coaching, when done effectively, can be quite an uncomfortable experience, it is hardly surprising that the system seeks to return to equilibrium. From these experiences, we captured a number of significant ground rules for embedding coaching within work teams.

IF YOU ARE GOING TO CHANGE THE SYSTEM, YOU HAVE TO CHANGE THE WHOLE SYSTEM

Change one part of the system, and it will resist. Change the whole system and you have a high chance of making the change stick.

Offering training on coaching only to the team manager is like teaching the steps of a dance to only one of the dancers – the chances that the couple will do well on the dance floor are very slim!

In the team context, it is critically important to engage everyone in the team – the manager and all their direct reports – to understand and support the change to a coaching culture. In a team with a coaching culture, everyone understands the basics of coaching and can coach everyone else. That includes, on occasion, the line manager being coached by a direct report. Equally, everyone needs to know how to be coached, so they can help the coach help them.

ACQUIRING THE COACHING MINDSET TAKES TIME

Coaching is both a mindset and a skill set. An intensive workshop can provide basic knowledge, skills and some opportunities to practise in a safe environment outside the team. However, the impact of coaching occurs between coaching conversations, when the learner reflects on insights, ideas, issues and intentions. It seems that learning to coach and be coached is most effective when broken up into relatively small chunks, with sufficient space (at least a couple of weeks) to reflect, absorb and practise using what has been learned.

THE LINE MANAGER AND THE TEAM NEED TO HAVE CLEAR EXPECTATIONS OF EACH OTHER

Research identifies a long list of potential barriers to effective coaching by line managers, from managers being perceived to have their own agenda, to finding it hard to break out of parent–child behaviours. All of these can be overcome if the line manager and the team have a clear understanding of the nature and purpose of coaching. One of the big shifts that needs to happen is replacing the belief that the role of line manager is to 'do coaching to team members' with a different one - that their role is to create an environment where coaching can happen on day-to-day basis.

THE CHANGE PROCESS NEEDS TO BE SUPPORTED

Within the team, developing an environment of psychological safety is closely correlated with speed of acquiring a coaching culture. At the same time, teams progress more confidently if they feel that their learning journey is supported from outside, for example, by senior management. External support may take the form of a specialist team coach or facilitator – an outsider with the skills to help the team deal with issues such as unsurfaced conflict, or clarifying the team purpose.

LEARNING NEEDS TO BE RELATED TO CURRENT ISSUES FOR THE TEAM

Teams focused on delivering demanding targets don't have a lot of time for the abstract and theoretical. They do want to know what the benefits of achieving a coaching culture will be (both individually and collectively), but, for the most part, they want to see how what they are learning can be applied to practical and relatively immediate issues the team faces in delivering results.

A number of large UK and multinational employers, including organisations in retail and the education sector, have already experimented with an approach based on the above principles. A series of up to nine modules consisting of podcasts, self-diagnostics and background reading was created and each team member was expected to work through the materials (taking typically no more than one hour) before the team met for a coaching conversation – a session, often attached to the end of a regular team meeting, where they explore their learning from the pre-work together and discuss how they can apply it in their work environment.

These sessions may be facilitated by an outsider, or by the team leader. Over the course of the modules, the team is expected to gradually become more confident and capable of using coaching processes; the coaching mindset becomes engrained in the way they think about work issues.

First measures from this new approach are very positive, but we require more verifiable data before drawing clear conclusions. What we have learned is that a requirement of this form of learning – which, if not unique, is certainly uncommon – is a high degree of flexibility about how the materials are structured and presented, what order the team works through them, the pace and timing of the team's learning, and how it applies learning to work issues.

There are also other organisations, such as PwC, who developed and very successfully implemented a similar approach without explicitly referring to it as building a coaching culture within the work teams. You can learn more about it in 'PwC and team-based learning' in 'Stories from the field' in this chapter.

Our expectation is that the development of coaching cultures within work teams will be highly instrumental in stimulating an overall organisational coaching culture. This is likely to be the subject of future research, using diagnostics of progress towards a coaching culture, at both team and organisational levels.

STORIES FROM THE FIELD

PWC AND TEAM-BASED LEARNING

PwC's approach to organisational learning has long been informed by the 10/20/70 model, which indicates that only 10 per cent of workplace learning should take place through formal instruction, 20 per cent through coaching and learning from others, while the remaining 70 per cent should happen in the course of day-to-day work. When designing development programmes, PwC ensures that all three elements of the 10/20/70 model are included and appropriately leveraged. PwC's team-based learning (TBL) is a good illustration of that approach.

So what exactly is TBL?

TBL aims at embedding continuous learning in the course of work to achieve better business outcomes and higher performance. It encourages all team members to look at every work situation as a learning opportunity, either for them or for someone else.

Maria Symeon, PwC Global Coaching leader, said: 'TBL has been a very effective vehicle to leverage that critical 70 per cent of on-the-job learning. Through giving people an easy to understand and implement framework, it has also been extremely supportive in instilling coaching and high-performance culture in our work teams. Essentially, TBL is a way of improving teams' work practices and to a great extent, although not exclusively, it is achieved by using core coaching principles, mindset and skills.'

How does TBL work?

TBL is a framework which is based on four principles and five routines.

The guiding principles of TBL are:

- teach don't tell – using questions to teach rather than just give answers to solve an issue
- own the client – a commitment to deliver quality client service
- on–the-job problem-solving – using real job-related problems to help increase skills and performance
- delegate for development – a challenging opportunity combined with supporting the learner to accelerate their development.

The five routines used in TBL are:

- Shadowing – for example, a less experienced team member accompanies a more experienced one to a meeting they normally wouldn't attend. There is a specific learning objective set for the meeting and a debriefing takes place afterwards.
- Observation and feedback – continuous observation and performance feedback on the job, so that team members can improve before the end of the project.
- Team workshops – a team member leads a session or a meeting focused on a specific technical or professional development topic in the context of a project, using the 'teach don't tell' principle.

- Lessons learned – the team uses a mistake, a 'near miss' or a successful experience in their work as a learning opportunity at relevant points throughout the project.
- Stretch assignments – an opportunity for a less experienced team member to take on new experiences, challenging projects and tasks that are beyond their current knowledge or skills to 'stretch' developmentally and provide their point of view on issues, decisions or challenges, with support from more senior team members.

TBL implementation – lessons learned

When asked about lessons learned from the implementation of TBL, Cristina Amador, the PwC director leading the TBL roll-out in Europe, mentioned the following.

Piloting

Probably the best strategy to roll TBL out is to start with a pilot in a supportive environment, where both the team and the leader are willing to experiment with new ways of working and feel motivated to enhance the team's work practices to achieve better results.

Ownership

In order to succeed, an initiative such as TBL needs to be owned by the business. That's why we make sure that the key people who support and drive TBL are those who either belong to the team or are amongst its leadership.

Whole-team engagement

A key pre-requisite for successful TBL implementation is a good understanding of its underlying principles among all team members. Each team member and the team as a whole needs to be clear about their role in the learning and coaching matrix, their responsibilities and mutual expectations. Both less experienced and the most senior team members have to identify equally with both roles – that of a coach and that of a coachee.

Measure, measure, measure

One of the key factors in the success of TBL is careful baselining, finding the right metrics and making a link to the key KPIs that enable measurement and demonstrate impact on business. Thanks to our measurement, we have been able to identify that TBL has significant positive impact on employee engagement and project margins. Being able to demonstrate these results has been a great help in promoting TBL throughout the firm and convincing even the more sceptical stakeholders.

Allowing time and supporting the change

Behavioural change requires time to take root in a team. We learned to have realistic expectations as to how quickly we can expect consistency in the implementation of desired practices and how long it will take to make them a part of a team's DNA. We also know that change will require significant support and, therefore, we invest a lot in creating a toolbox, e-courses, even a mobile app. We also foresee having the role of performance facilitator, who will help their team to implement their action plans and embed the behaviours.

Creating and maintaining a pool of champions to drive TBL implementation

Finally, what offered invaluable support in the implementation of TBL was creating and maintaining a pool of committed champions. Their role is to encourage teams to identify ways TBL can help them achieve better business results and stick to TBL principles and routines.

INTERNAL SEMI-PROFESSIONAL OR PROFESSIONAL COACHING POOL

The past decade saw a growing trend of developing pools of coaches and mentors within the organisation, able to operate more widely than just within their own teams. One of the reasons for this is economic: the crisis of 2009 caused organisations to explore less costly approaches than hiring external professional coaches. Another reason was to spread the use of coaching, so that it would reach larger numbers of employees. According to the most recent ICF survey on coaching culture (2014), 50 per cent of surveyed organisations employ internal coaches. This number is even higher (coming up to 65 per cent) in companies which already offer coaching by external practitioners. We believe that this trend is going to grow further, especially in large, multinational organisations.

However, let's start with the basics: who is an internal coach? An internal coach is an employee of the organisation who is a professional or semi-professional coach practitioner and works as a coach either on a part-time or full-time basis. Part-time coaches can come from any part of the business, including, but not limited to, HR/L&D. They are often leaders who came to coaching through their interest in a more coaching and collaborating style of management and subsequently gained professional coaching qualifications. Although the part-time coaches are employed by the organisation that they coach in, they are outside of their coachee's hierarchy and are fully disassociated from managing their coachees. Full-time coaches tend to be a part of HR/L&D and, apart from being professional coaching practitioners, they often have an HR, psychology or consulting background.

For a lot of organisations we interviewed, deploying internal coaches was a result of a spontaneous, organic process. It often involved a leadership development programme, which offered coaching or coaching skills training to a group of executives. As a result of this exposure to coaching, some of the executives decided to pursue a practitioner coaching training. Having coaching practitioners amongst their employees, these organisations seized the opportunity and proceeded to create an internal coaching scheme.

The second path to internal coaching that emerged from our interviews had a more intentional nature from the start – a number of organisations consciously decided to employ or develop internal coaches to serve clearly defined developmental needs of specific populations, for example, their more junior talent.

Irrespective of how organisations use internal coaches, the perceived benefits are similar and include:

- relatively low cost, especially when compared with external coaches
- reduced time spent on resourcing coaching engagements
- a deeper understanding of company culture and business
- developing a skill set (especially in the case of part-time coaches) that can be used as part of the coach's 'day job'
- possibility of observing the coachees on the job and to offer feedback based on these observations.

The downsides of having internal coaches, identified in our interviews, include:

- credibility issues, when coaching someone hierarchically more senior than themselves
- greater likelihood of being less challenging and of deferring to power (however, we could find no evidence of this in practice)
- higher potential for conflict between responsibilities to the client and to the organisation (although, again, we were unable to unearth any direct evidence of this happening)
- less commitment to professional development than external coaches (again, we found no evidence for this and some anecdotal evidence to suggest the opposite).

MAKING EFFECTIVE USE OF INTERNAL COACHES

Most of the steps to making effective use of external coaches which we described in the previous chapter will be highly relevant to internal coaches as well (see Chapter 7, Figure 7.1 for an overview of key steps). Some additional considerations, mostly relevant to part-time internal coaches, are summarised below.

INTERNAL COACHING ROLE IS INCLUDED IN THE JOB DESCRIPTION

For those internal coaches who devote just a small portion of their time to coaching, it is important to make sure that internal coaching is part of their job description and is acknowledged and rewarded in their performance evaluation. Sometimes it might also be necessary to review and adjust the main responsibilities of the coach so that they have the space and time to perform their coaching duties.

TRAINING AND CONTINUOUS DEVELOPMENT

While most organisations limit development and training support to group supervision meetings, internal coaches require more active organisational support to keep their coaching skills up to date and to remain aligned with the needs of the organisation. Some organisations have a database of reading materials and practical guidance, usually held on the HR intranet. This can be supplemented by video demonstrations of coaching and mentoring good practice and 'on demand' training and further education, via webinars and other electronic media. Coach development centres, in which internal coaches can have their skills expertly assessed and be helped to create and pursue a personal coach development plan, are an innovation we expect to see more of.

COMMUNITY OF PRACTICE

Building a community of practice can be key here. A lot of organisations organise quarterly meetings, where external and internal coaches come together to get an update of the organisation's strategic priorities, exchange experiences and best practices and gain new skills and knowledge.

Moreover, smaller peer support groups, often in the form of action learning sets, can promote continuous learning in the coaching role. Some organisations invite both external and internal coaches to their coaching supervision groups to facilitate consistency of coaching standards and encourage cross-pollination between both groups.

STORIES FROM THE FIELD

BUILDING AND MAINTAINING A POOL OF INTERNAL COACHES IN EY

Dedicated internal coaching teams are currently in existence in both EY UK&I and EY Americas to drive the delivery of formal executive coaching internally, and this is seen as best practice across the firm globally. The specific stories regarding how these teams were formed in EY UK&I and EY Americas follow below.

How EY Americas invested in an internal coaching practice

In 2009, EY Americas launched the first of its formal coaching initiatives through the Americas Executive Coaching Team (AECT), an internal team of full-time coaches whose purpose is to be both a catalyst for successful leadership transitions and to build coaching capabilities within the firm. The investment in an in-house coaching team was viewed as a strategic advantage, in addition to the significant cost advantage, because internal coaches:

- know EY as they are a part of the culture, understand the firm's values and purpose and know what it takes to succeed as a leader, both internally and in the market
- are strategic partners who are at the table during the creation of executive development programmes, which gives them direct insight and understanding of the bigger picture context of the investment being made in their leaders
- use a customised approach.

While EY Americas has signature programmes and approaches that have consistency, the internal coaches are able to customise each individual's coaching experience. Many vendors and external coaches have programmes they are selling which may not fit EY leaders' needs or are not in alignment with EY's values, culture or processes.

Similarly to the UK&I Coaching Centre described later in this section, the AECT was initially created to support newly promoted partners during their first two years in the role. An investment in this population was made based on the need to successfully support EY leaders through one of the most critical transition points in their career. EY found that a difficult or unsuccessful transition to the role of partner came at a high cost to the firm and to the individual. Voluntary turnover increased, team and individual productivity was delayed or diminished, and future career transitions and knowledge-sharing were impaired. Because the business environment demanded nothing but the highest level of performance from EY and its people, it was deemed imperative to provide coaching for new partners to transition them effectively at this pivotal junction in their careers. Based on the success and impact of the coaching efforts with new partners, the demand for coaching has increased significantly. Since its inception, the AECT has more than doubled in size (from eight coaches in 2009 to 19 coaches in 2015). However, the scope of coaching services remains with leaders in transition, including direct admit partners, ex-patriates/repatriates, newly titled leaders, new and expectant parents, partners approaching mandatory retirement, and teams. In addition to taking leaders to the next level through transitions coaching, the AECT expanded its focus to advance the coaching culture through coaching skill development for client-serving staff and internal talent team (HR) professionals. A Coaching Certification Programme (CCP) was developed, which has been accredited by the International Coach Federation (ICF), to target talent team professionals within EY Americas with the idea that they would help meet growing demand to provide coaching for the levels directly below partner. This internal community of practice now has a membership of over 80, along with the 19 members of the AECT. The next step is to roll out the Coaching Certification Programme globally.

How EY UK&I invested in an internal coaching practice

In July 2011, UK&I followed suit and their Coaching Centre was launched to consolidate all the coaching and mentoring activity taking place across the business:

The Coaching Centre has two dedicated coaches who provide around 60 per cent of the executive one-to-one coaching; the remainder is delivered by 18 internal coaches who work in different parts of the business (both client-facing and non-client-facing roles). They commit to between four and twelve coaching relationships at any one time depending on their role. This is often on top of their day job and is heavily dependent on their discretionary effort and passion to coach and develop others. This is an extremely cost-effective model as it can flex depending on the demands of the business and economic climate. In return, they benefit from quarterly continuing professional development sessions to further their coaching capability and quarterly supervision provided by both internal and external supervisors. This team now handles around 400 coaching relationships a year (45 per cent of these are with partners).

To manage this volume and ensure administration is efficient, as mentioned earlier, both EY UK&I and EY Americas have invested in a software tool (CoachNet) which manages the capacity of each coach and the matching process of coach to coachee. It also handles quarterly reporting and the annual evaluation process, so that EY can formally evaluate the return on investment for the business.

Since the development of their internal coaching offer, EY UK&I has significantly reduced its reliance on external coaching. Less than 5 per cent of all coaching is now delivered by external providers. This has significantly reduced the costs to the business and enabled them to make this bespoke development offering available to a much greater number of senior people to support them with the complexity and challenge of their individual roles.

During spring 2015, EY UK&I also launched a new service called the 'Talent Centre', which provides career guidance and confidential coaching to the firm's client-facing 'seniors'. These individuals will typically have been with EY for around three years and are soon to or will have recently completed their qualifications. They are therefore starting to consider their longer-term career plan and the options available to them. The Talent Centre aims to support EY newly qualified employees as they consider their career plan as well as keep them engaged with the firm.

The main services offered by the Talent Centre include a website with useful career-related resources and information, as well as the opportunity to have a one-to-one confidential career coaching conversation with one of the Talent Centre coaches.

These coaching sessions focus on areas such as career motivators, goal-setting, strengths/development areas and personal brand. There is also the opportunity for coachees to be referred to contacts and mentors in the business. The coaching session is suitable for people at any stage in their career, from those who know exactly what they want to achieve through to those with no idea what direction to take next.

Feedback from coachees to date has been very positive, and many individuals are now being referred to the Talent Centre through word-of-mouth recommendations. The following are some example quotes from coachee feedback:

- 'Very friendly, easy to talk to. Encouraged open and honest communication, which led to clearer goals and motivators.'
- 'Helped me understand what is important to me in a role and how my current role fits in with that.'
- 'Asked excellent and pertinent questions which made me pause and reflect.'
- 'Helped me to identify what I really wanted.'

In 2011, to support and enable on-the-job coaching as part of the culture at EY to help people achieve their full potential, EY UK&I also established a Coaching and Mentoring Network (CMN) – a community of line managers who are interested in managing and leading with a strong coaching style. This is another big influencer that drives coaching behaviours throughout the business, and these managers can draw on their coaching skills to support their teams with skills and performance coaching as required in a more informal capacity.

The network provides members with the opportunity to keep abreast of leading practices within the coaching world, and also offers a platform for discussion and interaction with other line coaches working in UK&I.

The quarterly network newsletter shares success stories as well as useful resources. Quarterly training webinars provide the network with access to the latest coaching and mentoring techniques. EY UK&I's annual coaching and mentoring conference gives members an opportunity to stay connected with the strategic importance of coaching for the business and its people, it develops their skills as a coach and provides the opportunity to network with other colleagues and get support and ideas from their peer group.

The network now constitutes of a mix of members from client-facing teams as well as from the Talent team. While the network started small, with around 10 members, it has now grown substantially and currently has over 600 members.

INTERNAL COACH CAPACITY-BUILDING IN THE NHS

This story was contributed by Anthony Owens, Leadership & Organisational Development Consultant, Yorkshire and the Humber Leadership Academy

Context

For several years organisations that make up the English National Health Service (NHS) have invested in coach training to create internal coaching services. Factors informing this intention include:

- unsustainable costs of externally commissioned training
- variable quality of coach training in terms of skill development and accreditation pathways
- staff capacity to undertake internal coaching (most trained coaches report less than five client relationships per year)
- low access and uptake of coaching supervision and continuing professional development
- low numbers of coaches as organisations struggle to train new coaches to replace those who leave.

Moreover, all organisations responding to a 2015 survey indicated a wish to maintain or increase their coaching capacity.

Approach

Sustained demand for coach training led Yorkshire and the Humber's Leadership Academy to design its own programme. Through consultation with stakeholder organisations and wider research, the following specifications were created.

Table 8.1 Programme elements and characteristics

Element	Characteristics
Strategic alignment	Consultancy with organisational strategic leads helps fine-tune marketing, recruitment, programme content and participant support.
Recruitment and selection	Applicants to the programme are interviewed and must demonstrate capacity to take on the role of coach, alignment with coaching values and the use of coaching skills in their everyday life.
Cohort configuration	Final selection of participants takes into account a number of factors to purposefully create a diverse cohort.
Line manager commitment	Managers commit to release staff to attend training and to monitor and manage future coaching activity and the application of coaching skills in the applicants' substantive role.

Training	Training is delivered over six days with each day themed to reflect a specific coaching context, eg career, performance, team coaching, etc.
Practice	Participants evidence coaching practice, learning and development with at least three clients.
Supervision	Participants must access group supervision of practice over the course of the programme.
Assessment and accreditation	The programme is accredited by a local university at level 5. A 360-degree feedback instrument has been developed to assess the competence of coaches and will form part of an ongoing quality assurance approach.

Programme experience

Individuals accepted to the programme join with a sense of accomplishment and commitment. As participants meet, they realise they are a group of talented people with great potential.

The programme is highly experiential, with strong focus on creating a learning community. Participants develop trust and rapport, while supporting and challenging each other and developing their community of practice. This is often positively contrasted with the climate experienced in day-to-day work.

By day three, participants have commenced coaching practice with three clients and report examples of using coaching approaches in their wider roles. What was a cohort of 12 has now engaged 36 more as coaching clients experience and learn about coaching as well.

As the programme progresses, participants' coaching skills and confidence develop. Strategic leads continually acknowledge the cohort as leaders of an important cultural shift in the organisation.

Diversity is cultivated by enabling each person to find and develop their own coaching model. Participants are encouraged to challenge each other, take risks and give and receive feedback.

The cohort access supervision during the programme. This is established as a norm for their ongoing practice.

The programme utilises existing internal coaches who support skills practice and, in turn, gain further development of their own practice whilst extending the coaching community.

Programme consolidation focuses on the development of coaching services by drawing on the everyday roles of participants to help raise organisational awareness, alignment and connection with coaching.

Outcomes

Cohorts consisting of executive directors, senior professionals and staff develop a strong identity as a community of practice and model coaching in the organisation.

The systemic nature of this approach, combined with the fact that leaders use coaching skills in their day-to-day work, supports the development of coaching culture within their organisations.

As new coaches gain competence and confidence, their development is often observed by their line managers. Awareness of coaching is raised by coaches actively seeking clients (for example by mentioning coaching in their email signature).

Moving forward, the focus will widen to train the trainer programmes for team leaders in one-to-one and team coaching. This will spread coaching skills and the ability of leaders to utilise trained coaches.

SUMMARY

It would be impossible to move beyond the tactical stage of coaching culture development without cultivating internal capacity for coaching. Internal coaching, in its various modalities, is already the most common form of coaching used in organisations and is expected to grow even further in the future. The three main pillars that will support the development of a coaching culture in an organisation are leaders using a coaching style as part of their daily management and leadership practice, teams using coaching skills to interact and improve their work practices, and internal coaches offering professional coaching to selected populations.

?

FIELDWORK

Reflect on the following questions:

- How can you demonstrate that using a coaching leadership style will be beneficial for your organisation (or an organisation that you are familiar with)?
- To what extent are managers currently supported in developing the skills, mindset and confidence to successfully implement a coaching leadership style?
- If the current support is not sufficient, what learning and support would be most effective?
- How could your organisation instil a coaching culture in work teams? Which part of the organisation would benefit most?
- Does your organisation have a pool of internal coaches? If not, would it be useful to have one?

CHAPTER 9

Team Coaching – Fad or Future?

'A good team, like a good show, comes into being when the separate individuals working together create, in essence, another separate higher entity – the team – the show – which is better than any of those individuals can ever be on their own.'
Gary David Goldberg

OVERVIEW

A lot of teams fail to achieve true synergy, in spite of the fact that they often comprise highly competent individuals. That is one of the main reasons why team coaching has been gaining more and more traction in the corporate world in the past few years. This chapter examines the still relatively new discipline of team coaching. We start off with key reasons to focus on teamwork and team coaching and move on to define the key terms around the subject. We explore the role of a team coach, as well as the competencies they need to acquire to be effective. We also present a typical team coaching process and share our thoughts on the future of team coaching.

WHY FOCUS ON TEAMS?

Teamwork amongst humans is as old as our species itself. In his book *Social Intelligence: The New Science of Human Relationships*, Daniel Goleman (2006) reflects on the new research in brain science and summarises it in one simple phrase – humans are wired to connect.

Our brain's evolutionary design allows us to adjust to the perspectives and emotions of others so that we can collaborate with them (Wolpert and Frith 2004). Numerous studies and experiments suggest that collaboration is our default response in a number of situations (Camerer 2003; Warneken and Tomasello 2007; Gurven 2004).

As far back as 2001, research has already identified that 82 per cent of organisations with 100 employees or more reported using team structures (Offerman and Spiros 2001). And while social and management trends change continuously, the need for teamwork in organisations prevails. In fact, there are hardly any organisations that don't rely on teams to deliver at least some of their key outputs.

SO WHAT IS A TEAM?

Academic literature offers a great number of views on what a team is. Two of the most popular definitions of a team are those by Katzenbach and Smith (1999) and Kozlowski and Bell (2003).

Katzenbach and Smith define a team as:

'A small number of people with complementary skills, who are committed to a common purpose, performance goals and approach, for which they hold themselves mutually accountable.'

Kozlowski and Bell, on the other hand, describe teams as:

'Collectives who exist to perform organisationally relevant tasks, share one or more common goals, interact socially, exhibit task interdependencies, maintain and manage boundaries and are embedded in an organisational context that sets boundaries, constraints the team, and influences exchanges with other units in the broader entity.'

The definitions above capture a number of important characteristics that define a team and differentiate it from a group:

- A relatively small size – research indicates that the larger the team size, the more challenging it will be for the team to maintain its effectiveness.
- A level of interdependence between its members – it is not possible for team members to achieve their individual goals independently of others.
- Shared goals and purpose – all team members are aligned around common objectives.
- Accountability – team members hold each other accountable.
- Clear boundaries – it is clear who is and who is not included in the team.
- Social interaction – team members need to interact with each other to accomplish their tasks.
- Being set in a specific organisational context – the team has been commissioned to contribute to a larger organisational purpose.

We present these definitions here because team coaching is different from group coaching and it only works when applied to a real team, as opposed to a group of individuals. Being clear on what a team is can help avoid unnecessary investment of energy and resources in applying a team coaching approach where it doesn't stand a chance of being effective.

WHY TEAM COACHING?

The vast majority of people interviewed for this book experienced the transformational power of one-to-one coaching either first-hand or through testimonials of those who worked with a coach. However, there were also quite a few stories of how one-to-one coaching failed to bring about the desired change. This was often because focusing on the individual was simply not enough.

For coaching to be truly effective, it needs to address not just the individual but also the systems of which they are a part. Sustainable individual change can often only be achieved if the systems around the individual also change to support and reinforce new behaviours, priorities and ways of thinking.

Research consistently shows that individual performance is far more dependent on the team environment than had previously been thought. Moreover, high individual performance by one or more people in a team doesn't necessarily lead to high performance overall – indeed, sometimes the opposite may be the case.

As Ruth Wageman et al note in their book *Senior Leadership Teams*: 'A surprising finding from our research is that teams do not improve markedly even if all their members receive individual coaching to develop their personal capabilities. Individual coaching can indeed help executives become better leaders in their own right, but the team does not necessarily improve. Team development is not an additive function of individuals becoming more effective team players, but rather an entirely different capability' (Wageman et al 2008, p161).

Of course, teams are also part of yet larger and even more complex systems, but it seems that the team provides a bridge between individual and organisational learning. Teams are the most practical unit to integrate the individual and systemic perspectives and to manage the complexity of co-working. It's not surprising, then, that team coaching has emerged as a growing practice and is perceived as a great means towards enhancing a coaching culture within an organisation.

Although the evidence-based literature on team coaching is still relatively thin, it clearly indicates that team coaching has a significant positive impact on team performance and processes. Some of the documented benefits of team coaching include improvement in team effectiveness through increased effort, skills and knowledge (Liu et al 2009), as well as enhanced innovation, safety and learning (Buljac-Samardzic 2012), improved relationship dynamics, team behaviours and skills, thinking and their decision-making (Claxton, et al 2015).

The above findings are often confirmed by the anecdotal evidence from organisations that use team coaching. The benefits of team coaching often quoted by these organisations include:

- increased productivity
- higher engagement
- more-innovative solutions to complex problems
- increased team coherence
- improved communication amongst team members
- higher levels of trust within the team
- improved relationships with external stakeholders (within and outside of the organisation)
- greater familiarisation with coaching
- instilling a coaching culture within the team.

The last point is consistent with our research and observations, which indicate that one of the most effective ways of cultivating a coaching culture in an organisation is to embed coaching in the way teams work and collaborate. Team coaching seems to be a powerful tool to achieve that, as it helps the teams to arrive at tangible results through the use of coaching skills and learning dialogue.

WHAT IS TEAM COACHING?

Team coaching has emerged in recent decades as a practical way to apply the principles of coaching to the team as a whole. It enables the team to focus on what Peter Hawkins refers to as the five disciplines of high-performing teams: commissioning, clarifying, co-creating, connecting and core learning (Hawkins 2011) and can include elements such as:

- developing a stronger sense of shared purpose
- gaining greater clarity, coherence and consistency around priorities – what's most important for the team to achieve collectively. One of the signs that a team is successful in this is that individuals routinely put the team priorities ahead of their own personal task priorities
- a better understanding of the processes that underlie how the team works and identifying ways to improve these – team coaching helps the team question and validate its own assumptions, with the result that radically new ways of working frequently emerge
- managing all three types of conflict (task, process and relationship) constructively – so that conflict becomes a driver of performance, rather than a barrier
- understanding and valuing the contribution each member can make at their best, and how to support each other in creating circumstances, where they can play to their strengths
- exploring the team culture and helping it evolve in line with a changing environment while still enabling everyone to retain their personal authenticity

- increasing the level of creativity and innovation
- managing the team's reputation within and outside the organisation
- improving the effectiveness of communication, both between team members and with external stakeholders
- becoming more resilient to setbacks
- developing a climate of psychological safety, conducive to collective learning – team members learn to have open dialogue, to share concerns and fears and to work with constructive, empathetic challenge. As a result, they build deeper levels of trust and higher quality of collaboration
- adjusting the team's temporal orientation (achieving a better balance between attention to the past, present, near future and long-term future).

As team coaching is still a relatively new form of coaching, it is not particularly surprising that there is no clear consensus about what it actually is. A quick Google search reveals that a number of team coaching offerings available in the market are actually a form of team -building, team facilitation, process consultancy or coaching a number of individuals belonging to the same team.

The descriptions in Table 9.1 give some flavour of the range of interpretations in the literature on the subject. For example, some emphasise achieving specific team goals, others improving performance and others the learning process, by which the team builds sustainable capability.

Table 9.1 Team coaching definitions

Zeus & Skiffington (2000)	'Facilitating problem solving and conflict management, monitoring team performance and coordinating between the team and a more senior management sponsor.'
Hackman & Wageman (2005)	'A direct intervention with a team intended to help members make coordinated and task-appropriate use of their collective resources in accomplishing the team's work.'
Clutterbuck (2007)	'A learning intervention designed to increase collective capability and performance of a group or team, through application of the coaching principles of assisted reflection, analysis and motivation for change.'
Thornton (2010)	'Coaching a team to achieve a common goal, paying attention to both individual performance and to group collaboration and performance.'
Hawkins (2011)	'A process by which a team coach works with a whole team, both when they are together and when they are apart, in order to help them improve their collective performance and how they work together, and also how they develop their collective leadership to more effectively engage with all their key stakeholder groups to jointly transform the wider business.'
Britton (2013)	'A sustained series of conversations, supported by core coaching skills. The focus is on goal setting, deepening awareness, supporting action and creating accountability. The focus of the coaching may be on the team as a system and/or individuals within the team. Team coaching links back to business goals, focusing on results and relationships.'

A common theme that emerges from these otherwise diverse definitions is that team coaching addresses the team as an indivisible unit, not a loose collection of individuals. That means that in essence team coaching works with the collective dynamics (the team system), which emerges as a result of individuals coming together and working towards the achievement of a common goal.

Given the range of definitions, it is to be expected that team coaching can be applied in a wide range of circumstances. The most common appear to be:

- when a new team is being created and needs to hit the ground running (intact, virtual or a project team)
- when an existing group of leaders needs to evolve into a team
- when an existing team isn't performing as well as it could
- when a team wants to reinvent itself to meet challenges in its environment
- when the team acquires a new leader or changes membership significantly
- when a team is currently highly effective and successful and wants to keep ahead of the game.

The great majority of team coaching interventions appear to be at leadership team level, though this has not been validated by research. Next most common are project teams, particularly those concerned with major product launches or large-scale technological or cultural change. However, there is no reason – other than cost – why it cannot be equally helpful at any level.

THE ROLE AND COMPETENCIES OF A TEAM COACH

THE ROLE OF A TEAM COACH

So what does a team coach actually do? Based on dozens of interviews and workshops with practising team coaches around the world, we have been able to identify the following areas:

- helping the team become honest with itself
- facilitating true alignment around the team purpose and priorities
- supporting the team to understand its environment
- catalysing understanding and improving team processes
- helping identify and tackle barriers to performance
- supporting in building the capacity to manage conflict positively
- helping to draft the team learning plan
- facilitating building of team trust and collective self-belief
- enabling the team to coach itself.

Helping the team become honest with itself

At the very basic level, this is about helping the team recognise how much of a team they really are. Many leadership teams are a bunch of individuals with divergent agendas, little interchangeability of roles and minimum dependency on each other. Establishing why and when they need to be a real team provides clarity and the basis for more effective collaboration. Team coaching helps the team become more self-aware and authentic. As one manager put it: 'It's about helping us to have the courage to see ourselves as we are, and to behave as who we are, rather than feel we have to put on an act.'

Facilitating true alignment around the team purpose and priorities

Mission statements and other strategic paraphernalia can often give a gloss of purposefulness, which often hides what is at best an uneasy consent. An example is a leadership team of a public organisation where everyone had signed up to a strategy document that was about to go public. However, the chief executive was far from sure they were actually aligned as a team in how they interpreted the words. Team coaching helped them open up sufficiently to bring these differences into the open and to gain a much deeper level of agreement about the priorities for each of them personally and for their departments.

Supporting the team to understand its environment

Much of the work of team coaches relates to helping the team understand internal and external systems. For example, who are the hidden influencers and stakeholders? Managing team reputation is a common theme here. So is helping the team face up to threats it has avoided acknowledging, such as competition or a rapidly changing business environment.

Catalysing understanding and improving team processes

Once a team has been together for a while, it is inevitable that routines develop. Gradually, they become so ingrained in the thinking and behaviour of the team that they are never questioned, sometimes not even noticed. Team coaching shines a light on how the team functions, on its unwritten rules and behavioural norms, and hence creates opportunities to bring about conscious change.

A good example is a project team meeting, which routinely takes place without a clear agenda and is mostly limited to progress reporting. By observing and feeding back the processes at work, the team coach can help the team work out ways in which it can build genuine dialogue and thus improve the quality and outcomes of the meeting, consequently leading to a more successful outcome of the project.

Helping identify and tackle barriers to performance

One of the classic dilemmas for teams is that recognition and reward tend to be based on individual performance, but that a lot of great individual performances can add up to relatively poor collective performance. Groupthink, lack of key skills, dysfunctional behaviours that no one is prepared to confront – the list of barriers is endless. Team coaching encourages the honest conversation that allows the team to identify and challenge its performance barriers and agree on the way of overcoming them.

Supporting in building the capacity to manage conflict positively

Conflict about task and process can be destructive or productive, depending on how it is managed. Relationship conflict is always destructive. Team coaching not only surfaces but also, where possible, defuses hidden conflict. It also equips the team with the tools and skills to use conflict to generate dialogue and hence improve performance.

Helping to draft the team learning plan

The team learning plan defines what the team and its individual members need and want to learn and how this will contribute to the business purpose. It is as important a document as the business plan, because it underpins targets and goals with practical ways of developing capability and capacity.

Facilitating building of team trust and collective self-belief

High levels of mutual trust and collective self-belief are hallmarks of a high-performing team. Neither happens overnight. Team coaching helps people articulate and align their personal values with the team values. It also helps the team develop more effective habits of collegial supportiveness.

Enabling the team to coach itself

Whereas facilitation or consultancy tends to focus on solving a specific problem, some forms of team coaching aim to leave the team significantly better equipped to solve future problems without external intervention. A challenge here for the team coach is not to let the team become dependent on them.

THE COMPETENCIES OF AN EFFECTIVE TEAM COACH

A member survey by the Institute for Employment Studies in the UK (Carter 2010) revealed that 60 per cent of organisations surveyed believe that their internal coaches are equally well equipped to coach teams as they are to coach individuals. Our experience shows that in most cases this is simply not true: team coaching is considerably more complex and an arguably more demanding arena. Team coaches need to have a good understanding not just of coaching basics, but of team dynamics and team psychology, of collective decision-making, of systems theory and a variety of other topics not needed in one-to-one coaching (Clutterbuck 2013). A few examples of additional challenges that a team coach will have to face are:

- managing varying paces of learning
- managing sub-groups
- managing more complex confidentiality issues
- facilitation.

Managing varying paces of learning

In team coaching, it is common for some members of the team to come to conclusions about the way forward while others are still at the early stages of thinking it through. The team coach has to have processes that prevent this difference in pace from becoming a cause of conflict and use it constructively to help the team come to better decisions overall.

Managing sub-groups

Many teams divide into sub-groups. These sub-groups can sometimes vary according to the topics under discussion or the nature of perceived threats. Being aware of these sub-groups and preventing them from hijacking the coaching conversation requires a good understanding of group dynamics and how allegiances change. In order for the coach to make the team aware of these behaviours (so they can consciously seek to change them), the coach has to be hypersensitive to them first!

Managing more complex confidentiality issues

What gets said one-to-one often isn't appropriate to say in front of the whole group. Yet the coach will typically be privy to a number of individual confidences from members of the team. Managing this takes delicate judgement and skill.

Facilitation

While the role of team coach is not the same as that of a facilitator, he or she does need a good grasp of facilitation skills and a toolkit of team facilitation techniques and methods.

Moreover, many of the standard approaches and qualities of one-to-one coaching are also essential in team coaching, but they tend to demand a higher level of skill. For example:

- **Listening is a core competence for all coaches**. However, the team coach needs to listen both to the person talking and to everyone else in the room. Being aware of their silent conversations, through observing body language and intuiting the mood of the listeners, isn't easy – especially if the speaker is particularly passionate or persuasive.
- **Using silence effectively is a sign of a confident and mature coach**. But creating silence in a group situation, especially when the team is composed mainly of activists, is much more challenging.
- **Powerful questions are often at the core of coaching**. In one-to-one coaching, the emphasis is usually on the coach finding the right question at the right time to stimulate learning in the client. In team coaching, the emphasis is more firmly on helping the team find its own powerful questions.
- **Identity**. Coaches help individuals articulate and understand their own identity. Achieving this awareness as a team tends to be more complex.
- **Conflict management**. The one-to-one coach frequently helps clients to work out strategies for dealing with conflict in the workplace (or elsewhere). Those strategies are 'opaque', in the sense that they are known only to the coach and the client. In team coaching, conflict management strategies usually have to be transparent, because all the players are in the room and part of the conversation. Handling the emotional energy in such situations requires a high level of skill.

These differences make it essential that coaches, whose experience has been mostly in one-to-one environments, preface any move into team coaching by undertaking additional training to equip them for the extra demands of this more complex role. In doing so, they often find that those extra skills add to the impact of their one-to-one coaching as well.

A question that might arise here is whether it is possible for a leader to be a team coach. Our view, just as in the case of one-to-one professional coaching, is that while a team leader cannot fully step into the role of an independent professional team coach, they can effectively use some of the skills and practices of team coaching.

HOW DOES TEAM COACHING WORK?

We talked to dozens of practising team coaches about what makes team coaching effective. One of the main themes identified in these conversations was the importance of employing a powerful yet flexible process. The synthesis of the most important elements of these varied approaches led to the creation of the team coaching process presented in Figure 9.1.

Figure 9.1 Key steps in team coaching conversation

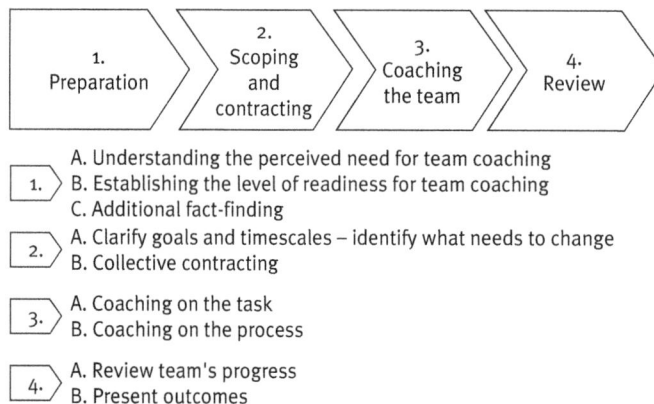

PREPARATION

One of the main activities in the preparation stage is connecting with the key stakeholders and discussing what their expectations, concerns and aspirations are, as well as what the context for team coaching is. Many coaches have short meetings with the team coaching sponsor (the person commissioning coaching), the team leader and individual team members before the commencement of the team coaching engagement.

There are two main objectives of these meetings: understanding the perceived need for team coaching and establishing the team's readiness for coaching.

Understanding the perceived need for team coaching

When a team or its sponsor comes to a coach with a request for team coaching, there is usually a specific reason to do so. The coach needs to understand the perceived need for team coaching, as seen by various stakeholders. Other important questions to answer at this stage are:

- How does the team/sponsor understand team coaching and what makes them think that this would be an appropriate intervention?
- Does the team have experience with team coaching? What is it?
- What would the success of team coaching look like?

Establishing the level of readiness for team coaching

Not all teams are ready to embark on a team coaching journey. As a minimum, the team should have the basic characteristics of a true team. Moreover, a number of factors such as previous experience with coaching, willingness to change, or the level of commitment to becoming a high-performing team will play a major role. In Exhibit 9.1 we give a set of questions that can be helpful in reflecting on the team's readiness for coaching.

Exhibit 9.1 Examples of questions to establish readiness for team coaching

Do the team members have positive experience and expectations of coaching?
Does the team see team coaching as both urgent and important?
Does the team have an appropriate mix of complementary skills, relevant to its expected outcomes?
Are the team members genuinely committed to becoming a high-performing team?
Are the team members – including the leader – committed to open and honest dialogue?
Are they – including the leader – willing to challenge themselves and each other?
Are the team leader's motivations for introducing team coaching transparent and accepted by the team members?
Is it clear who is in the team and why?
Is team membership likely to change during the period of the team coaching?
Is the team willing to address and review its purpose and priorities?
Do team members genuinely want to collaborate rather than work in silos?
Does the team meet at least monthly?
Do team members accept responsibility for their own and their colleagues' learning and development?
Is the team adequately resourced (in terms of money, time, information, etc) to achieve its goals?
Is the team prepared to invest time into coaching sessions and into implementing necessary changes?
Is the team willing to address internal conflict?

Is the team prepared to address poor performance by individual members?
Is the team manager prepared to undertake personal change, to better support team performance?
Is team coaching supported by key stakeholders outside the team?
Are there any other significant barriers to making team coaching work?

Additional fact-finding

In many cases it is helpful to use additional tools and assessments to gain deeper insight into the potential barriers and drivers of the team's performance. This can be done through a range of tools and methods, such as team effectiveness questionnaires, 360-degree assessments, psychometrics or interviews.

Data gathered through these tools will be helpful not just in establishing the gap between the current and the desired state, but can also serve as a baseline against which progress can be measured in the future.

A word of caution, however. It is advisable not to overload teams with questionnaires – that can create unnecessary resistance from the start. Better to start with one or two general ones, to pinpoint issues to work on, then to use other diagnostics to help the team understand its own dynamics later on in the assignment, when the questionnaires can be related to specific issues that are being addressed.

SCOPING AND CONTRACTING

Clarify goals and timescales – identify what needs to change

The data from the previous stage will be very helpful in the first attempt to identify the main focus and timescales of the team coaching intervention. However, this will need to be reconfirmed with the team both at the individual and collective level during the contracting stage.

Collective contracting

Collective contracting usually takes place when the whole team comes together as part of a team coaching intervention for the first time. Typical steps of the kick-off team coaching session are:

- arriving at the common perception of the team's starting point
- creating a consensus around what success of the team coaching looks like – what will change by the end of the coaching engagement
- agreeing areas of focus for coaching – identifying specific goals.

A central issue in team coaching and essential in contracting is clarity of responsibility. There are typically four major stakeholders in externally resourced team coaching:

- the team
- the team leader/manager
- other team members (i.e. apart from the manager)
- the sponsor.

Issues that need to be foreseen and managed include:

- The team leader's behaviour or competence may be one of the primary reasons for poor team performance – hence, there is a potential for conflict of loyalty.

- The team and the leader may have different agendas, as may the sponsor.
- Many teams are in fact composed of sub-teams, with considerable variation in their willingness and ability to collaborate – and with different agendas and priorities.

COACHING THE TEAM

The team coaching sessions tend to follow a clear structure. One that provides consistent and thoroughness is described in the nine steps below:

1 Contracting for the session: what responsibilities do we have to each other?

2 Overarching goal: how does this issue fit with our team mission or purpose?

3 Define the issue: why is it important now?

4 Context: understand the system(s).

5 Redefinition: how has our understanding of the issue changed?

6 Seeking individual and collective mind-shift: what do we need to let go of and embrace?

7 Alternative ways forward: what [additional] options do we have?

8 Decisions: including deciding not to decide.

9 Re-contracting: what has changed in our understanding of how we need to work together on this issue? How will we keep on top of this issue in the future?

Additionally, what emerged from our conversations with team coaches is that their interventions are focused on two broad areas: coaching on the task (to help the team achieve its goals), and coaching on the process (to support the team to acquire the skills of learning dialogue).

Coaching on the task

Having established specific objectives for team coaching, the task of the coach is to support the team in achieving them. This, not unlike in individual coaching, will involve supporting the team in creating an appropriate action plan, foreseeing and overcoming potential barriers towards goal achievement, developing the necessary skills, offering feedback, creating accountability, and so forth.

Coaching on the process

It often happens that a team turns up for team coaching with the expectation that the coach will be doing most of the work. Coaching the team on the process addresses the skills that will be needed by the team to make the most of the team coaching session. Effective team dialogue involves:

- preparation – everyone needs to reflect beforehand on:
  - the significance the topic has for them individually and as a team
  - their experience and the learning they take from that experience
  - the evidence they have for the assumptions or conclusions they make about the issue (How substantial is it? Of what quality? How current?)
- intensive listening and a genuine interest in other people's opinions
- avoiding 'groupthink' (where people suppress their own views in order not to confront, or to lose face)
- constructive, considered, and empathetic challenge
- clarity about decisions made and where accountabilities lie for acting on decisions.

After every two or three sessions, it is important to review with the team how it has absorbed the team coaching mindset and behaviours.

Many coaches consider their responsibility to ensure that the team gradually takes over the management of the coaching conversation. Failure to do this can make the team dependent on the coach and push the relationship towards consulting facilitation.

REVIEW

Reviewing is an important part of the team coaching process. Every team needs a sense of whether they are making progress. The act of measurement stimulates reflection on the process and often re-energises change. It indicates when new approaches or new thinking are needed.

Review team's progress

In our work with various kinds of team, a pragmatic approach to measurement has emerged that makes it possible to assess both short-term actual outcomes and propensity for change. It does not necessarily lend itself to tick-box measures, nor to numbers-based analysis. Rather, it relies on the quality of narrative in relation to five key questions:

1   Does the team have a greater understanding of its internal and external context/dynamics, in so far as it affects performance?

2   Does it have greater clarity of what it wants/needs to do as a result?

3   What actions have they taken? What are they doing differently?

4   What impacts can they define and attribute to those changes?

5   Can these impacts be assessed from multiple perspectives?

A simple yes or no answer isn't acceptable here. What's required is detailed evidence through example (a coherent narrative of change) and input from as many sources as possible – the team itself, its key stakeholders, the coach and interested observers.

Appropriately, these questions are highly compatible with the team coaching process itself, so they can be built into the team coach's interventions and become a significant part of the team's learning about itself and its environment.

Present outcomes

A good practice at the end of a team coaching engagement is to document and present the outcomes to the team, as well as to the key stakeholders. Positive results and success stories tend to have significant positive impact on the cultivation of coaching culture within the organisation.

TEAM COACHING SUPERVISION

As we are working on this book, the world of professional coaching is only just getting to grips with team coaching. The need for specialist team coach supervision is evident. However, there are relatively few coach supervisors who have the relevant experience and/or qualifications to work in this more complex environment. The leading professional associations for coaches and, in particular, the European Mentoring and Coaching Council and the Association of Coaching Supervisors, are looking at standards for team coaches and team coach training, and for team coach supervision. In the absence of a clear theory or substantial body of knowledge about what good team coach supervision looks like, we suggest that a starting point is to build upon and extend existing approaches within one-to-one supervision.

THE FUTURE OF TEAM COACHING

One sign that team coaching is joining the mainstream is the arrival of professional development programmes to help experienced one-to-one coaches step up into team coaching. A set of competencies can be expected for this role before too long.

It is also predictable that companies, which have so far mainly just talked about adding team coaching skills to the portfolio of their professional and lay internal coaches, will take the plunge and invest in relevant training and support. When this happens, team coaching will become much more widely used across those organisations.

Here are some of the emergent trends which are likely to shape team coaching in the coming decade (Clutterbuck 2013).

A gradual movement towards professionalisation of team coaching. This can be seen in discussions within the European Mentoring and Coaching Council and elsewhere about standards for team coaching, and in the rise of academic accreditation for team coaches. It is too soon to see team coaching as a required element of coach training, even at master's degree level, but it is probably only a matter of time before this becomes common practice.

Increasing clarity about what team coaching is, for both providers and purchasers. It will become less tenable to label team facilitation, management consultancy or team-building as team coaching.

Team coach supervision. There is, at present, only a handful of qualified (i.e. formally accredited to at least postgraduate certificate level) supervisors with credible team coaching expertise. In countries such as the UK and Germany, where there are well-established communities of qualified coach supervisors, this transition is likely to be relatively smooth. In countries where supervision for one-to-one coaching is less entrenched, this is likely to take longer.

Increased emphasis on team coaches' knowledge and competence in systems theory and managing systems dynamics. Peter Hawkins' book *Leadership Team Coaching* (2011) has been useful in extending the boundaries of systems thinking in team coaching. However, the toolkit of tools and techniques for addressing systems issues – especially where they concern the team's relationships with its external environment and other teams – could be expanded considerably, with further scavenging from the worlds of family therapy, social mapping and chaos studies.

Research and writing. A search on any of the internet book distributors quickly reveals how few books on team coaching there are. Similarly, the academic literature is relatively thin. The list of topics that can be explored is vast but falls conveniently into two categories: fundamental studies of key aspects of team dynamics and how the coach can assist (eg how teams make decisions); and applications of schools of one-to-one coaching practice to the team environment. The late Richard Hackman, whose research and writing informed much of our current thinking about team effectiveness, nurtured a caucus of US researchers who continue his work. Some of these are interested in the team coaching dynamic. There is also research interest in Europe and Australia.

Expanding scope of team coaching. Most team coaching is targeted at top teams or enterprise-critical teams. In part, this is because team coaching is a relatively expensive, medium-term investment. However, some organisations, which have benefited from team coaching at the top, are examining how to spread team coaching throughout their structure, for teams at any level. This will in most cases involve developing a team coaching capability internally. Managers who have demonstrated good coaching skills one-to-one within their teams have the potential to continue their development and take on team coaching roles for other teams within the business.

Team coaching is becoming a de facto element of creating a coaching culture, quietly added to the list of factors which will encourage and reinforce a coaching mindset.

Pharma company uses team advantage™ coaching model to transform culture

Contributed by Darelyn 'DJ' Mitsch, MCC, creator of Team Advantage™ President, The Pyramid Resource Group

> 'In my decades in business, I have never seen a company so decisively execute a plan to change the culture . . . thank you!'
>
> Employee comment from a 2013 engagement survey, one year post-team coaching programme

In November 2011, a new president of the North American region of a global pharma company planned her next year's strategy, noticing not only the company's robust therapy pipeline but also the really low employee engagement scores. Employees had experienced numerous mergers and realignments in less than two years, creating heightened anxiety. Energising the workforce became the top priority for 2012 and the president hired Pyramid Resource Group to design a change initiative powered by the signature team coaching process, the Team Advantage™. The goal was to engage 60 teams, or 25 per cent of the workforce, and produce a tipping point for the entire organisation.

The first step was to train 25 first-line leaders to become 'change agents' – a dedicated team of people whose role was to embed skills for change leadership, team coaching and continuous improvement. Pyramid Resource Group's master coaches trained the change agents in core coaching skills in three intensive weeks to deliver on the first two components in the design model – change agility and team coaching – which jump-started the first 90-day plan to change the water cooler dialogue from 'I can't' to a more hopeful 'together, we can!' Two surveys were launched during the initiative: one to measure engagement at the beginning and a follow-up to measure impact one year out to assess sustainability.

Bottom-line impact

The company made dramatic organisational changes and achieved unprecedented results in both engagement and core leadership competencies as a result of this initiative, moving from 61.4 per cent to 90.4 per cent engagement in just one year and significant improvements were made in leadership capabilities measured.

Exhibit 9.2 Engagement index score

Engagement Index Score

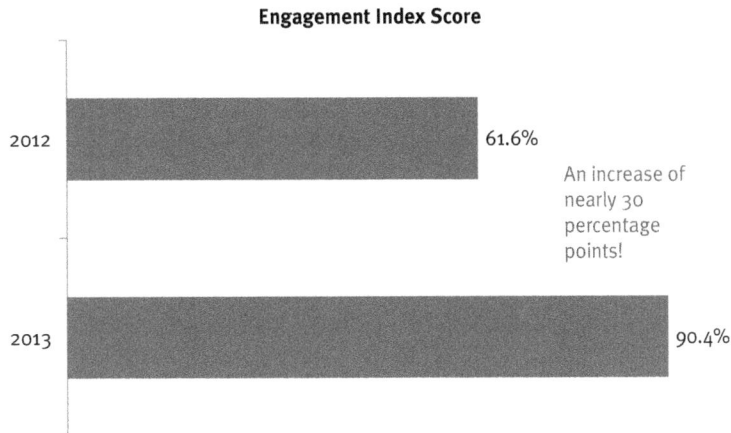

2012 — 61.6%

An increase of nearly 30 percentage points!

2013 — 90.4%

Pyramid's design and development model uses coaching as the conversational skill set used to drive all culture change processes for leaders and teams. Of the three design elements, the Team Advantage™ team coaching process was the accelerator in this initiative. The process worked to shift company culture, with a specific focus on coaching three types of teams: teams with new managers, high-performing teams that needed to stretch, and mid-level performing teams with potential for more business impact.

Exhibit 9.3 Pyramid's Change Initiative Development Model

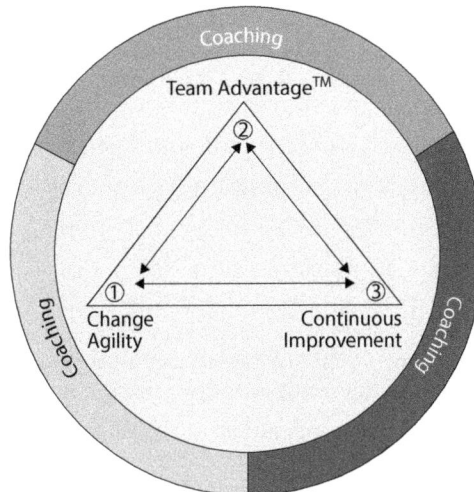

Pyramid's Change Initiative
Development Model

An ambitious series of programmes (referred to as 'games' because of the team bonding focus and disciplines common to sports, such as a specific time limit for the process, roles and responsibilities for winning) were conducted concurrently. Team Advantage™ is a 16-week team coaching process that accelerates team cohesiveness and performance by establishing team charters, setting an extraordinary but tangible goal, coaching through breakdowns and team dynamics and celebrating daily successes, as well as the attainment of the extraordinary goal.

Pyramid's principal coaches partnered with change agents to coach the teams in pairs. More than 60 Team Advantage games were conducted throughout the enterprise from April to October 2012, impacting many more as energised teammates promoted the shifts they were making. While invigorating the participants, team coaching helped employees build the skills to problem-solve more effectively, work toward innovative and far-reaching goals, and communicate and collaborate across work groups and departments.

The Team Advantage™ 16-week coaching process:

- facilitated business game plan creation around the extraordinary goal
- coached teams in one-hour sessions over 16 weeks to attain the goal, focusing on team dynamics
- conveyed real-time coaching skills during the team coaching sessions, including prep and debrief for the team leader
- challenged team members to participate fully, take ownership of outcomes, and to have more fun.

The research conducted for Team Advantage™ is based on a simple principle: *individual and team behaviour changes are at the heart of significant organisational change*. Transformation isn't achieved by reviewing theory-based slide decks to define change. Culture change is achieved when people choose to give discretionary effort and shift their mindsets to perform during a constant and chaotic state of change. That principle is core to the Team Advantage™ coaching process.

The client-approved white paper is available for download from www.team-advantage.com for more information about both sets of results.

TEAM COACHING CAPACITY–BUILDING IN THE NHS (UK)

This story was contributed by Anthony Owens, Leadership & Organisational Development Consultant, Yorkshire and the Humber Leadership Academy

Background

Yorkshire and the Humber's Leadership Academy is part of the English National Health Service (NHS). The academy supports the development of strategically aligned, sustainable coaching capability. This reflects a wider commitment to developing coaching cultures that energise and engage staff and the public to create better care.

Annual NHS staff surveys indicate that 90 per cent of respondents work in teams. The percentage of effective teams falls to around 40 per cent. As studies indicate, a 5 per cent increase in staff working in effective teams is associated with a 3.6 per cent decrease in patient mortality (West et al 2015). Consequently, a sustainable approach to applying coaching for team effectiveness is compelling.

Towards a meta-model for team coaching

An organisational programme for 25 staff from seven diverse organisations looked at how perspectives on coaching and team effectiveness could be combined and applied in context. Organisations deployed participants as team coaches alongside supervision of practice. The Leadership Academy hoped to gather and share learning to help organisations develop bespoke models and approaches to team coaching.

Organisational programme

Yorkshire and the Humber's Leadership Academy partnered with an international coaching organisation (The Performance Coach) to create a programme with the following elements:

Table 9.2 Team coaching programme elements

Organisational recruitment, assessment and commitment
Briefing programme participants
Programme delivery (seven days)
Team coaching practice (three teams over four sessions and consultancy work with team leaders)
Supervision (closed group supervision for each organisation)
Supervision of supervision
Consolidation and inquiry (conducted by a local university)

A meta-model for team coaching

The programme brought experiences and dilemmas to the surface, illuminated important questions and informed the development of a team coaching meta-model, shown in Exhibit 9.4.

Exhibit 9.4 Anthony Owens team coaching meta-model

Anthony Owens ©

Table 9.3 Team coaching meta-model

Strategic Alignment and Consultancy
Establishing and maintaining commitment and priorities for team coaching. This element provides a credible connection between team coaching, organisational strategy and delivery along with feedback that informs strategic learning.

Developing Team Disciplines

Patrick Lencioni described five naturally occurring dysfunctions arising in teams. Five disciplines were proposed for teams to overcome or reduce the risks of dysfunction:

- vulnerability-based trust
- engagement in productive conflict
- commitment through vision and decision-making
- accountability through feedback
- focusing on team results

Supporting evidence was found for each discipline (West and The Work Foundation 2012). The concept found good resonance with team coaches and their clients.

Developing Change Methodology

Most organisations invest in improvement approaches and supporting resources. The degree to which these become integrated in everyday team life varies. Team coaching helps a team critically reflect on what it wants to change and how it goes about this with organisational improvement approaches. This component provokes organisations to evolve improvement approaches using a coaching mindset and approaches.

Developing Systems Thinking

This is a significant challenge for politicised sectors dominated by short-term thinking and emphasis on compliance and control. Systems thinking shifts the focus to relationships, patterns, connections and appreciation of the whole rather than analysis of its parts. System working involves focusing on the aspirational questions of the whole team and its connection with the people who constitute the system to which these questions belong.

Coaching Mindset and Approaches

Coaching holds a belief in the potential of the client and their ability to learn and perform. Raising non-judgemental awareness, along with trust in the client's learning capability whilst following their interest, are examples of a coaching mindset. This contrasts the more deficit-based mindset found in many organisations. This is a key shift for team leaders and members if team coaching is to be sustainable.

Moving forward

Components of the meta-model are interdependent and seldom fulfilled by one person. The Academy offers a systemic approach to team coaching rather than team coaching as an intervention. The meta-model is a framework for consultancy and planning with client organisations or systems wishing to develop team coaching capability. A range of resources provides bespoke support. These are pragmatic and adaptable for incorporation in the everyday life of teams.

The work described highlighted the importance of a systemic approach to team coaching. It also uncovered the need to develop team coaching skills among team leaders. Deploying team coaches without awareness or engagement of team leaders was invariably less effective.

Inquiry highlighted overwhelming enthusiasm for team coaching. However, organisations appear slow to invest in this capability without support, further emphasising the need for a systemic approach.

The team coaching model helps organisations identify existing enablers and development support needed. Examples of application include:

- team coaching skills development for all staff, focusing mainly on the team disciplines element (one-day programme for smaller organisations)
- team coaching as an extension of existing skills and approaches (three-day programme for large organisations)
- training managers and potential team coaches together with main focus on team leaders and their collaboration (three-day programme for large organisations)
- team coaching supervision training as a means to help coaches shift to practice in team coaching (for organisations with experienced team coaches).

As a regional organisation Yorkshire and the Humber's Leadership Academy role is to support organisations in their use of the model. While some require no support, others rely on the Academy to create collaboration with other organisations or to provide the needed interventions.

SUMMARY

High-performing teams are more critical to the success of organisations than ever. Therefore it is not surprising that the demand for various forms of team development, including team coaching, is on the rise. This, in turn, leads to an increased interest in developing the field of team coaching, on the part of both practitioners and professional bodies.

Team coaching is more complex than individual coaching and calls for additional competencies on the part of the coach, such as managing varying paces of learning, sub-groups, managing more complex confidentiality issues, and facilitation. Core coaching skills required by one-to-one coaching are relevant too, but are usually practised at a higher level of difficulty.

Most of the team coaching practitioners rely on a robust coaching process that is often tailored to specific client needs. The stages of that process most frequently mentioned by coaches include planning, scoping and contracting, coaching the team, and review.

We believe that team coaching will keep growing as a discipline, something that will lead to its professionalisation, broadening of its scope and possible expansion of relevant research.

?

FIELDWORK

Think of your organisation or an organisation you are familiar with:

- How could team coaching be introduced there?
- Where would be a good place to start?
- Would you use internal team coaches, external ones, or a combination of both?

Think of a team you are familiar with:

- Does the team have the characteristics of a 'true' team presented in the chapter? If not, what is missing?
- How could this team benefit from team coaching?
- Consider how you might use the questionnaire on the readiness for coaching presented in the chapter with this specific team:
  - Would you ask them to complete the questionnaire as it is?
  - Adapt it (if so how)?
  - Discuss the questions in an open forum?
  - Work through the questions in one-to-one interviews?
  - Not use it at all?

CHAPTER 10

Formal and Informal Mentoring

'The delicate balance of mentoring someone is not creating them in your own image, but giving them the opportunity to create themselves.'
Steven Spielberg

OVERVIEW

In this chapter, we look at mentoring and how it can contribute to the development of a coaching culture within an organisation. We start with a short history and definition of mentoring followed by an examination of the similarities and differences between the two closely related disciplines of developmental coaching and developmental mentoring. The chapter also describes various applications and forms of mentoring and looks at how to make the best use of formal and informal mentoring in an organisation.

As we will demonstrate later in this chapter, mentoring and coaching are not that different from each other. They rely on a number of similar skills and approaches to offer developmental support to individuals. Therefore, introducing mentoring into an organisation can have a significant positive impact on further enhancing the coaching culture.

A VERY BRIEF HISTORY OF MENTORING

The first known direct reference to mentoring is 3,000 years old and comes from Homer's epic poem, *The Odyssey*.[1] The original Odyssean Mentor had two personas: an old courtier to whom Odysseus entrusted the kingdom of Ithaca when he had to leave for the Trojan war, and Athena, the goddess of courage, war, civil administration and wisdom. Athena frequently guided the story's two main characters – Odysseus and his son Telemachus. Disguised as Mentor, Athena encouraged Telemachus to set out on a journey to find his father.

Telemachus's voyage was filled with trials and extreme challenges; his mission to find Odysseus turned into a journey of self-discovery and coming of age, at the end of which Telemachus found his power and became a man in his own right.

In the late 1940s, Joseph Campbell, a mythologist, proposed a now widely accepted thesis that this scenario has been present in myths since the dawn of culture. He argued that all the myths, regardless of their cultural origins, share the same underlying pattern, which he called the monomyth (Campbell 1972).

According to Campbell, the archetype of a mentor, to whom he refers as a 'wise old man' or 'wise old woman', has been present in all the important stories of humanity. It was

---

[1] The story was extended by the French cleric, Fenelon, in the 17th century.

often expressed in characters who encourage and support the hero to set out on a journey into the unknown. They advise, challenge, teach and protect the hero. They also provide valuable gifts for what inevitably becomes a journey of personal growth and self-discovery.

With the mentor archetype so deeply ingrained in our collective psyche, it is not surprising that various forms of mentoring relationships have been present throughout history, from trade craftsman–apprentice to religious master–disciple (Gay and Stephenson 1998).

However, while informal mentoring goes back millennia in human history, with known examples of mentor–mentee relationships such as that of Socrates and Plato, its formalisation is a relatively recent phenomenon. One of the earliest organisations to formalise mentoring is Big Brothers, Big Sisters, a non-profit organisation founded in the US in 1904 to offer mentoring to children at risk.

Later, in the early 1980s, a number of American companies decided to formalise the mentoring which was already taking place informally. This led to the crystallisation of the American model of mentoring, sometimes referred to as 'sponsorship mentoring', which is based on an older, more powerful individual 'adopting' someone who is much younger and just starting in their career (protégé) to help them succeed (Clutterbuck 2013). This model was not fully embraced in many European countries, including the UK, Holland and Scandinavia, where the cultural and philosophical underpinning of mentoring was culturally more associated with learning dialogue. What emerged in Europe was what we now call 'developmental mentoring', based on two-way learning and aimed at helping the more junior partner with the quality of their thinking about themselves and their career goals. These two models of mentoring can be related to different aspects of Athena. Sponsorship mentoring derives primarily from her role as protector (she hides her protégés under her aegis or cloak of invisibility) and intervenes on their behalf. Developmental mentoring derives from Athena's role as the goddess of wisdom.

Nowadays, there is evidence that mentoring in the US is also evolving towards the more developmental end of the spectrum (Kram and Chandler 2005).

DEVELOPMENTAL MENTORING DEFINED

So what is developmental mentoring?

Since the late 1980s, there have been many attempts to define mentoring. Some of these definitions talk about 'passing on of wisdom', which is a fundamental misconception. Wisdom is something that you acquire for yourself; a mentor helps you in this process, by employing their own wisdom to challenge your thinking.

A definition that withstood the test of time, first published in *Everyone Needs a Mentor* (Clutterbuck 1985), states that 'mentoring is off-line[2] help by one person to another in making significant transitions in knowledge, work or thinking.'

We also like the following definition by Lois Zachary: 'Mentoring is best described as a reciprocal and collaborative learning relationship between two (or more) individuals who share mutual responsibility and accountability for helping a mentee work toward achievement of clear and mutually defined learning goals' (Zachary 2005).

What these definitions capture are some of the key characteristics of developmental mentoring, such as:

- It is an off-line relationship. The mentor is typically a person outside of the reporting line of the mentee. They can be from the same organisation, industry or networking organisation. Mentoring in the reporting line can introduce too many conflicts of interest and may divide teams into those who receive mentoring and those who don't.

---

[2] 'Off-line' means here outside of the reporting line.

- Developmental mentoring helps the mentee to improve the quality of their thinking so that they can increase their knowledge, enhance their career, or improve their life in general.
- It is mutually beneficial. Although the emphasis is on helping the mentee grow and develop, it is often reported that mentors experience substantial benefits as well. Some of the most frequently quoted ones are: developing their mentoring, coaching and leadership skills; gaining deeper insights into their own work; obtaining a new, fresh perspective on things; achieving personal satisfaction; and creating a legacy.
- It is focused on specific goals. The mentor helps the mentee to identify what their key goals are (they may typically be emergent and evolve as the person evolves) and encourages and supports them to achieve these goals.

HOW IS DEVELOPMENTAL MENTORING DIFFERENT FROM DEVELOPMENTAL COACHING?

A review of available books on the subject or even a quick Google search reveals that there are a lot of conflicting views as to what differentiates mentoring from coaching. Particularly strong opinions come from the various providers of coaching or mentoring services, both of whom claim the superiority of one form of developmental support over the other.

Approaching the differences between mentoring and coaching as something that can be easily and clearly defined leads to dubious conclusions. In our experience, the issue is really complex. The existence of many different types of coaching and mentoring contributes to this complexity. For example, where coaching sits on the 'directive versus non-directive' continuum will affect its characteristics to a great extent. Therefore, we can't help but see many shades of grey in an issue which some practitioners and writers tend to approach with black and white certainty.

Table 10.1 Similarities between developmental coaching and developmental mentoring

Both create a reflective space and rely on the Socratic method (powerful questioning) to support the quality of thinking of the coachee/mentee.
Both have developmental character.
Both might offer advice in certain circumstances, although directive guidance is not a default mode of either of the two.
A significant amount of the learning occurs in the reflections of the coachee/mentee between or long after their meeting with the coach or mentor.
Coach and mentor have a duty of care towards the coachee/mentee.

As illustrated in Table 10.1, developmental coaching and mentoring share many common characteristics. They require a very similar mindset and almost the same set of skills and behaviours and are guided by broadly the same principles. Mentoring provides a safe space in which line managers can practise the skills of developmental conversations, and hence transfer these into coaching their direct reports.

Differences are fewer and can be summarised as follows:

- A mentor is typically required to have context-specific expertise or knowledge, whereas such a demand is rarely placed on a coach.
- Mentors will often guide their mentee through the organisation's, profession's or industry's political maze.
- Mentors are more likely to be role models.
- Coaches are more likely to observe and give feedback on performance issues.

Because of those similarities and the fact that developmental coaching and mentoring rely on virtually the same skillset, developing a mentoring scheme can be yet another way of supporting what we call 'a coaching culture' within an organisation. One manifestation of this is that line managers who are also mentors to people outside their teams can practise developmental behaviours with their mentee that they might hesitate to use with their direct reports. Mentoring, therefore, provides a safe haven for developing their developmental skills.

APPLICATIONS OF MENTORING

The first applications of structured or supported mentoring date back to medieval times, when the concept of apprenticeship was born and supported by craft guilds and town governments. In the 1970s, it was initially used to acclimatise young graduate recruits into an organisation's culture.

Since then, the range of applications has significantly expanded, with mentoring being used within organisational, educational and community settings.

ORGANISATIONAL SETTING

In the organisational setting, mentoring is often used as a supportive tool to:

- achieve diversity objectives – for example, equal opportunities or leveraging diversity in the workplace
- help people in making significant role transitions (for example, first supervisory job or moving from the role of functional head to general management)
- support people who are fast-tracked to more senior leadership roles
- enable people with disabilities to find work or create their own businesses
- change organisational culture
- embed new skills and behaviours
- improve retention
- support talent pools
- support diversity management and equal opportunities objectives
- facilitate mergers and acquisitions
- support parents returning to work after a period of maternity or paternity leave.

One of the most interesting recent developments is ethical mentoring, in which experienced internal coaches or senior managers with mentoring experience are additionally trained in the psychology of ethicality. These ethical mentors help people work through complex ethical dilemmas, build ethical resilience and act as a conscience to other executives and leaders. They also provide a resource to which potential whistleblowers can go, to think through how they raise concerns in ways that will be least damaging to themselves and to the organisation, and most likely to achieve positive change.

COMMUNITY SETTING

From its earliest days, modern mentoring has been used to address social issues. Below are some of the most common applications:

- programmes to help young people at risk keep out of trouble, stick with their studies, identify and pursue their purpose in life
- re-integration of ex-offenders into the community and the workforce
- supporting people with learning disability
- supporting the integration of immigrants into their host society
- helping professionals better understand their clients (for example the expert patient programme)

- helping a disadvantaged social group, such as single mothers, to discover ways of coping with practical and social challenges.

EDUCATIONAL SETTING

Mentoring is also finding many applications in education, for example in:

- prevention of bullying in schools
- preventing dropouts from school or tertiary education
- transition into the role of head teacher
- encouraging participation in higher education by people with disabilities
- helping research or teaching staff gain academic tenure
- achieving professional status (for example Chartered Engineer or Accountant)
- helping undergraduates studying in a foreign country to appreciate the host culture.

LIFELONG MENTORING

An interesting concept that has recently emerged is that of the 'lifelong mentoring', which takes the perspective that we can be mentor or mentee (or both at once) at any stage of our life, from the earliest age. Some of the key transitions at which mentoring can be particularly beneficial are:

- starting school
- starting secondary school
- puberty
- leaving school
- going to university
- entering the workplace
- marriage
- parenthood
- mid-life transition
- leaving prison, or the armed forces
- first time managing other people
- other transitions in 'the leadership pipeline'
- setting up a business
- moving job roles
- retiring
- end of life – mentoring the dying and their families.

You might be wondering at this point: how is mentoring in a community or lifelong mentoring relevant to creating or sustaining a coaching and mentoring culture within an organisation?

While the link might not be that clear at first glance, many organisations which include mentoring for vulnerable social groups or talented students in their corporate social responsibility (CSR) agenda testify that the link is surprisingly strong. This is mostly due to the mutual learning nature of mentoring relationships – mentors who offer support to vulnerable social groups, talented students or non-profit organisations get a lot out of those relationships as well. Community mentoring is often reported to have a ripple effect which affects the sponsoring organisation in often unexpected ways. Its indirect benefits can range from improved leadership skills to increased commitment and engagement of the participating managers and their team members. Moreover, managers who act as mentors tend to transfer the skills they developed into their daily work practices, something that greatly contributes to the development of a coaching and mentoring culture in their organisation. Some internal mentoring programmes expect mentees, after six months or so, to become mentors in a community-focused programme. One of the benefits of doing so is that the experience helps these relatively junior employees become more effective mentees because they are better able to see the relationship through the mentor's eyes. (See cascade mentoring later in this chapter.)

There are numerous examples of interesting mentoring programmes that illustrate the various applications of mentoring in the organisational context. Here are just a few of them:

- A major London solicitor's practice uses mentoring to help people make the transition to partner. What it takes to be considered partner material is so difficult to explain or demonstrate that formal training doesn't help. Mentoring provides a useful way of passing on this largely intuitive understanding.
- For many multinational companies, a major challenge is how to speed up the development of local nationals to take over from the expatriate engineers and managers. Mentoring provides a practical and culturally acceptable route to making this happen.
- The Institute of Chartered Accountants in England and Wales has a programme of 'ethical mentoring'. Mentors are experienced financial services people who help mentees tackle acknowledged ethical dilemmas and also help them develop their ability to recognise and work through ethical dilemmas and become agents for change in their organisations.
- The Institute of Practitioners in Advertising created a programme in which relatively young (under 40) entrepreneurs in the field were mentored by successful peers, mostly 15–20 years older, on issues such as how to sustain their businesses, or build greater value in the business.
- A division of British Telecom (BT) selected a number of small businesses with high growth potential to take part in a programme with a dual purpose. On the one hand, the small businesses, which were selected through a competition process, gained access to the professional expertise of the mentors, who were all on the leadership team or one level below. On the other hand, the BT executives learned a great deal about the issues that small business customers faced.

DIFFERENT FORMS OF MENTORING

Being essentially a relationship of mutual learning, where the mentor's power or authority is not substantially relevant, developmental mentoring may take many different forms. Some of the most common ones are:

PEER MENTORING

A professional exchange, where both parties support each other in personal growth and achievement. Peer mentoring relationships typically work better when one or both parties have had prior experience of more traditional mentoring.

REVERSE MENTORING

Reverse mentoring takes place when the junior person mentors the senior. It has evolved in response to two organisational needs:

- changing cultures to make them more diversity-friendly, by educating leaders about diversity issues
- helping leaders to catch up with technology or areas of specialist knowledge.

For the junior person acting as a mentor, the relationship provides opportunities to improve their visibility to leaders, and to gain insights into how leaders think. For the senior mentee, diversity-oriented reverse mentoring provides a safe space to explore their assumptions and concerns and to develop greater comfort in having meaningful conversations with someone different.

GROUP MENTORING

Group mentoring typically occurs when there are not enough mentors to meet the demand from mentees. A mentor might work with a group of three to eight mentees at a time, in a group setting, Both mentors and mentees require additional training above and beyond standard mentoring training, to cover the requirements of the group dynamics. Typically, some one-to-one mentoring also occurs, as mentees have specific issues they want to discuss outside the group setting.

SHADOW BOARDS

Shadow boards are a particular type of group mentoring. Typically, junior managers in an organisation are selected to form a shadow board. They receive the same documentation as the real board or leadership team, a few days ahead. They meet to discuss these documents, under the chairmanship/mentorship of a member of the real board/top team. In some cases, the same person acts as a mentor; in others, the role rotates amongst leaders, to give them all an opportunity to work with the shadow board.

The aims of the shadow board are to:

- introduce junior managers to more strategic thinking and what it means to be a leader
- expose leaders to the realities of how people in lower ranks of the organisation perceive planned changes

SPEED MENTORING

Speed mentoring is a method of providing rapid, focused access to knowledge and experience. Typically, speed mentoring involves bringing a group of mentors together with a group of learners who have specific needs. Each pair works together for a defined period (up to 15 minutes) before one of them moves on to a new partner.

This approach to mentoring (if it is really mentoring at all, given that it lacks the essential element of a learning relationship) tends to be shallower and more advice-heavy than normal mentoring. However, it has a role to play in, for example, helping people explore a variety of different career options or in gathering multiple perspectives on one issue.

NETWORK MENTORING

Network mentoring describes a growing trend for people to have more than one mentor at a time. For example, they may work with one mentor on long-term career issues and with others over shorter periods on transferring specific skills and knowledge. A practical way to initiate this is for mentors in a formal programme to encourage and support their mentees in creating and developing such networks.

CASCADE MENTORING

Cascade mentoring is based on the principle that mentees can be more effective if they experience mentoring from the mentor's perspective. So, for example, young graduate recruits being mentored by a junior or middle manager would be encouraged to become a mentor to someone in the community. The experience typically helps them better appreciate their own mentor's role and gain clarity about how they can help the mentor help them.

FORMAL MENTORING, INFORMAL MENTORING – OR BOTH?

There is an ongoing debate on the merits of formal versus informal mentoring, fuelled by conflicting views and data that continually emerge from academic literature and mentoring practitioners alike. A question that sparked this debate is: which is better – formal mentoring, where an organisation intervenes to create, guide and support relationships, or informal mentoring, where the organisation does not intervene at all, except perhaps encouraging people to develop spontaneous relationships?

We will resist plunging into the rabbit-hole of analysing the pros and cons of formal and informal mentoring. Instead, we just present the key differences between the two (see Table 10.2).

We also intend to shift the focus and, instead of asking: 'Which of the two is better?', in the next part of the chapter we attempt to answer a different question: 'How can both formal and informal mentoring work well in an organisation?'

Table 10.2 Main differences between formal and informal mentoring

	Formal mentoring	Informal mentoring
Relationship duration	Relationship length is clearly defined, with an agreed on beginning and end.	Emerge gradually and can last for much longer.
Matching	There is support around matching and mentees may have no choice or a selected choice.	Requires mentee to find their own mentor.
Meetings	Meetings take place regularly based on the guidance received in training.	Meetings take place on 'as and when needed' basis.
Training	Both mentors and mentees are trained for the role.	Formal training doesn't take place.
Impact on diversity	Frequently used to achieve diversity objectives, by matching for difference.	Tends to occur between people who are similar in background, gender, race, sexual preference and so on.
Support	There is a programme manager to provide advice and help relationships which are struggling. There may also be support for mentors from more experienced mentors, and, in some cases, supervision.	Relationship is left to its own devices – if there is a problem, it drifts away.
Goals	Organisation encourages individuals to set goals and there may be organisational goals too.	Less clearly defined goals.
Contracting	Pairs are encouraged to discuss their expectations of each other and how they will work together.	Expectations are generally less clear within informal relationships.
Measurement	Build in measurement and evaluation, which is helpful in encouraging participants to review the relationship together.	None.

	Formal mentoring	Informal mentoring
Organisational outcomes	Within formal programmes that have an established purpose this will ideally have a positive outcome for the organisation.	Outcomes could be positive or negative for the organisation.

MAKING FORMAL MENTORING WORK – INTERNATIONAL GOOD PRACTICE

Being up to date with good practice in formal mentoring has never been easier; an impressive amount of research, resources and publications, as well as the existence of accreditation bodies such as the International Standards for Mentoring Programmes in Employment (www.ismpe.org), can help organisations design and run effective mentoring schemes.

However, in spite of this wide availability of knowledge, resources and support, a significant percentage of mentoring programmes don't deliver on at least a portion of their objectives. For us, these failures have been a rich source of learning; talking to organisations whose programmes ran into difficulty – or even completely failed – enabled us to identify the chief pitfalls of mentoring in organisations. Based on these conversations, we identified three broad themes amongst the reasons why mentoring programmes fail:

- lack of clarity
- inappropriate level of direction, instruction or training
- improper matching

LACK OF CLARITY

Clarity is key in getting a mentoring programme off the ground and sustaining it. There are a few aspects of clarity that we want to discuss here: clarity of purpose; clarity around the type of mentoring that is expected to take place; and clarity around the benefits of the mentoring programme for the key stakeholders.

Clarity of purpose

Programme clarity of purpose – why it is being done, what is expected of participants, what the respective roles and responsibilities of mentor and mentee are, and what the desired outcomes are – is directly correlated with the clarity of purpose in the individual relationships. Most relationships require a clear sense of purpose and a defined transition which the mentee wishes to achieve. The clearer that transition is, the more focused the discussions and the easier it is to relate day-to-day issues to the larger goal. Even in relationships where the primary objective is for the mentee simply to have an occasional sounding board, unless that is agreed up front, one or both parties will often feel dissatisfied.

Clarity on the expected type of mentoring

The second main problem is that companies often assume that perceptions of mentoring are pretty standard. In reality, as we mentioned before, there are at least two major schools of mentoring – developmental mentoring and sponsorship mentoring – and failure to clarify which is intended can cause confusion, arguments and major misalignments of expectations between participants and the organisation. Multinational companies which have attempted to introduce mentoring around the world without taking these differences in mentoring style properly into account are surprised when they meet resistance.

Clarity on the benefits of the mentoring programme

The third pitfall linked to clarity is failure to engage line managers and promote to them the benefits of the programme. It is not surprising that many line managers fear being exposed by discussions between their direct reports and other, possibly more senior managers. Involving line managers in the design and overall management of the programme helps, as does briefing them about the advantages to them of having someone with whom the mentee can discuss in confidence how the mentee manages their key working relationships.

INAPPROPRIATE LEVEL OF DIRECTION OR INSTRUCTION

Problems can arise when there is an inadequate level of direction or instruction, either on the side of the organisation, or the mentor. For example, we often see programmes that are heavily over-managed. In one case, mentors and mentees were given discussion sheets to create uniformity in what was discussed in their meetings. This excessive level of direction smothered the spontaneity and individual focus of effective mentoring. In another case, the opposite occurred. An enthusiastic HR function simply told people they were to be mentor and mentee and left them to it, without any instruction or training. When relationships ran into difficulty, or participants needed advice, there was no provision to support them and the HR professionals were too busy running the next initiative.

At a relationship level, mentors sometimes fail to establish an appropriate balance between being directive and laissez-faire. Indeed, a core skill for a mentor is to recognise when to lead and when to enable the mentee to lead discussions. One of the most frequent complaints by mentees is that the mentor talks *at* them, instead of engaging them in a reflective dialogue. Less common, but equally dysfunctional, is the mentor who never gives guidance and is unable to adapt their style to the mentee's needs at the time.

Similarly, if you don't train mentees, you reduce the effectiveness of the programme dramatically. This isn't surprising, given that we expect the mentee in developmental mentoring to play an active role in relationship management.

Another issue relates to the duration of support for participants. The international standards, which are based on wide experience across the globe, emphasise the importance of continued support for mentoring pairs over their first 12 months. The forms of support available include professional supervision, oversight by members of a steering committee (who are experienced mentors), formal collective review sessions, measurement and monitoring, additional training to embed good practice and widen participants' toolkits, and online databases to answer participants' queries and concerns.[3]

IMPROPER MATCHING

One of the key success factors in mentoring relationships is rapport, the amount of trust and the quality of the relationship between the mentor and the mentee. Equally important is for the two parties to be sufficiently different from each other, as a difference in perspectives, personality, or even background will have a positive impact on the couple's ability to solve problems, learn and develop. That is a difficult balance to strike and a lot of organisations gravitate to one of the extremes, either making the matching process too rigid or too laissez-faire. For example, a global IT company was proud to create a mentor–mentee matching system supported by highly sophisticated technology. Complex algorithms analysed data and suggested the most appropriate match. Neither the mentor nor the mentee had an opportunity to influence that matching. Although the organisation initially believed that the process worked, the programme started to die off within a few months of its commencement. What the organisation eventually found was that while the

---

[3] Useful resources can be found at www.coachingandmentoringresource.com

'shotgun marriages' generated by the matching system looked compatible on paper, it was not the case in real life. As a result of this finding, the organisation further improved its matching system, but also proceeded to give people a shortlist of three mentors to choose from after having 'a chemistry meeting' or a call with each of them.

A positive sign, however, is that more and more HR professionals are becoming knowledgeable about mentoring and recognise the value of anchoring it firmly in priority business needs. In addition, many of those companies which have experienced initial failure are now taking a more considered, mature look at the process and resourcing it properly.

HOW TO AVOID THE MAJOR PITFALLS

Although a few years have passed since some of the suggestions below were first formulated by David Clutterbuck (2011), our experience shows that they are still valid.

Planning and preparation

Time spent thinking through what the programme is meant to achieve and how each aspect of it should be managed, supported and measured is an investment that will pay its dividends later. Engaging the stakeholder group in the planning identifies barriers to success and occasionally radically changes the nature of the programme. There had been cases when feedback from the intended beneficiaries significantly changed the programme scope or even led to turning it on its head – for example when the intended mentees became mentors instead!

Selection and matching

It can be dangerous to assume that a good leader or manager will make a good mentor. In reality, many managers lack the required self-awareness or find it extremely hard to engage in a learning dialogue and avoid giving advice.

In terms of matching, good practice steers clear of 'shotgun marriages'. It does not give people a completely free choice of a mentor, but it offers a selection from which the mentee can choose. In this way, the mentee feels some control over the matching process and ownership of the relationship. Selection by mentors is best avoided. Our research indicates that mentees are keener to influence matching than are mentors.

Training and ongoing support

Companies that have the most success with their in-house mentoring programmes invest in training both mentors and mentees. They also provide a detailed face-to-face briefing for line managers and other stakeholders who might be affected by the programme. Data shows that without any training at all, less than one in three pairings will provide significant benefits for either party. Training mentors alone raises the success rate to around 65 per cent. Training both mentors and mentees in combination with educating line managers about the programme pushes the success rate above 90 per cent, with both parties reporting substantial gains.

Initial training is rarely enough to give mentors more than a basic level of competence and confidence. The experience of hundreds of programmes in more than three dozen countries shows that they both want and need access to continued expert advice on how to perform the role and develop their skills and that they greatly value the opportunity to share their experience with other mentors.

Process ownership

It is critical that the mentee acquires the confidence and skills to manage the relationship, and this is when training them can be highly supportive. Developmental mentoring, in particular, demands that the mentee helps the mentor to help them, by understanding the process and contributing to it.

Measurement

Effective, appropriate measurement, especially at key points in the first 12 months, not only helps keep the programme on track, but also stimulates mentor and mentee to good practice, for example, reviewing the relationship and what each is gaining from it. Many companies have adopted a 'balanced scorecard' approach to measuring their mentoring programmes.

The above suggestions are also reflected in the International Standards for Mentoring Programmes in Employment (ISMPE), which have been generated to fill a gap in the evaluation of mentoring programmes, with particular emphasis on programmes in adult employment and development. Six core standards outlined by ISMPE are as follows:

- clarity of purpose
- stakeholder training and briefing
- processes for selection and matching
- processes for measurement and review
- maintains high standards of ethics
- administration and support.

For more information refer to the ISMPE website: www.ismpe.com

MAKING INFORMAL MENTORING WORK

One of the goals of many formal mentoring programmes is to bring the organisation to the point where the majority of mentoring is carried out informally, without the need for substantial, structured support from HR and elsewhere.

Our discussions with informal mentoring pairs and with HR professionals who have experience of both formal and informal mentoring suggest that the key lies in creating an environment where effective mentoring can flourish. Such an environment would contain some elements of structure, in the form of support available, but require no third party intervention in pairings. Rather, it would allow market forces to drive both the matching process and the quality control of the mentoring provided.

One organisation that adopted this approach to mentoring is Vodafone Turkey. You can find more information on their mentoring scheme in the 'Stories from the field' section of this chapter.

Based on their experience, as well as our own understanding, the essential elements in establishing a positive climate for informal mentoring include:

- An on-line registration and matching system, where people can seek and make their own pairings. The system needs to have clear guidance as to how to go about selecting an appropriate partner and, ideally, a resource which prospective mentees can go to for personal advice.
- Sufficient, visible role models of good mentoring practice to demonstrate what quality mentoring looks and feels like and to provide a voluntary, informal advisory resource for mentors. If top management can be among those role models, it gives a very strong message to the organisation.
- A mixture of voluntary training resources. These might include: a regular open training programme, run in-house or externally with a consortium of other organisations; an e-learning package to run on PC or online; and a library of wider reading materials on mentoring and related disciplines. It may also be useful to provide an option for people

who have a strong interest in developing their mentoring skills to take a certificate or degree course through one of the several providers now available.

- An understanding that the quality of mentoring rests to a considerable extent on the amount and relevance of the training both parties have received. While an informal process can't insist that mentors and mentees are trained, the desire to have an effective relationship should drive both parties away from matching with someone who is not sufficiently committed to being trained in the role.
- An opportunity for mentors (or developers in general) to meet informally as a mutual support and learning group through an online chat room or self-organised gatherings. In this scenario, mentors may request some help from HR in arranging venues and perhaps finding external speakers on specific learning topics, but the impetus has to come from them. Some organisations already run 'lunch and learn' events – in one case monthly – along these lines.
- Good practice 'snippets', sent monthly to all managers (or indeed all employees), on developmental behaviours, from both the learner and the developer perspectives. This is perhaps the closest to a formal arrangement the organisation may go. These short advisory bulletins (no more than a few hundred words each time) would be generated by HR, with the aim of stimulating awareness, discussion and incremental improvements in people's behaviour to mentor and be mentored, coach and be coached and so on.

It should be obvious by now that all of these elements may also be useful in helping a formal mentoring programme to deliver results for both participants and the organisation. Our thinking increasingly is that the mentoring 'package' that will give organisations greatest value is one that integrates both formal and informal mentoring so that they become mutually supportive.

STORIES FROM THE FIELD

Vodafone turkey – a self-managed, mentee-led mentoring programme for vodafone turkey

Contributed by Tim Bright, a Partner in OneWorld Consulting, and Sanem Celikyilmaz, Vodafone Leadership & Talent Development Manager.

Background

Vodafone is a leading mobile communications operator in Turkey with over 21 million customers and more than 3,300 employees.

Driven by a strong need for more developmental conversations to happen across the organisation, Vodafone decided to add a formal mentoring scheme to the portfolio of various development offerings already available to employees. Vodafone wanted to create a programme that would be available to everyone, operate on a voluntary basis and be sustainable across the organisation.

It was clear at the outset that a 'typical' programme might not meet the organisation's needs. Vodafone Turkey is an extremely fast-paced organisation, with all employees striving to achieve multiple goals under significant pressure and amidst almost constant change. Historically, senior leaders struggled to commit sufficient time to development initiatives. Faced with pressing issues on the business agenda, personal and people development became an item of secondary importance. Adding to the issue, Vodafone employees at all levels have often been very selective in committing to time-consuming development initiatives.

Additionally, based on the experience of other organisations, Vodafone was wary of numerous risks around matching, selecting and maintaining a pool of mentors.

The design

Keeping the above considerations in mind, OneWorld Consulting and Vodafone developed an innovative, voluntary-basis, mentee-driven mentoring programme with the following parameters:

- Any employee can be a mentee.
- Anyone who wants to be a mentee needs to select a mentor from within the company and approach them. The mentor can't be in their own reporting line.
- People who are approached to be mentors can accept or reject the invite as they wish.
- Each mentor can work with a maximum of three mentees at any one time.
- Once a pair is established, the mentee should inform their HR partner or the Mentoring Programme Manager.
- Information on the programme and e-learning tools for mentoring (videos, presentations, methodology) are provided to everyone in the company.
- Half-day training workshops for mentees and mentors are offered to all participants.
- Mentoring pairs are recommended to meet once a month over 12 months.
- HR will support mentors or mentees who approach them for input or guidance. Participants can also reach out for support to the external consultant.
- Two-hour follow-up/supervision sessions are run periodically (two to three times each year) separately for mentees and mentors. Attendance is voluntary.
- Short 'pulse check' email surveys are sent to mentors and mentees, with a maximum of five questions, to get feedback on their participation in the programme.

The formal programme in terms of HR support and follow-up ends after a year. After that, mentees are encouraged to choose a different mentor to work with if they want to continue in a mentoring relationship.

Principles

The programme was designed to be as 'light touch' as possible and to put the responsibility for the mentoring relationship fully on the mentee. It is also completely voluntary so there is no requirement for HR to select mentees or mentors or to follow up on whether they are meeting or not. This avoids many of the challenges of selecting and matching mentors with mentees and managing the pool.

The scheme design is very transparent and all participants have access to the same tools and materials. Participants are encouraged to be open about their mentoring relationships. Cascade mentoring is happening as well, as a number of participants are simultaneously mentors and mentees, and as such they are free to attend either the mentee or mentor workshop or both.

Outcomes

At the time of writing this case study, the Vodafone mentoring programme is now in its second year. The participation in the programme has been much higher than expected. Consequently, three 'waves' of training had to take place to accommodate over 200 mentoring pairs, who now continue to work together. If the organisation worked with a typical approach to selecting a pool of mentors, it could not have had more than 20 or 30 pairs active at this stage.

There has been a great deal of enthusiasm for the programme, with many participants acting as both mentors and mentees. Mentees have a great sense of ownership as they have volunteered for the programme and pick their mentor themselves.

Challenges

The implementation of the programme has not been without its challenges. A number of senior leaders have been approached by a large number of potential mentees and have found it difficult to choose who to work with and how to reject others. The limitation of having a maximum of three mentees at a time, as well as the guideline of the maximum duration of a mentoring relationship being 12 months, have proven helpful in facing this issue.

There have also been significant demands on the time of the HR team, with mentees and mentors asking for support over issues such as choosing a mentor or how to manage the process effectively. These conversations have also given the HR team an opportunity to work effectively with their internal clients and contribute to their development.

Some participants (mentees and volunteer mentors) didn't immediately find a partner, and the HR team has helped them find a match.

A number of mentees chose mentors from departments that they think they might want to work in in the future. At first, the concern was that this could present a potential conflict of interest. However, the outcomes so far indicate that there were no such issues.

Lessons learned

An important learning was that it is absolutely critical to make the purpose of mentoring as clear as possible at the outset of the programme. Many mentees were looking for sponsorship, and while some mentors were prepared to offer it, this was not the aim of the programme.

Vodafone and OneWorld Consulting were careful to differentiate sponsorship from developmental mentoring and made it clear that the programme focuses on developmental mentoring, not sponsorship.

The self-service nature of this programme has generally been effective. Although initially there was a plan to run full-day workshops to present and discuss a range of material, it was soon clear that half-day workshops have much higher attendance rates and other materials have been provided via Vodafone's e-learning portal.

The role of the internal programme manager has been critical to success. Also important is the role of front-line HR business partners, who all need to be comfortable talking about the programme and dealing with questions.

Based on Vodafone's experience so far, the programme appears to be a good fit for the organisation's particular context and culture; it has led to a huge number of development-focused conversations that probably wouldn't have happened otherwise. It also unleashed a great deal of energy and focus on people development, increasing effective cross-functional communication within Vodafone Turkey.

ENHANCING COACHING CULTURE IN BRISA

(Bridgestone Sabanci joint venture: http://www.brisa.com.tr/)

Contributed by Tim Bright, a Partner in OneWorld Consulting and Neslihan Eroglu, Brisa Human Resources Manager

Brisa is a joint venture between the Sabancı Group of Turkey and the Bridgestone Corporation of Japan. Brisa is the market leader in the Turkish tyre industry and the seventh biggest tyre manufacturer in Europe. It has an internationally recognised record of achievements in total quality management and has many awards in the field of business excellence. The company produces the Bridgestone and Lassa tyre brands, and also markets other customer-oriented service brands into many international markets and has over 2,500 employees.

Brisa has set an explicit goal of developing a coaching culture in line with their strategic objective to 'become employer of choice'. All executives are measured using the Hay Group's leadership styles tool each year, based on subordinate feedback, and one shared goal is to increase the usage of the coaching style, which has a primary objective of long-term development of others.

Brisa has implemented a number of initiatives directly aimed at strengthening the coaching culture:

- coaching skills workshops on 'Manager as coach'
- mentoring programme
- executive coaching.

All have been led by corporate HR, with strong buy-in and support from the CEO and leadership team. These programmes have been presented in a coordinated way as part of an effort to build a learning- and innovation-focused culture, where managers at all levels are encouraged to use a coaching style of management.

A goal within most of the executive coaching assignments (supported by the Brisa mentoring programme) has been to encourage senior executives to develop and use their own coaching style more within the organisation.

Key success factors

Key role of HR

The HR team has strong credibility in the company as it knows the business well and displays great commitment to continuous improvement and development. HR had an active role in the programme's design and implementation and in coaching planning, assessment and review meetings (alongside the coachee's line manager and the coach).

Positioning mentoring as an opportunity for people to practise their coaching skills

It can be difficult for managers to implement coaching skills immediately after they participate in coaching training. Years of habits, potential resistance from team members and being responsible for team members' business results do not help.

Mentoring gave executives in Brisa an opportunity to practise their coaching skills in a less challenging but more learning-oriented environment. Establishing a new relationship with their mentee, which was free of habitual ways of working and responsibility for the mentee's business results, allowed Brisa executives to focus on developing each other and practising their coaching skills, including listening, effective questions, summarising and use of silence.

It was clear that as managers developed their coaching skills and confidence as mentors, they started applying a coaching style more frequently in their daily work with their own teams.

Annual coaching style assessment results demonstrated an increase when executives were focused on using and implementing coaching methodology.

Consistency of skills and tools across the programmes

Participants have seen models and skills being used in one-to-one coaching, as well as mentoring and coaching workshops. This consistency and frequent exposure to coaching facilitated behaviour reinforcement and encouraged the use of skills. Mentoring supervision meetings with the executive team have also been used as an opportunity to discuss participants' own use of coaching with their direct reports, to update the senior leadership of the business on the 'Manager as coach' programme and to encourage them to support their subordinates as they use the coaching style more.

Observations

Brisa has a strong and successful engineering culture (multiple quality award winner, influenced by Japanese approaches through the Bridgestone partnership). There is a commitment to developing people and continuous improvement, the 'apprenticeship' type culture is strong, and people are very open to feedback and learning.

Also, managers tend to look for root causes (Toyota's 'ask 5 why questions to get to the root cause' is influential) and for gaps and weaknesses to be improved. To counterbalance these elements of the approach, participants have been encouraged to focus more on strengths and solutions instead of fixing the deficits.

Also, since there can be a strong desire to quantify and measure issues and outcomes, Einstein and William Bruce Cameron were frequently quoted: 'Not everything that can be counted counts, and not everything that counts can be counted.'

Since there is a very strong results and achievement-orientation (most managers are achievement oriented according to Hay Group's PSE), it can be important to emphasise that in coaching conversations the coach won't be achieving things directly themselves, but needs to take on a more facilitative role instead.

Brisa managers work as mentors both within their own Brisa programme and in the Sabanci Group programme in which mentors and mentees are paired across different companies.

Mentors find it easier to mentor someone from a different group company, rather than from their own company. The distance from the issues and people involved means they feel they can, in their words, do 'pure mentoring' and stay away from advice and conflicts of interest.

However, overall both programmes have been perceived as very useful. The cross-company programme gives participants exposure to a completely different sector and builds a sense of belonging and ownership across the Sabanci Group, while the single company programme helps strengthen company culture and builds useful connections across functions and locations.

SUMMARY

Developmental mentoring is an invaluable tool for supporting a coaching culture within an organisation. A well-designed and well-implemented mentoring programme leads to an increased number of powerful developmental conversations taking place in the organisation – something that often results in increased employee engagement and talent retention. Mentoring also enables both the mentor and the mentee to develop and use the mindset and skills that they can find useful in a variety of different contexts, from coaching and managing people to interacting with external stakeholders.

Mentoring is a very flexible tool that can be used to serve a number of different organisational objectives, from talent management through diversity management to change management. Currently the use of mentoring focuses on aligning mentoring with the wider organisational goals and maximising the potential positive impact it might have on the bottom line.

?

FIELDWORK

Think of your organisation or an organisation that you are familiar with and answer the following questions:

- What is the current mentoring state of play? Is there a formal mentoring programme being implemented at the moment?
- If yes, what is it? How effective is it, based on the ISMPE criteria?

If there is no formal mentoring scheme:

- Is there informal mentoring happening? With what result?
- How could the organisation benefit from a mentoring scheme?
- What would be the objectives of the mentoring programme?
- How would you ensure that it is fit for purpose and achieves the desired results?

PART FOUR

MOVING BEYOND THE BASICS

CHAPTER 11

The Unsung Heroes of Coaching Culture

'Never doubt that a small group of thoughtful, committed citizens can change the world; indeed, it's the only thing that ever has.'
Margaret Mead

OVERVIEW

To a great extent, this chapter is intended as an homage to the 'unsung heroes of coaching culture' – the people who make daily contributions to cultivating a coaching culture in their organisations. While many individuals contribute to that task, we will focus on just a few of them – those who have specific, identifiable roles, such as HR, coaching or mentoring managers, executive sponsors and champions of coaching. All of them play a crucial role in implementing coaching strategy and leading their organisation towards achieving the embedded stage of coaching culture.

'Looking at the visible manifestations of coaching culture is like watching a performance on stage; the quality of the final product is directly proportional to the amount of toil and the dexterity level of a small army of people – the producers, the playwright, the stage director, the set and costume designer, and the lights technician. They are all indispensable and yet invisible to the spectator,' said Claire Davey, Head of Coaching and Leadership Development in Deloitte.

We refer to this invisible 'army of people' as the 'unsung heroes of coaching culture', mainly because the literature on the subject has not given them due credit, nor has it explored the impact they have on the success rates of various coaching and mentoring initiatives.

While the hard data might not be there yet, anecdotal evidence strongly suggests that organisations that have made significant progress towards the embedded stage of coaching culture have one distinctive advantage – and to be absolutely clear, it has nothing to do with a generous budget or even an ideal, coaching-friendly environment! This advantage is a strong network of highly enthusiastic individuals who deeply believe in the developmental and transformational power of coaching and mentoring. These are the people who, either of their own accord or commissioned by the organisation to do so, envision and work hard towards creating a work environment where others can have meaningful learning conversations every day and with anyone. What makes their commitment particularly powerful is a deeply held belief that coaching can enable their organisation to fulfil its mission and create extraordinary value for all stakeholders.

THE KEY ROLES

HUMAN RESOURCES

A recent survey by the International Coach Federation (ICF 2014) indicated that 82 per cent of respondents identified human resources (HR) as responsible for developing a coaching culture, compared with the learning and development (L&D) function (59 per cent) or senior executives (43 per cent). While it is true that most initiatives aimed at cultivating coaching culture sit under the umbrella of HR, more and more companies make an effort to engage senior leadership and line-management representatives to ensure strategic alignment and buy-in.

Organisations which focused only on human resources development (HRD) as the driving force of coaching culture usually experience increased resistance. While the resistance mostly comes from the business, it is not uncommon for some of the reluctance to originate within HR as well (Clutterbuck and Megginson 2005). This is often because different parts of HR may view coaching and mentoring through dramatically different lenses. At best, such misalignment can lead to suboptimal results. At its extreme, it can hinder progress or even take an organisation a few steps back. An example of such misalignment is a manufacturing company which, after many years of consistent investment in building a coaching culture, managed to develop a large pool of highly qualified internal coaches and embed coaching in the way managers lead their people. However, during a recent period of a major business transformation, with a new CEO and a new business strategy, HR failed to make a compelling case for maintaining and further developing a coaching culture. As a result, a number of people responsible for the coaching programmes were made redundant, while coaching, which up to that point had a mainly developmental character, was recast to be a tool in the service of specific (and often unpopular) changes. It is too early to report on the results of this turn of events, but it is relatively easy to foresee their potential impact on the coaching culture in this particular organisation.

This cautionary tale illustrates that HR has a critical role in coaching culture development. A few key aspects of this role are:

- creating a compelling business case for a coaching culture
- promoting coaching to the organisational stakeholders
- protecting it from the destructive forces of sudden economies and changes of management fashion
- ensuring that the quality of coaching and mentoring initiatives is maintained, in spite of personal agendas or limited budgets.

Ideally, HR should be one (but not the only one) of the driving forces of a coaching culture and be involved in:

- coaching culture strategy creation
- strategy implementation, including support in coaching and mentoring capability development, good practice development and communication
- coaching culture measurement and identifying its impact on business results
- keeping coaching culture on the business agenda.

If an organisation is serious about embedding coaching and mentoring into the way it does its business, it will also need to make sure that, at the minimum, it has the right people in the following roles:

- head of coaching and mentoring
- organisational sponsors
- coaching or mentoring champions.

COACHING (OR MENTORING) MANAGER

When starting their journey towards a coaching culture, many organisations do not have a formal coaching or mentoring manager. Such a role is usually created at a stage when there are already a number of coaching engagements running in parallel or an extensive mentoring programme is being launched. At that point, it usually becomes apparent that setting up, running and properly supporting any coaching or mentoring initiative will take a great deal of time and effort.

A good coaching or mentoring manager is integral to the success of coaching or mentoring initiatives. It is their energy and enthusiasm for coaching or mentoring specifically and for developing others more generally that will drive the programme and keep momentum within it.

Depending on the size of the organisation and the number of initiatives taking place simultaneously, being a coaching or mentoring manager might be a part-time or a full-time job. Moreover, the degree of hands-on involvement will vary, depending on whether the manager has a team of people to support them or they are on their own. Based on our discussions with people in this role, it seems that their primary responsibilities may include those listed here.

Promoting the concept of coaching (and/or mentoring) and ensuring commitment from the business

Along with their enthusiasm, effective managers bring a strong sense of the pragmatic. They identify where coaching or mentoring will add the most value to the organisation, by addressing key business issues, and they build a solid argument around how it will do so. Wherever possible, they engage top management in a discussion to ensure that they are fully supportive and that they understand at both intellectual and emotional levels what a difference coaching or mentoring programmes will make. This includes making sure that senior management understands what coaching (or mentoring) is, how it works and why it can be beneficial.

Creating or strengthening the network of supporters

Support from top management helps to give efforts to build a coaching culture prominence and shape, but only rarely do the business leaders spend substantial amounts of time on specific initiatives. For that, the manager needs an active steering group of enthusiasts and a network of influencers who will promote coaching positively.

Facilitating the creation of a coaching culture vision

A coaching manager engages key stakeholders in identifying what kind of coaching culture is desirable for the organisation and makes sure that it is clear what success looks like.

Identifying, defining, designing and implementing initiatives that support the development of a coaching (and mentoring) culture

This will include: defining the objectives and success criteria for the initiatives; supporting the planning for recruitment, matching or training; identifying how the initiatives will be measured; and maintaining the momentum.

Guarding confidentiality

Ensuring information gathered as part of the coaching and mentoring schemes is secure and providing support to participants of various schemes around the issue of confidentiality.

Giving honest and constructive feedback to coaches and coachees (or mentors and mentees)

This may take place at any stage of coaching (or mentoring) engagement and particularly when the relationship faces difficulties.

Managing the expectations of all stakeholders

This involves ensuring that everyone involved in initiatives aiming to cultivate a coaching culture have sufficient initial understanding of their roles and responsibilities.

Providing appropriate resources or support

This entails understanding what each initiative requires in terms of resources or support and ensuring that all parties involved have the training, information, tools, guidelines and other forms of support that will enable them to be successful. In most cases, this will involve creating and getting a budget approved by the senior management.

Evaluating the schemes and programmes that are being implemented

The coaching or mentoring manager is responsible for ensuring that not only does measurement take place, but that the data is analysed, shared and responded to. A great manager is constantly assessing the status of the current initiatives and making adjustments, based on both the firm and anecdotal evidence they see. They also have a troubleshooting system in place in case relationships go wrong.

Keeping all stakeholders well informed

This involves sharing all evaluation data and detailing any challenges that they have encountered. Keeping any steering group or senior management close to the current programmes will give the manager more scope to enhance the initiatives, develop new ones and keep the stakeholders motivated to support them in the future.

Maintaining financial control over the coaching or mentoring programmes

The manager has to make sure that the programmes are within budget and that appropriate financial resources are available, as agreed with the senior management.

Setting up and maintaining administrative records for coaching and mentoring engagements

There is a great deal of data that needs to be gathered during the course of an engagement or a programme, such as:

- type of engagement (coaching or mentoring; one-to-one or team or group)
- coach and coachee/mentor and mentee details
- matching process
- date of first meeting
- mid-term evaluation results
- final outcomes.

A coaching/mentoring manager will ensure appropriate systems are put in place to track this data and will store and share this data safely. Many companies nowadays decide to use specialised software that enables efficient management of all ongoing corporate coaching and mentoring engagements. By automating routine tasks and providing deep insight into various metrics, these tools can significantly aid the coaching or mentoring manager in their administrative duties.

Some of the critical skills and competencies that the role requires are:

- excellent interpersonal understanding
- political astuteness
- knowledge of the organisation and culture
- clarity around business priorities and politics of the organisation
- sound communication skills (both verbal and written)
- access to top management
- time to listen and become involved
- facilitation skills
- project management skills
- working knowledge of coaching and mentoring theory and practice
- experience of being a coach and a coachee.

The role of coaching or mentoring manager is a complex and demanding one. However, most of the effective coaching or mentoring managers consider their role as one of the most satisfying and personally fulfilling work roles they have undertaken.

SPONSORS

The latest compendium report on *Best Practices in Change Management* by Prosci (2014), one of the largest bodies of knowledge on change management, identified the greatest contributors and biggest obstacles to change. For the eighth consecutive study, executive sponsorship was recognised as the largest contributor to success. There was a direct correlation between sponsor effectiveness and meeting change objectives. What was the number one obstacle? Ineffective executive sponsorship.

It is not surprising – the majority of stories of successful progress towards a coaching culture feature committed, enthusiastic and visible sponsors. When senior leaders in an organisation are passionate advocates of coaching and mentoring, it is much easier to promote coaching and achieve the desired momentum.

An example is a manufacturing organisation which had been working on developing coaching capability as part of its leadership development programme for almost ten years. People experienced coaching and were encouraged to use it with their team members, but the change was erratic and slow. A major shift did not happen until the CEO changed. Being a strong believer in people's development, the new CEO was very vocal about the importance of coaching. He crafted and communicated a coaching vision and consistently used coaching with his direct reports. His commitment led to a number of initiatives that allowed the organisation to create and maintain its own pool of internal coaches and experience a gradual shift of leadership style. In a similar vein, some years ago one of us conducted a development climate survey in a professional services organisation, ahead of the launch of a mentoring programme. Presenting the results of the survey to the leadership team was a challenge – this was one of the most hostile developmental climates we had encountered. The CEO took it on the chin and asked what was needed from him to make the programme work. As a result, he attended almost every training session personally, talking about his own experience as mentor and mentee. This action legitimised mentoring within the organisation and, a few years later, the organisation was one of the first to achieve a gold award under the International Standards for Mentoring Programmes in Employment.

There are many reasons why an effective executive sponsor is crucial to building or sustaining a coaching culture. Apart from authorising budgets for coaching or mentoring initiatives, when effective, they build a coalition that ensures the necessary momentum is created and maintained. Their personal involvement sends a strong message to the rest of the organisation, demonstrating that coaching and mentoring are considered a priority.

When executive sponsors talk about coaching, or – even better – use a coaching approach in working with their teams, the rest of the organisation pays attention.

The lack of a visible sponsor, on the other hand, can lead to an even stronger resistance from those individuals who are not big believers in coaching. It will also be more difficult for the coaching culture steering committee or coaching or mentoring manager to overcome difficulties around resources or schedules.

Our research indicates that not all organisations are lucky enough to have a strong and committed leadership support. There are many reasons for sponsors lacking effectiveness, for example:

- **They lack positive personal experience with coaching** – while a sponsor may intellectually understand the importance of creating a coaching culture within the organisation, lack of coaching skills or personal experience with coaching can be a significant limiting factor. When this is the case, the sponsor's involvement may lack the emotional charge necessary for effective advocacy and consistent role-modelling.
- **They fail to see building a coaching culture as a priority** – when the business case is not clear to the executive sponsor, they tend to gradually lose their interest or even abdicate sponsorship and delegate it to someone else, for example HR or an external consultant.
- **They do not have a clear understanding of their role** – often executive sponsors think that their role is limited to signing off budgets and approving various initiatives. They are not entirely clear on what the active involvement should look like.

How to create and maintain strong executive sponsorship

There are a number of things that can be done to strengthen executive sponsorship. Below are the three top strategies organisations successfully implement to achieve that.

Creating, re-creating and regularly communicating a compelling business case for coaching culture

The first important step towards strong leadership support is creating and communicating a compelling business case for coaching culture. We already talked about this in detail in Chapter 3. However, creating and communicating a business case is not a one-off proposition. As with most change initiatives, the initial commitment has a tendency to dissipate (Clutterbuck and Megginson 2005) and will require regular reinforcement. We would therefore suggest continuously updating the business case for coaching culture and communicating it on a regular basis. Revisiting the business case not only helps to rekindle the executive sponsor's engagement, but also ensures the business relevance of various coaching initiatives.

Offering coaching and mentoring experience and developing capability among the executive sponsors

Many organisations discovered that providing positive experiences with coaching as well as developing coaching capability among the executive sponsors is extremely helpful in engaging executive sponsors and equipping them with the skills that allow for successful role-modelling. This is where an investment in the highest possible quality of executive coaching and coaching training pays off tenfold.

Educating, supporting and coaching for effective sponsorship

For many leaders, culture change sponsorship will involve developing an entirely new skill set. Even the term 'sponsorship' itself is often misunderstood and will require a clear definition of its key aspects and requirements. We have noticed that most executive sponsors will fulfil their role to their best abilities if they believe in the necessity of change and are entirely clear on what their role specifically calls for. According to Prosci's *Best Practices in Change Management* report (2014), there are three main activities involved in the role of an executive sponsor:

- **Active and visible participation.** For example, an executive sponsor in a large global hospitality chain always included the implementation of coaching culture-related initiatives on his management team meetings agenda and his video-recorded message was incorporated in all the coaching training materials used within an organisation. In another organisation, the sponsor kicked off all coaching-related awareness-building workshops for the employees.
- **Building sponsorship coalition and managing resistance.** An example is another executive sponsor in a professional services firm who regularly invited the coaching culture champion to management meetings to report on the success of coaching culture interventions and share good practices. This was aimed at softening the resistance from some of the management team members who saw coaching as a 'spend' rather than an 'investment'. It is worth remembering that resistance also means that the resisters care enough to put their head above the parapet. It is prudent to find out what the resisters are standing for and to seek to honour this impulse.
- **Direct communication with employees.** A director in a non-profit organisation would openly talk about his experience with coaching, referring to it as life-changing and transformational, and encouraged people to seek formal coaching, as well as coaching from their managers.

Sponsors are typically busy executives who might need significant support to perform their sponsorship role effectively. That support, often coming from HR or the coaching manager, can have a hands-on or coaching nature, depending on what is needed. Hands-on support will include helping the executive sponsor to identify the best opportunities to participate in coaching culture initiatives, schedule meetings with the key stakeholders, prepare their talking points for meetings, and identify the potential sponsorship coalition as well as primary sources of resistance to change. Coaching the sponsor involves helping them envision what success in their role will look like and creating a roadmap specifying actions they will have to take to achieve that.

CHAMPIONS

If anyone can make coaching or mentoring spread through an organisation fast, it will be the champions. In many organisations, champions were initially coaching enthusiasts, who spontaneously stepped into the role simply because they deeply believed in the benefits of coaching. However, as organisations progress towards building a coaching culture in a more systematic way, the role of a coaching programme champion is often becoming formalised, especially in organisations that aspire to enter the strategic and embedded stage of coaching culture development.

We can define a coaching culture champion as someone who is a passionate and vocal advocate for bringing coaching culture vision to life and who actively promotes coaching throughout the organisation while encouraging the desired behaviours and addressing any resistance to coaching or mentoring initiatives.

While one coaching culture sponsor can be enough (especially if their influence and decision-making power are strong enough), it takes more than one champion to embed and sustain coaching culture. In fact, many organisations recognise that it is necessary to identify and engage coaching champions in every department and in every team that is in the focus of coaching culture initiatives.

So what do effective coaching culture champions typically do? There are many different ways coaching champions go about performing their roles. These are some of the key themes that we identified.

Role-model coaching behaviours and encourage others to display similar behaviours on a daily basis

Most of the effective coaching champions are able coaches (and coachees) themselves. They are good coaching role models and can offer advice and guidance on how to take a coaching approach to various issues. They speak about coaching with passion and enthusiasm, encouraging others to experiment with the available coaching modalities.

Demonstrate core coaching principles

Good coaching champions walk the walk in terms of how frequently and how well they use coaching skills. However, perhaps even more importantly, they live and breathe the core coaching principles, such as attentiveness, collaboration, curiosity, ethicality, growth orientation, openness and honesty, reflection and respect (see Chapter 1 for more details on the core coaching principles).

Identify key issues on the ground

A good coaching culture champion is always tuned to what is happening within the teams that are implementing coaching or mentoring initiatives. They take note of the main systemic issues that impact the implementation, gather feedback on how things are going and accurately identify key sources of resistance. They also feed back these to the coaching culture steering committee or coaching manager. Champions can also support mentoring and line manager coaching initiatives by taking part in steering groups: helping to devise policy, identifying problems on the ground and being available for under-the-radar troubleshooting.

Use storytelling to illustrate the cultural beliefs linked to coaching culture

In Chapter 1, we talked about coaching culture having its roots in people's beliefs and mindsets. Therefore, any notable culture shift will have to address these. Storytelling can be a powerful technique to cultivate the desired beliefs and mindsets. An example is a story told in PwC about a client pitch during which a young and inexperienced team member completely froze during the presentation, temporarily unable to deliver their part. At that time, PwC was implementing the team-based learning (TBL) initiative, the guiding principle of which was seeing everything a team does as an opportunity for learning. A part of that scheme was for more junior team members to participate in the so-called 'stretch assignments', such as a client pitch. Being aware of TBL and its principles, the client offered the junior team member a glass of water and suggested a short break. After that, the presentation resumed and the young team member performed their part well. PwC won the client engagement, and one of the reasons quoted by the client was the firm's unwavering commitment to people development! This story is often used by TBL champions to illustrate cultural beliefs and principles linked to coaching culture, such as honesty, transparency and growth-orientation.

Identify and speak about business benefits related to coaching culture initiatives

One of the best ways of creating a momentum for coaching in the organisation is to demonstrate its clear business benefits and success stories. A good coaching champion has their eye set on success stories and benefits that coaching brings and often relates to them when interacting with various stakeholders. One of the particularly powerful stories that we hear quite often has a common theme: a sceptical (and usually senior) stakeholder refuses to engage with the coaching initiatives until they see tangible benefits, usually within their team. Another one that is often used by champions is about the tangible, measurable results that have improved as a consequence of a coaching intervention, such as team coaching.

Recognise and acknowledge progress towards coaching culture

A good coaching champion follows up on the progress made towards coaching culture and acknowledges people for good results. They inform the coaching culture sponsor or coaching manager about the progress they have noticed and ensure that all efforts are appropriately rewarded. The rewards do not have to be financial – recognition is an important reward too.

How to create an effective network of champions

When an organisation is considering whether to formalise the role of champions and create a strong champion network, it is good to consider the following:

- **Defining champions' responsibilities.** The first step towards creating a network of coaching culture champions would be identifying what their responsibilities should be. Discussing stakeholders' expectations (and managing them!) can be quite useful at this stage as it creates role clarity and allows the steering group or the person responsible for the particular programme to plan any support or training the champions might need.
- **Identifying criteria for selecting the champions.** Not everyone will make a good coaching champion. Clarifying the key characteristics of a good coaching champion can help organisational leaders to pick the right people for the job. Example criteria could be:
  - has had personal experience with coaching and believes that coaching can support the organisation to achieve its key objectives
  - acts, or has the capability to act, as a role model for the specific coaching initiative
  - is well established and respected within their department or business unit
  - has good communication skills
  - has participated or contributed to other coaching or mentoring programmes developed by the organisation.
- **Providing training and support.** No matter how self-motivated and committed your coaching champions are, they will require briefing or training to help them understand their role and key responsibilities as a champion, as well as the details of the initiatives they will be supporting. The most common training format offered to champions is a half-day workshop. A common agenda addresses:
  - the role of a champion
  - key attributes of an effective champion
  - potential challenges and ways of overcoming them
  - programme details
  - action planning – identifying key actions champions can take going forward. Beyond formal training, champions can also engage with L&D or HR if they face any issues or difficulties in their role.
- **Making it available to the rest of the organisation.** There won't be much use to the champion network if the rest of the organisation is not aware of its existence. Large organisations tend to post champions' profiles and contact details on the intranet so

that people can get in touch with them whenever support is needed. In smaller organisations or within divisions, champions are announced to the participating individuals or groups in face-to-face meetings. It helps when this is done by a senior executive, for example, the sponsor of the coaching or mentoring programme.

Having a strong, well-prepared and adequately supported network of coaching or mentoring champions has proven to be one of the key success factors in the roll-out of various coaching or mentoring initiatives. Champions also play a major role in sustaining coaching culture within the organisation.

HOW COACHING CHAMPIONS CONTRIBUTE TO CULTIVATING A COACHING CULTURE WITHIN SAVE THE CHILDREN AND BEYOND

This story is based on interviews with the following individuals:

Shola Awolesi – Global Leadership Development Manager at Save the Children

Gareth Owen, OBE – Humanitarian Director at Save the Children

Mavis Owusu-Gyamfi – Director, Programme Policy and Quality at Save the Children

As already described in previous chapters, Save the Children has greatly benefited from the existing pool of external coaches. Amongst the many benefits that the organisation reaped from engaging coaches in its leadership development programme and from launching developmental coaching was that a number of coaching recipients turned into exceptionally committed champions of coaching.

Shola Awolesi says: 'I believe that the key reason for some of our executives becoming such vocal champions of coaching is that their own personal experience with coaching was so powerful. We hear of people having major breakthroughs, gaining a series of vital insights or even experiencing the whole process as entirely transformational, both on personal and professional level.' Two coaching champions that we interviewed readily confirmed that.

Gareth Owen says: 'Three years ago, when I was asked if I wanted to be a beneficiary of coaching, I jumped at the opportunity. Back then, I was stuck and getting desperate, so coaching seemed like a great idea. The matching process worked really well judging by the outcomes; it resulted in three years of the most transformational experience. Coaching was an amazing gift for me and the organisation; it was an incredibly settling experience that allowed me to gain access to things I knew, but could never have reached on my own, without the help of a coach.'

For Gareth, who leads 250 staff and manages an operation with a turnover of £80 million to £100 million annually, coaching offered invaluable help in further strengthening the enabling environment necessary for his people to be effective. The 'distributed leadership' style that Gareth honed partially thanks to coaching resulted in his team's achievements, such as effectively forming partnerships with universities, building entirely new organisations, developing a relationship with the government, starting a consortium of 26 NGOs and many other positive disruptor projects. His passion for coaching did not only impact people within the organisation. He recalls: 'In my enthusiasm, I got into a conversation with the senior leadership of the United Nations, people reporting to the Secretary-General of the United Nations. One thing led to another and now they use coaching in their leadership development as well.'

Similarly to Gareth, Mavis Owusu-Gyamfi considers coaching an invaluable tool for a leader. Having had a very positive experience with coaching herself, she not only openly shared her experience with others but also sought to improve her department's engagement score by offering coaching skills training to her managers. When asked about the change she hopes for by equipping her managers with coaching skills, she said: 'I would like to see people become more self-aware and realise the impact their leadership style has on others. It would be good for my managers to fully see the value of diversity and learn to leverage it when working with people who have a different personality, a different view or preference.'

These two examples of coaching champions in Save the Children – Mavis and Gareth – illustrate how people who feel passionate about coaching can contribute to the organic growth of coaching culture, through their own leadership practices but also by advocating for coaching, within their own organisation but also beyond its boundaries.

COACHING CULTURE IN PWC: THE KEY PLAYERS

This story was contributed by Maria Symeon, PwC Global Coaching Leader/Partner Development

Context

In a professional services context, coaching is a core skill which starts being developed from day one in the firm. All professional staff are expected to use a form of on-the-job, performance or development coaching as part of their day-to-day work. Additionally, the more senior individuals will often experience increased focus on personal and career development of the people they work with. While a lot of coaching in PwC is part of the line management duties and interactions, there is a significant amount of peer coaching taking place as well. So how do people learn the range of coaching skills they need to be effective?

Key people

Learning and Development

In PwC coaching is formally 'owned' by the centralised Learning and Development function. The function is responsible for a range of activities: designing the strategy to enhance and sustain a coaching culture within the firm, providing a framework and supporting curriculum for coaching skills development and managing an external and internal executive coaching practice.

The wider network

While the firm relies on L&D to provide a core framework and best practices for coaching, it is clear that an organisation as large as PwC needs a much wider network to create and sustain a coaching culture.

Part of this supportive network sits within the human capital (HC) function of the firm, with a number of individuals who are directly involved in the day-to-day activities of the business. These people play a crucial role in promoting coaching and supporting any initiatives that are aimed at further enhancement of coaching culture. Also, being the first port of call for people experiencing a work-related or personal challenge, they are often the ones who role-model good coaching in the moment. Providing that kind of support as part of their duties led a lot of HC professionals within the firm to develop a deep interest and expertise in coaching. Therefore, they are often called upon to support the more specialist interventions (for example executive coaching), as well as supporting their business in developing the skills and conditions for coaching to be effective.

While L&D and HC practitioners often have a leading role in implementing coaching initiatives and have undoubtedly made a tremendous contribution to the enhancement of PwC's coaching culture so far, they are not the only ones at the forefront. A critical success factor for PwC has always been having a main executive sponsor and a network of champions of coaching. Leaders who can demonstrate the skills and behaviours, who believe in the value of coaching and who are open to being coached are the best advocates of coaching in PwC.

SUMMARY

Making even the slightest change to organisational culture is an immense undertaking; it requires a great amount of dedication and effort. Building a coaching culture would be a futile task without a committed, well-organised group of people. The key roles in cultivating a coaching culture are that of HR, coaching or mentoring manager, executive sponsor and coaching or mentoring champions.

?

FIELDWORK

Think about your organisation or one that you are familiar with and reflect on the following questions:

- What are the current coaching or mentoring initiatives that are being implemented?
- How are they being supported?
- Can you identify any of the roles mentioned in the chapter?
- If the answer to the previous question is 'yes', how could these people be further supported to maximise their contribution to developing the desired culture?
- If there are currently no clear roles of the executive sponsor, coaching or mentoring manager, or champion, which do you think would be most helpful to introduce at this stage? How would you go about it?

CHAPTER 12

Marketing Coaching and Mentoring

'Marketing is too important to be left just to the marketing department.'
Philip Almond, Marketing Director, Diageo

OVERVIEW

This chapter talks about the role of marketing in developing a coaching culture within an organisation. It describes the foundations and essential elements of an effective coaching or mentoring marketing plan and presents key themes that emerged from our interviews with organisations that are successful in marketing coaching.

WHY MARKETING?

We were not surprised when marketing and communication emerged as one of the four main areas of an effective coaching culture strategy (see Chapter 6).

Cultivating a coaching culture is, after all, an advanced juggling act. It requires a simultaneous focus on many different elements.

Literature often groups these elements into two broad categories, referred to as 'hard' and 'soft' aspects of change. The hard aspect is concerned with the supportive structures and systems, in this case with providing people with the appropriate tools and processes to enable coaching. Experience repeatedly shows that this tends to be the relatively straightforward part of the process. In contrast – and contrary to its deceiving label – the 'soft' aspect of building a coaching culture deals with the hardest part of the process – enabling, embedding and reinforcing the desired behavioural change. It focuses on creating the understanding and acceptance of coaching and its benefits. Ultimately, it is about shaping new habits – creating and sustaining new patterns of behaviour which are rooted in beliefs, mindsets and principles congruent with coaching. And this is where marketing proves to be an indispensable tool.

COACHING AND MENTORING MARKETING FUNDAMENTALS

In his seminal article, 'Marketing Myopia', Theodore C. Levitt described marketing as 'an effort to discover, create, arouse and satisfy customer needs' (Levitt 1960).

In this case, our customers are the employees, at all levels, including executives and subcontracted employees. The marketing of coaching and mentoring, therefore, aims to identify and demonstrate the link between people's expressed (or latent) needs and the benefits of coaching. Effective marketing convinces people to be open to persuasion, willingly experiment with and eventually fully embrace new behaviours. Viewed from this vantage point, marketing coaching emerges as an integral part of coaching culture strategy, rather than a standalone intervention.

The good news is that coaching does – directly or indirectly – contribute to satisfying a huge range of needs spanning from psychological to job-related ones. They include the need for belonging, esteem and self-actualisation (Maslow 1954); power, achievement, affiliation or even avoidance (McClellan 1989) and the needs commonly generated by the demands of the business, such as creating high-performing teams, achieving objectives, increasing efficiency and so on. From this point of view, coaching and mentoring are potentially highly 'marketable' offerings and the high uptake of coaching and mentoring services in most organisations featured in this book consistently confirms that.

Why then is it that marketing efforts related to coaching often don't bring about the desired results? Coaching marketing campaigns frequently fail in the absence of the necessary groundwork, when they are either premature or based on a host of inaccurate assumptions. Our observations lead us to the conclusion that in order to market coaching or mentoring effectively, three key elements need to be in place. They are illustrated in Figure 12.1.

Figure 12.1 Marketing coaching and mentoring fundamentals

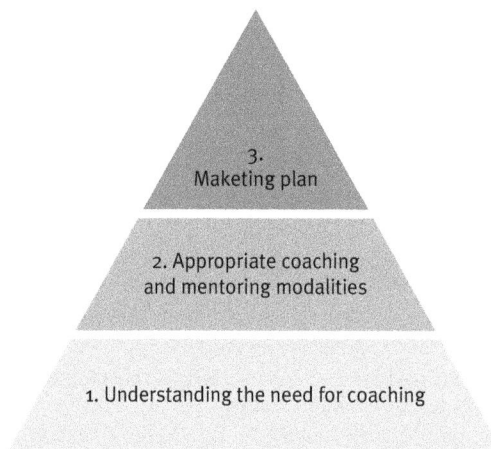

3.
Maketing plan

2. Appropriate coaching
and mentoring modalities

1. Understanding the need for coaching

UNDERSTANDING THE NEED FOR COACHING

We have already talked a lot about the importance of perceived relevance of coaching and the necessity to create a robust business case for coaching, where the link between 'what do we need to achieve as a business?' and 'how can coaching support us in this?' are crystal clear.

It is, however, equally important to understand the individual needs of various demographic groups, such as those of people at different hierarchical levels, in career transitions, new-joiners, mothers returning to work after maternity leave and so on. There are many potential sources of information to explore:

- employee surveys
- informal conversations with various groups
- events that open up channels of communication, such as employee forums or meetings
- coaching and learning needs analysis
- Organisational learning from existing coaching engagements (as described in 'Stories in the field' in Chapter 2)
- communities of practice (such as EY's Coaching and Mentoring Network, where line managers and coaches meet and exchange experiences).

APPROPRIATE COACHING AND MENTORING MODALITIES

Seth Godin, a well-known American author and marketer, is often quoted as having said: 'Don't find customers for your products. Find products for your customers.'[1] This customer-centred approach resonates particularly strongly with the philosophy of cultivating a coaching culture. Understanding both business and individual needs for coaching is a prerequisite for identifying the most appropriate modalities of coaching or mentoring in each particular context. This is closely linked to another area of an effective coaching culture strategy that we mentioned in Chapter 6, accessibility and relevance of coaching, and specifically to ensuring that the portfolio of coaching and mentoring modalities on offer is sufficient and appropriate for the target groups. Even the most ingenious marketing tactics will not work if the offering does not match the demand.

MARKETING PLAN

Promoting coaching and mentoring in an organisation becomes easier with a robust marketing plan in place. It allows for alignment with the overall business and coaching strategy and helps avoid overlaps, duplications or even conflicts with the already existing initiatives or messages. It also enables you to customise the messages and approaches to specific target groups.

ELEMENTS OF AN EFFECTIVE MARKETING PLAN

The coaching culture marketing plan is an integral part of coaching culture strategy. Its purpose is to support the achievement of the overall coaching culture objectives.

Examples of how marketing activities can be aligned in order to support coaching culture objectives are presented in Table 12.1.

Table 12.1 Examples of aligning marketing with coaching culture strategy

Coaching culture strategy pillars	Coaching culture objectives	Coaching culture marketing objectives	Coaching culture marketing activities
Increasing coaching and mentoring accessibility	Launching a mentoring scheme available to everyone in the organisation with a minimum of 100 mentoring pairs in the first year.	Making everyone in the organisation aware of the potential benefits of the scheme. Convincing a minimum of 100 leaders across the organisation to offer mentoring and a minimum of 150 employees to seek a coach in the first year. 10 per cent increase in selected questions of the employee survey linked to having meaningful career conversations and support.	Email communication campaign. Setting up and regularly updating online information library. Organising 'mentoring days' where people can come and learn more about mentoring. Including mentoring in the annual coaching and mentoring conference. Bringing in an external speaker to talk about mentoring.

---

[1] Source: http://www.goodreads.com

	Offering group coaching addressed to leaders facing work–life balance issues.	Increasing awareness of group coaching by 20 per cent (measured by a spot survey). Launching five groups of eight participants in the first year. 10 per cent improvement in work–life balance related questions in the employee survey.	Email campaign. Organising group coaching open days. Uploading information to the intranet. Featuring group coaching in the company-wide newsletter. Videos with testimonials of participants who have benefited from the programme.
Broadening the portfolio of coaching and mentoring modalities	Adding team coaching to the existing portfolio of coaching modalities.	Increasing awareness of team coaching by 20 per cent (measured by a spot survey). Increasing the number of people working in effective teams by 5 per cent (measured by employee survey questions). Having 20 teams go through a team coaching programme in the first year.	Presenting team coaching at the managers' meeting. Email campaign featuring success stories from the pilot run of team coaching. Recording and disseminating testimonials. Identifying champions and informal networking.
	Launching maternity mentoring programme.	Reaching all employees leaving on maternity leave to inform them of the possibility of benefiting from maternity mentoring. Raising the awareness of maternity mentoring by 80 per cent in the main target group and 20 per cent in the wider population. Creating at least 20 mentoring pairs. Increasing the number of returning mothers who have the same or higher performance rating as the one they had before maternity leave.	Identifying potential mentors and mentees and approaching directly through email and face-to-face contact. Informing all managers of the maternity mentoring scheme and its benefits. Publication in internal and external media. Video testimonial from the first pairs. Featuring maternity mentoring in the annual coaching conference.
Integration – making coaching part of the way	Reinforcing the use of a coaching approach among	Increasing the awareness and understanding of what	Creating an e-learn with useful coaching techniques.

'we do business around here'	the line managers.	line manager coaching looks like. Increasing the percentage of employees who receive frequent coaching from their line manager – from 60 per cent to 75 per cent.	Creating a line managers' community of practice. Including coaching in all leadership development programmes. Video testimonials on intranet.

An effective coaching and mentoring marketing plan usually includes the following elements:

- baselining and context
- objectives
- target audiences
- messages
- communication methods
- budget
- implementation plan
- evaluation.

BASELINING AND CONTEXT ASSESSMENT

Before putting a new coaching culture marketing plan together, it can be helpful to explore what is already there and what the starting point is; being aware of the existing communication and marketing initiatives aimed, directly or indirectly, at promoting a coaching culture will help avoid duplication, overlaps or conflicting messages.

Even revisiting an organisation's values, mission, vision, or competency framework can be helpful at this stage: it is important to make sure that coaching culture messages are congruent with these.

Evaluating other (unrelated to coaching) communications and marketing initiatives in the organisation can pay off, too. It will allow you to gain useful insights into which formats and channels of communication are a good cultural match. For example, while a campaign using the intranet and an online internal social network can be very effective with a young, technically savvy population, it might have very limited reach and impact in a more traditional environment, where face-to-face contact is the preferred form of communication.

Involving corporate communication and marketing (C&M) departments early on in the process can be very useful. In most organisations, communication or marketing initiatives have to be aligned with the corporate guidelines. Additionally, the C&M department – usually the best source of information on the existing marketing initiatives – will be able to assist with audience segmentation, crafting of marketing messages and media, and timing (it's usually best to avoid a campaign on coaching when people's attention is likely to be focused on major changes with more immediate impact, for example).

Questions to explore here

- What marketing initiatives promoting a coaching culture are already under way? How do these align with other current corporate messages?
- Which have been particularly well received? Why?
- What typically tends to work in our organisation when it comes to internal marketing and communication?

- What are the organisational messages that we need to be aligned with in promoting coaching or mentoring?

OBJECTIVES

Marketing objectives need to be aligned with the coaching culture objectives, as well as the wider business goals. Setting clear objectives at the outset is important not only to give the right direction to marketing activities but also to establish a basis on which to measure results.

Examples of coaching marketing objectives from a number of organisations that we interviewed include:

- increasing the awareness of coaching in our organisation by 20 per cent (survey based) by the end of the year
- improving the overall understanding of the benefits of coaching by line managers by the end of the next quarter
- demonstrating that team coaching is an extremely useful tool for improving team performance
- 90 per cent of target audience visits the online coaching and mentoring library at least once by the end of the year
- 85 per cent of visitors to a coaching fair would recommend their colleagues to visit in the future (based on a spot survey on the day).

Questions to explore here

- What are we hoping to accomplish through our marketing activities?
- What will the success of our marketing efforts look like?
- How will we know that the campaign/marketing activities have the desired impact?
- How will we measure success?

TARGET AUDIENCE

The amount of work that goes into understanding the target audience is the best predictor of how effective the marketing efforts will be. A potential audience could encompass all employees or be more targeted and comprise senior leaders, all managers in the organisation, key talent, coaching champions, mothers preparing for their return to the workplace and so on.

Questions to explore here

- Who are our target audiences?
- What are each target audience's needs/priorities/motivations (both voiced and implicit)?
- What do they already know about coaching/mentoring/coaching culture/specific scheme or programme that we are launching?
- What are the most likely points of resistance in each group?
- What are the concerns of each target audience?
- What do we want them to know as a result of our marketing/communication campaign?
- What is the most effective way to communicate with each target audience?
- Who do they look up to? Who could easily influence them?
- How can we involve them in designing the right marketing approach?
- Which of our target groups is most likely to actively promote coaching and mentoring?

The analysis of the target audience will enable to identify what kind of messages might convince people to engage in industry coaching initiatives or embrace coaching in their daily work. It is very likely that senior executives in a non-profit organisation will be sensitive to a different message than Generation Y individuals in an accounting firm. Populations within the same organisation can differ significantly, too – your target group for a maternity mentoring programme will not only require a different message but a different tone than, for example, sales team leaders whom you want to attract to a team coaching programme.

One thing particularly worth stressing here is that for marketing messages to be effective, they need to speak not only to people's heads, but also – and perhaps far more crucially – to their hearts. As Kotter and Cohen said in the *The Heart of Change* (2002): '. . . the core of the matter is always about changing the behavior of people, and behavior change happens in highly successful situations mostly by speaking to people's feelings. This is true even in organizations that are very focused on analysis and quantitative measurement, even among people who think of themselves as smart in an MBA sense. In highly successful change efforts, people find ways to help others see the problems or solutions in ways that influence emotions, not just thought. Feelings then alter behavior sufficiently to overcome all the many barriers to sensible large-scale change.'

Questions to explore here

- What are our key messages?
- How can these messages be 'packaged' to:
  - resonate with our target audiences' key concerns, motivators, needs and feelings
  - help overcome key points of resistance?
- What would be the most appropriate tone of our key messages for the particular audiences (a few examples of key-message tone are: playful, inspirational, formal, informal, youthful, challenging, or conservative)?
- How can we test the clarity and effectiveness of our message?

Our experience shows that the budget for marketing coaching and mentoring can be limited. This calls for identifying creative methods of communication and marketing (see communication methods below).

Questions to explore here

- Is there a budget available already or will we have to obtain financial resources for this?
- Who are the key decision-makers?
- How do we present the expected benefits of marketing coaching and mentoring to convince key decision-makers?
- How can we make the best possible use of the available resources?

As soon as we are clear on the message, and know that resources (financial and other) will be available, it is time to identify the most appropriate methods to present it to the target audience.

In our interviews and work with various organisations, we have come across the following methods:

- newsletters
- intranet – an internal webpage where relevant information (for example articles, blogs or videos) is posted and updated with news
- email
- open days (where people can come and experience coaching or get the information they need)
- team meetings
- annual conference on coaching and mentoring
- community of practice meetings
- publications in newspapers or industry magazines[2]
- flyers and other printed materials
- informal networking
- division or department meetings
- social media (especially group forums).

Questions to explore here

- What communication methods have been successfully used with my target audience?
- What hasn't worked with the target audience in the past?
- How technologically savvy is my target audience?
- Which spots does the target audience frequently visit (online or offline)?
- What/who is the best source of information regarding target audience preferred methods of communication?
- What method will have the biggest possible reach?
- What method is likely to have the biggest possible impact?

IMPLEMENTATION PLAN

At the minimum, coaching or mentoring marketing implementation will include:

- marketing actions
- timelines
- people responsible.

Our experience shows that it helps to schedule regular communication to build the momentum and keep coaching initiatives on people's radar.

Questions to explore here

- What is the right timing and frequency of our marketing activities?
- Who are the best people to take responsibility for each activity?
- How will we follow up on the implementation?

EVALUATION

A good marketing plan looks at how all marketing efforts will be evaluated. It outlines how to measure the value and effectiveness of the marketing campaign. In planning how to evaluate coaching marketing initiatives, it can be useful to consider measuring success or failure against the predetermined set of objectives.

A useful approach is the three Os (Lindenmann 1997), focusing on:

---

[2] Industry magazines and newspapers have a wider reach than internal communication methods. External publications can benefit employee branding, attract more desirable job candidates and help enhance reputation both with internal and external stakeholders.

- *Outputs* – measuring specific actions taken to promote coaching or mentoring, for example, the number of updates in the coaching and mentoring online library, the number of events that have been organised to promote coaching or mentoring, or the number of management meetings that had coaching or mentoring on the agenda.
- *Outtakes* – looking at how well the messages were received and retained by the target audience. Examples of outtakes measurement are the percentage of people who clicked on the provided link, visited the online coaching library or the percentage of managers who can clearly articulate what line manager coaching is.
- *Outcomes* – exploring whether the marketing activities have resulted in any behaviour, attitude or belief change in the target audience, for example, the percentage of managers who incorporated coaching into their leadership styles portfolio or the number of people who have been convinced that coaching techniques can be included in their sales process. Some of the most popular ways of measuring outcomes that we have come across are 360-degree surveys, focus groups and interviews.

Questions to explore here

- What actions, activities or events can we measure to follow up on our marketing plan progress?
- How will we know that people have received and understood the message? What are the measurements that can capture that?
- How will we know that people have changed their attitudes, mindsets, beliefs or behaviours? What methods will we use to measure that?

STORIES FROM THE FIELD

HOW ORGANISATIONS SUPPORT THE IMPLEMENTATION OF COACHING AND MENTORING CULTURE STRATEGY THROUGH MARKETING AND COMMUNICATION INITIATIVES

Looking at the interview material we gathered for this book, we realised that while the content of marketing messages may vary, a few common themes emerge. We present these themes below to illustrate good marketing practices we came across.

Educating the organisation about coaching

When we asked an executive coach how she would know that the organisation she was working with was making progress towards a coaching culture, she said without hesitation: 'The first clear sign will be when my coaching clients stop asking me for advice so much. Instead, they will say: "Here are the challenges I'm facing – and I need your help to work through them."

Educating people about what coaching is and how it works prepares the ground for coaching culture to take root. What seems to open people to coaching is positioning it as a developmental intervention; it tends to have a much better resonance than the old model of remedial coaching which stigmatised people as low-performers or troublemakers.

Demonstrating the benefits of coaching – both on the individual and organisational level

Most of the organisations that had success in promoting coaching didn't just limit themselves to stating what the potential benefits of coaching and mentoring could be. Instead, they continuously searched for existing success stories or for people who would be willing to share their experiences and demonstrate what the actual benefits have been so far. Examples include video-taped testimonials, publishing results of teams who benefited from team coaching, success stories passed on informally by coaching champions or presented during annual meetings of coaching and mentoring network, demonstrating the impact of managerial the coaching on the engagement index in the teams where managers used a coaching style or illustrating the correlation of engagement index and high performance with strong coaching culture.

Identifying and using the most user-friendly channels of communication

No matter how obvious the need for communication channels to be user-friendly is, it turns out it is not common practice. We know of communication emails with links that did not work or coaching sites that required a complicated registration process, discouraging people from signing up. Companies that have success in marketing coaching always make sure to utilise user-friendly media to convey their messages. While many organisations rely on electronic media to support their coaching culture strategy implementation, our observations indicate that often there is nothing more powerful than face-to-face interaction. This is closely linked to the point presented below.

Lowering the threshold for change

While in most organisations various communications about coaching reach large numbers of people, only a small fraction embraces coaching immediately. This is not unusual, as research indicates that early adopters of change amount to not more than 15 per cent (Rogers 1995). Change can be hard and the majority of people will initially experience fear, lack of self-confidence or resistance.

Many organisations working on developing a coaching culture notice that they have a few islands of good practice, where coaching principles guide the way people work and interact with each other on an everyday basis. While the appearance of these islands of good practice can be encouraging at the beginning, it quickly leads to frustration when the desired beliefs, attitudes, mindsets and behaviours do not seem to spread to the remaining parts of the organisation.

So what do successful organisations do differently from others in order to help a coaching culture spread and reach larger parts of the organisation?

First of all, they work on the assumption that most people usually follow the lead of those they know and trust when deciding whether to change or adopt a new behaviour. They focus on identifying, engaging and encouraging the best coaching champions and, by doing so, they lower the change threshold for the vast majority.

We already talked about the importance of champions in the previous chapter, and it is hard to overestimate their role in marketing coaching culture. Truly effective coaching champions are typically early adopters in the process of developing a coaching culture. They embrace the coaching philosophy first and become the role models for others. Typically, they are natural-born networkers, well respected in the organisation and often highly charismatic and influential. Successful coaching marketers identify these people early on in the process and bring them on board by giving them an opportunity to learn about, use and benefit from coaching. In many respects, the endorsement of a respected, vocal and passionate champion is to a coaching culture what a celebrity endorsement is for commercial products – it inspires instant credibility and trust, but also provides a positive role model that people aspire to emulate.

SUMMARY

Marketing plays a significant role in developing a coaching culture within an organisation: it provides crucial information, achieves the desired exposure and allows people to understand what coaching is, what its benefits can be and how to start using it or adopt coaching philosophy in their everyday work.

Two main prerequisites for an effective marketing plan are understanding business and individual needs for coaching and making appropriate coaching and mentoring modalities available. An effective coaching or mentoring marketing plan will involve the following activities:

- baselining and context assessment
- setting the objectives
- identifying the target audience and key messages to be communicated
- deciding on the right communication methods
- establishing the available budget
- creating an implementation plan
- deciding on how to evaluate progress.

Organisations that are successful in marketing coaching or mentoring tend to focus on educating the organisation about coaching, demonstrating its benefits, identifying and using the most user-friendly channels of communication and lowering the threshold for change.

FIELDWORK

Think about your organisation or one that you are familiar with and answer the following questions:

- What communication and marketing support is in place to develop coaching culture?
- What seems to work well? What requires improvement?
- Who are the key target groups at this stage of coaching culture development?
- How can the messages be better tailored to these particular groups?
- What would be the most appropriate channels of communication?
- How can the organisation demonstrate the value and benefits of coaching?
- How can the organisation lower the threshold for change through engaging effective champions of coaching?

CHAPTER 13

Cross-Cultural Issues

'Every view of the world that becomes extinct, every culture that disappears, diminishes a possibility of life.'
Octavio Paz

OVERVIEW

This chapter talks about the new multicultural landscape that has been emerging with heightened intensity in the past couple of decades, putting new demands on coaching and mentoring. It tackles questions such as:

- Is coaching appropriate in all cultural contexts?
- What are the skills and characteristics of an effective cross-cultural coach or mentor?
- How can organisations develop cross-cultural competencies amongst their coaches and mentors?
- Does coaching culture help organisations leverage cultural difference?
- Is there a universal formula to use across cultures to develop a coaching culture?

The global balance of power is shifting. In 2014 China surpassed the US as the world's largest economy (measured by purchasing power), with India forecasted to follow suit. The unprecedented growth of the BRIC countries,[1] combined with the growth forecasts of the Next Eleven[2] and ASEAN Five[3] are all clear indications that the era of Western economic dominance is rapidly coming to its end.

Additionally, the old barriers, borders and demarcation lines are giving way to continuously growing globalisation, migration, international mergers, acquisitions, integration, cross-border relocation and virtual businesses. Supported by social media, increased mobility, telecommuting and ease of travel, these trends expose us to a multitude of cultures and diverse worldviews every single day.

In this new context, organisations and individuals face the challenge of navigating an increasingly complex territory, where bridging the differences between cultures and leveraging diversity becomes the new business imperative. In fact, business is increasingly seen as one of the change agents in promoting intercultural understanding. As Cly Wallace Aramian (2009) said: 'Because of its bottom-line imperative to bring people together to achieve a common goal, business can act as an important "connector" across divides, providing a forum for overcoming stereotypes, "demystifying" the other through

---

[1] The BRIC countries comprise Brazil, Russia, India and China, which are considered as the fastest growing economies and forecasted to be the largest world economies.

[2] The Next Eleven are Bangladesh, Egypt, Indonesia, Iran, Mexico, Nigeria, Pakistan, Philippines, South Korea, Turkey and Vietnam.

[3] The ASEAN Five are Indonesia, Malaysia, Philippines, Singapore and Thailand.

dialogue, building trust and creating a sense of common purpose. Because of the growing need to manage diversity in a globally interconnected world, business is in some cases leading the way in learning to value difference and to create inclusive mindsets that reflect the perspectives of its diverse employees, customers and other stakeholders in society.'

If businesses are indeed to play such a role, they will need to develop a brand new skill set. According to Hay Group's Leadership 2030 research (Hay Group 2014), leaders of tomorrow will have to be 'multilingual, flexible, internationally mobile, adaptable and culturally sensitive'.

Predictors of workplace success such as IQ and EQ are now joined by the CQ, which measures cultural intelligence, defined as the 'capability to function effectively across national, ethnic, and organisational cultures' (Ang and Van Dyne 2008). Building international management experience is seen as a must for global organisations' talent – in fact, it has appeared for the first time as one of the top two reasons for sending employees on international assignments in the Global Mobility Trends Survey[4] (Brookfield Global Relocation Services 2015).

All of the above changes place new requirements on coaching. It is not surprising that the Association for Coaching listed cross-cultural coaching as one of the hottest trends (Carter 2008; Plaister Ten 2009), especially when it is considered to be any type of coaching that takes place in a 'cross-', 'multi-' or 'inter-' cultural context, such as mergers and acquisitions, international projects, joint ventures, expatriate assignments, multicultural teams, coaching relationships involving people from different cultural backgrounds and so on (Abbott 2010).

Based on our observations, cross-cultural coaching continues to increase in frequency, and it looks like coaches will be required to work across cultures more often than ever before (Rojon and McDowall 2010). However, a number of questions arise:

- Will coaching, which is largely dominated by Western perceptions, turn out to be a suitable tool in the multicultural world we live in?
- What are the skills and characteristics of effective cross-cultural coaches?
- How can an organisation help its coaches (and people in the organisation in general) to develop cross-cultural skills?
- Can cultivating a coaching culture help an organisation to keep up with the times and thrive because of (and not in spite of) the unprecedented, all-encompassing cultural diversity of the modern world?
- Finally, can the same approach to building a coaching culture be used irrespective of cultural background?

These are the questions we want to examine in this chapter.

COACHING – A WESTERN APPROACH OR A UNIVERSAL TRANSCULTURAL TOOL?

While the exact origins of coaching might still be a subject of academic dispute, scholars and practitioners alike agree that coaching as a business discipline was developed in the Western world.

Many writers (Brunner 1998; Krohn 1998; Hughes 2003; de Hahn 2008) maintain that coaching originates from Ancient Greece, considering Socratic dialogue to be one of the earliest forms of coaching. This, however, is disputed by other observers, who maintain that the reductio ad absurdum of Socratic dialogue is not compatible with a coaching style; and that the style of non-directive questioning associated with modern coaching originates from mentoring and, in particular, the writings of the French cleric Fenelon (Garvey et al 2008).

---

[4] See more at: http://globalmobilitytrends.brookfieldgrs.com/#/keytrends

The first direct mentions of coaching were noted in the academic context (coach as a tutor) and the world of sports. They date back to 19th-century England (Garvey et al 2008). In its modern form, coaching can be traced back to the US (Rosinski 2010).

It is not just the origins of coaching that contribute to its Western character: a vast majority of coaching tools and models are derived from Western thought. This leads to understandable concerns that coaching might not always be appropriate or effective in diverse cultural contexts (Handin and Steinwedel 2006; Verhulst and Sprengel 2009).

Unfortunately, research is still not sufficient to reach clear conclusions as to the efficacy of coaching in non-Western cultural contexts.

However, literature review reassures us that coaching in the world of cultural diversity can offer unprecedented opportunities. One of the pioneers of cross-cultural coaching,[5] Philippe Rosinski, argues that cultural diversity can generate significant benefits for the coach, the recipient of coaching and their wider system. Rosinski talks about 'leveraging cultural differences', where 'the riches appear in the form of useful insights, alternative perspectives on issues, and can be collected from human wisdom accumulated through space and time' (Rosinski 2003).

Other authors share that optimism, simultaneously warning coaching practitioners against being too rigid in applying Western coaching tenets and highlighting the importance of making coaching culturally congruent.

For example, in their study on the impact of social hierarchy on coaching relationships, Lina and Ajay Nangalia (2010) found that some of the universally accepted tenets of coaching simply do not hold true in Asia. The coaching principles in question were:

- Coaching is a partnership among equals.
- The coach should restrain from advising the client what to do.
- The coaching process relies on the use of powerful questions.
- The client already has all the answers within them.

The Nangalia study found that a coach in Asia is far from being seen as an equal. Rather, he or she is treated as a respected elder or a teacher whose advice and guidance are highly sought after – a model that in the West is more reminiscent of North American sponsorship-based mentoring than of coaching.

Similarly, in the book *Diversity in Coaching*, Passmore (2009) suggests that an approach to 'culturally appropriate coaching' has to be based on the social, historical, economic, political and racial context.

In the light of the above, the answer to our initial question 'is coaching an exclusively Western approach or can it be a universal, transcultural tool?' can only be: 'It depends on how it is applied.' Coaching across cultures or the larger task of developing a coaching culture in a multicultural environment involves a major paradox: it requires a higher level of coaching proficiency and greater flexibility in implementing it. As Pablo Picasso once said: 'Learn the rules like a pro, so you can break them like an artist.'

SKILLS AND CHARACTERISTICS OF AN EFFECTIVE CROSS-CULTURAL COACH

While interviewing coaches who work across cultures, we realised that not all of them were fully aware of the cultural differences that might come into play in their relationships with clients. Based on our observations, the most common pitfall that coaches fall into is trivialising or dismissing the cultural differences by holding a belief along the lines of: 'we are all human so we are all the same.'

---

[5] Plaister Ten (2009, p77) offered a useful definition for cross-cultural coaching: 'Cross-cultural coaching is working with awareness of cultural difference and facilitating culturally determined steps.'

Rosinski would classify that as an 'ethnocentric pitfall' stemming from an assumption that our own culture is central to the reality (2003). While the ethnocentric view is certainly a risk in the case of different national or ethic cultures, it is also possible to underestimate other cultural differences, such as those originating from a different organisational culture or different social background.

So what are the skills and characteristics of an effective cross-cultural coach?

After reviewing the existing literature and drawing conclusions from our own research and observations, we have been able to identify four key skills and characteristics of an effective cross-cultural coach:

- cultural awareness
- proficiency in using a multifocal perspective
- ability to work with paradox
- knowledge and skill in dealing with cross-cultural issues.

The above points are equally relevant for external and internal coaches, as well as leaders who use coaching skills as part of their leadership portfolio.

CULTURAL AWARENESS

All researchers and writers on the subject agree that the elementary prerequisite for effective cross-cultural coaching is the coach's ability to understand their own culture and how it might facilitate or interfere with their ability to support their client in achieving what they want (Handin and Steinwedel 2006; Peterson 2007; Rosinski 2010). Carr and Seto (2013) go a step further and suggest that apart from their ethnic, national or organisational culture, a coach often brings the inherent bias of the coaching profession into their relationship with the client. And, as we have already mentioned, while the non-directive approach or future- and action-focus are widely accepted tenets of coaching, they might not work for certain clients, in certain cultures.

It is worth noting here that cultural self-awareness is not enough. A good cross-cultural coach understands and educates themselves about the culture of their coaching client as well. They strive to comprehend how their client's culture may influence the way they perceive reality, their effectiveness and the level of congruency with the system in which they operate.

Cultural awareness can be developed and improved by the coach's personal experience with cultural adaptation (Abbott et al 2006). In fact, we believe that personal experience of adapting to other cultures can hardly be substituted by reading about cross-cultural theories and models (although they are important – more on this later). Working on a multicultural team, immersing ourselves in a different culture during our holidays, cultivating friendships with people from different cultural backgrounds, being part of a merger or even changing an organisation can all be hugely enriching experiences that help develop cultural awareness.

PROFICIENCY IN USING A MULTIFOCAL PERSPECTIVE

This is one of the many paradoxes of coaching in a cross-cultural environment.

On the one hand, a good cross-cultural coach needs to be well tuned in to how cultural issues might play into their client's perspectives or contribute to their challenges. This is a complex task in itself and requires looking through such a multiplicity of lenses that it conjures an image of a kaleidoscope (Plaister Ten 2013).

On the other hand, while being culturally sensitive, cross-cultural coaches do not allow the focus on culture to turn into an idée fixe, which would obscure other aspects of the coachee's situation or hinder the holistic view of the client as a person (Abbott 2010; Peterson 2007; Plaister Ten 2013).

In that sense, being an effective multicultural coach requires an ability to discern which perspective or tool is most appropriate in the particular context. The cultural focus should not be more than just an additional lens through which to view the client and their situation. A prerequisite here is a high level of coaching mastery. That is because in order to pick the right tool (or perspective), the coach needs to have it in their toolbox in the first place!

ABILITY TO WORK WITH PARADOX

One of the key skills to leveraging cultural differences is the ability to hold and manage paradox. At its fundamental level, this skill is linked to how the coach shows up in the coaching relationship. It involves their ability to manage the paradox they face – of letting go of themselves, their own preferences and culture and yet maintaining their personal and cultural identity at the same time. This ability is critical not just from the point of view of coaching technique but also because of its role-modelling value. A client who is struggling with cultural dilemmas or polarities will find it easier to manage paradox if they have observed their coach doing so throughout the coaching engagement.

The next level of this skill is linked to the coach's interaction with their client, and more specifically to how well they are able to facilitate synergistic approach towards cultural challenges (Abbott 2010). It is the ability to allow the client to make a shift from an ethnocentric to an ethnorelative approach, as well as from 'either/or' thinking to 'both/and' thinking. In other words, it is the ability to support the client in the exploration of many paradoxes that are inherent in differing cultural perspectives, such as individualism versus collectivism, being versus doing or hierarchy versus equality. We will talk more about these seeming opposites, called cultural orientations, later in this chapter.

KNOWLEDGE AND SKILL IN DEALING WITH CROSS-CULTURAL ISSUES

An aspiring cross-cultural coach has access to knowledge that they can easily integrate into their coaching practice. The work of Hofstede, Kluckhohn, Schwartz, Trompenaars, Hampden-Turner, Rosinski, Berry, Harrison and Harrison, and Plaister Ten (to name but a few) provides a wealth of knowledge on the subject. However, as Rosinski pointed out: 'We still have a long way to go before culture is systematically integrated into coaching' (Rosinski 2010, p123), and, therefore, keeping up to date with the current developments in the field is one of the key requirements for a cross-cultural coach.

DEVELOPING MULTICULTURAL SKILLS

It is worth noting that when we refer to coaches and mentors within an organisation, we include both external and internal coaches and mentors. In organisations that have reached relatively advanced stages of coaching culture development, that population will be quite large and comprise professional and semi-professional coaches as well as managers and, on occasions, even team members, especially if peer coaching or coaching within work teams is common practice.

It is probably safe to assume that by supporting such a large population in developing cross-cultural skills, an organisation will significantly increase its capacity to effectively address cross-cultural issues in general.

SO WHAT CAN BE DONE TO DEVELOP CROSS-CULTURAL COACHING AND MENTORING SKILLS?

There is wide agreement amongst scholars and practitioners that cross-cultural skills are something that can be developed. Organisations can support their internal and external coaching pools in developing these skills through many different means, which we set out here.

Cultural awareness training

Training is definitely not enough to develop cross-cultural skills but it can provide a useful foundation. At a minimum, it should provide the participants with:

- in-depth cultural awareness and understanding of the impact of cultural differences
- a sound understanding of key challenges facing multicultural workplaces
- the basic tools to become culturally competent.

Peer coaching

Coaches or managers who have cross-cultural experience can be assigned to coach or mentor their peers on various issues linked to cultural diversity. This is a particularly good idea in organisations which have a lot of expat assignments and want to support their executives in the faster and more effective assimilation into their new environment.

Incorporating cross-cultural issues sessions into coaching supervision or coaching network meetings

We have already talked about the importance of supervision and coaching network meetings for the continuous professional development of coaches and mentors. A possible way of improving cross-cultural competency is to incorporate a session on cross-cultural issues into the coaching supervision or coaching network meetings. Apart from sharing challenges and experiences around facing cross-cultural issues, coaches could also benefit from short presentations and lectures from experts on the subject of cross-cultural coaching or cultural diversity.

Creating a cross-cultural resources platform

Some organisations create a web library or a list of suggested resources to develop cross-cultural awareness. Often this can be enough to bring cultural issues to the forefront of people's mind and encourage them to explore the subject. Even reading anthropological literature about specific cultures and one's own culture can be highly beneficial. For example, the book *Watching the English*, by Kate Fox (2008), raises awareness of how perspectives and behaviours that are considered normal by English natives can be confusing to people from other cultures.

Matching of coaches or mentors with their clients across cultures

What we have noticed while interviewing various organisations is that mentor–mentee or coach–coachee matching is often based on the similarity of cultural backgrounds, not the differences between them. However, in some situations, especially when cross-cultural issues are likely to arise as a subject of coaching or mentoring (such as expat assignments, working on multinational teams or assimilation after a merger or acquisition), it might be a good idea for the coach or mentor to bring a different cultural perspective into the relationship. If managed well, this approach has the potential of offering a richness of insights and learning for both of the parties involved.

An example of how this is already applied by some organisations is reverse mentoring. By becoming the learner, the more senior person opens themselves more thoroughly to the perspectives, experience and culture of the younger generation.

DOES DEVELOPING A COACHING CULTURE HELP LEVERAGE CULTURAL DIFFERENCES?

There has not been sufficient research to prove that the answer to this question is a resounding 'yes' and that organisations who have a strong coaching culture can benefit more than others from operating in a highly multicultural environment (internally and externally).

However, if we use our definition of coaching culture presented in this book – 'a coaching culture is one where the principles, beliefs and mindsets driving people's behaviour in the workplace are deeply rooted in the discipline of coaching' – and remind ourselves that reflection, openness, curiosity, respect and growth are among the core coaching principles, we cannot help but be hopeful that coaching culture should be able to help leverage cultural differences.

But first, let's look more closely at what we mean by 'leveraging cultural differences'. In Rosinski's words, it is about 'looking for gems in your own culture(s) and . . . treasures in other culture(s)' and synthesising them for a result that exceeds the sum of its parts (Rosinski 2003). In very simple terms, it means getting the best of both (or all) worlds.

But what exactly are these different cultural 'worlds'? Many scholars have attempted to answer this question (Hofstede 1980; Rosinski 2003; Trompenaars and Hampden-Turner 1997; House et al 2004). As a result, many cultural orientation frameworks have been created to help us describe and understand cultures. While it is not within the scope of this chapter to review these frameworks, it might be useful to understand their basic premises:

- There are certain dimensions of culture worth investigating in order to better understand key cultural differences.
- Each of these culture dimensions has a positive as well as a negative side.

For example, one of the cultural dimensions described by Rosinski (2003) is the 'notion of territory and boundaries with two seeming opposites: the protective and the sharing approach'.

In cultures characterised by the protective approach, people like to keep their personal lives private and seek to minimise intrusions to their physical space. Sharing personal information or physical space can make them feel uncomfortable, vulnerable or even threatened.

By contrast, in cultures characterised by the sharing approach, people enjoy sharing both psychological and physical domains and are uncomfortable and distrustful towards people who don't, mostly because, without sharing, it is difficult for them to understand who others really are.

Developing a coaching culture and cultivating coaching principles such as reflection, openness and honesty, curiosity, respect and growth should help leverage cultural differences.

Using the above example of the protective and sharing approaches, we could expect that in an organisation with a strong coaching culture, we would be more likely to:

- *Reflect* on our experiences and behaviours and ask ourselves how our cultural preference might be influencing our interactions with others. For example, if we exhibit more of a sharing orientation, reflection might help us realise why a colleague was so withdrawn and quiet when we were sharing the excruciating details of our recent root-canal treatment. Or, if we are of the protecting orientation, it might become clearer why our colleague has the irritating habit of storming into our office without knocking and gets offended when we don't encourage them to hang around for too long.
- Be *open* to different perspectives and points of view and recognise and perhaps even internalise the 'gems' of the opposing cultural orientation. For example, even if we are of the sharing orientation, we might acknowledge that protecting our physical territory can be very useful to do work that requires mental focus. We might even adopt this practice from time to time and experience its benefits first hand. And if our cultural orientation is protecting, we might be open to sharing our views or personal information when we want others to get to know us better and strengthen our

relationship. Eventually, we might decide to experiment frequently with appropriate sharing and experience further benefits. We would also be open and honest about communicating our cultural preference, something that would encourage understanding and perhaps even cross-pollination between the different orientations.

- Be *curious* and engage in a dialogue to co-create meaning and synthesise the differing approaches, instead of relying on our culturally biased assumptions. If we have protective orientation, people storming into our office without knocking will seem to be lacking manners or even respect for our privacy. Allowing ourselves to be genuinely curious about why people behave a certain way allows us to discover a more accurate meaning of that behaviour (which could be, in this case, that our colleague simply had really important news to share and was too excited to knock – plus that they don't value privacy as much as we do).
- *Respect* others, irrespective of differences of opinion or culture. This leads to an understanding that there is no right or wrong in how we approach the issues of psychological and physical privacy. It would be easier for us to respect others' choices for more or less sharing and avoid judgement.
- Be driven by the need to *grow* and learn from each other (instead of being driven by the need to be right). When growth and learning are one of our key driving principles, being right becomes far less important than enriching our internal landscape. This would make us more open to seeing cultural differences as a factor that has a potential to enrich dialogue, produce more insights and lead to better, more sustainable results. We would be more prone to ask ourselves questions such as: 'What can I learn from the fact that this person's oversharing makes me want to hide somewhere where they will never be able to find me?'

It seems, therefore, that in an organisation with a strong coaching culture people would be more likely to think and act in a way that leads to leveraging cultural differences.

This is further supported and facilitated through ongoing coaching or mentoring conversations. For example, one of the coaches we interviewed said: 'A client of mine has operations in Germany, Myanmar and Cyprus, with a number of global functions where people need to collaborate across cultures. Many challenges that we discussed with my coaching clients were directly linked to the differences in people's cultural orientation, for example, individualistic versus collective or directive versus participative preference. Putting these issues in the cultural context, helping clients develop cultural awareness and supporting them in exploring how to leverage these differences led to more open dialogue and specific changes in how the individuals communicated and took decisions.'

DOES ONE SIZE FIT ALL?

Based on our conversations with a number of international organisations and their experiences in implementing coaching culture strategy in various geographical territories or even just across various business units, it is clear that the cookie-cutter approach does not work.

Based on the analysis of interviews and case studies, it seems that the organisations which have success in implementing their coaching cultures across cultures tend to adopt what we referred to in Chapter 2 as a 'coaching culture on the edge of chaos' approach. They found the right balance between providing enough structure and support for coaching or mentoring to maintain its key qualities and enough freedom for various territories or business units to customise strategies to their needs. For example, a global manufacturing organisation provided its various geographical territories with a framework for developing coaching culture but left it to the territories how to populate that framework with culturally congruent details. The differentiations were present even at a very basic level, for example the definitions of coaching and mentoring differed slightly to resonate with the culture context of the territory.

EY – USING COACHING TO LEVERAGE CULTURAL DIFFERENCES AND EASE CULTURAL ADJUSTMENT

As an organisation that operates globally, as well as one with increased acquisition activity, EY recognises the importance of supporting its people in dealing with cross-cultural issues. Below are two examples of how EY uses coaching to leverage cultural differences and support people's transitions from one culture to another.

Mobility coaching in EY Americas

Recognising that there are significant organisational, individual and family aspects to working abroad, EY Americas launched a mobility coaching model and programme in 2014 to support its expatriates/repatriates as they transition to/from their assignments abroad.

At the end of 2015, 50 people at the executive and senior manager level on overseas assignments were supported by internal coaches. With the help of their coach, programme participants learn how to navigate the process of adjusting to a new environment.

The EY Americas coaches not only work with expatriates before and during their assignment but also help them prepare for their return at least six months before their repatriation date, as repatriates often experience reverse culture shock. The focus is on helping people develop and articulate their value proposition so as to ensure the right fit for their return whereby they can truly utilise their skills and experience from the overseas assignment. This results in less frustration and increased job satisfaction upon repatriation. The coaches also continue to work with programme participants for up to a year so as to ensure that they are re-integrated into the culture not only at work but at home as well.

The programme focuses on the top three areas that expatriates/repatriates find most challenging:

- creating a professional support network
- defining objectives and linking them to a strategy
- clarifying personal brand and value from the overseas assignment.

However, the success of the transition is also dependent on the cultural competence of not only the coachee but also that of the coach. This means that they too must have a global mindset, self-awareness, and an understanding of cultural values, in order to examine a particular situation and take action (via their coaching) in culturally appropriate ways.

Merger coaching in EY Americas

Increased acquisition activity in EY is driving a greater number of experienced hires from different organisational culture backgrounds entering the firm at a rapid pace. While most partners, principals, executive directors and directors (PPEDDs) in this population receive individual coaching via the executive onboarding coaching programme for individuals, focused attention was not being paid to the unique cultural transition which faces acquired PPEDDs as a group (ie change of identity, new processes, etc.).

These executives as well as their staff have a limited network and tend to turn to their existing, established network to make sense of their new environment. In addition, while their firms are being acquired, so as to provide key new services to EY and their clients, existing teams within EY are hesitant to fully engage their services because they are an unknown or unproven commodity (fearing potential risk to existing client relationships, and infringement on their roles or 'turf').

Coaching plays a very important role in supporting the acquisition's unique onboarding needs and challenges by focusing on not only individual support (accelerating their unique transition journey into EY) but also by supporting the group's shared need to:

- acculturate into EY, helping them to begin to let go of their old world (independent company) and start to 'find fit' and succeed in the new one (EY)
- grow their network/brand internally by leveraging the power of the group to develop key relationships and become a known/trusted provider of value at EY.

Working with both the acquired and receiving executives, the coach facilitates a dialogue between them that:

- helps everyone to 'find fit' and contribute sooner/faster with fewer obstacles
- ensures greater harmony within the new organisation as they explore new ways to work together
- creates more mutual understanding and honouring of culture and values
- counteracts any 'winners/losers' mentality and builds a greater sense of 'we'.

SUMMARY

The current context of rapid globalisation puts entirely new demands on businesses, individuals and their coaches or mentors. These new demands call not only for a new skill-set (which includes cultural awareness, proficiency in using a multifocal perspective, ability to work with paradox and knowledge and skill in dealing with cross-cultural issues) but also challenge the widely accepted tenets of coaching. While it's important to differentiate the approach to developing a coaching culture, depending on the host culture, it seems that coaching culture can help most of the organisation to leverage the cultural diversity it experiences.

?

FIELDWORK

Reflect on your organisation (or one that you are familiar with) and answer the following questions:

- What are the cross-cultural issues that the organisation is experiencing at the moment?
- How are these issues being addressed?
- What about the cultural challenges that might appear in the future?
- How can developing a coaching culture support the organisation in addressing these issues and leveraging cultural differences?
- Is there a need to customise the approach to developing a coaching culture to achieve cultural congruence?
- If yes, how would you go about it?

Epilogue

HOW WILL ORGANISATIONS CONTINUE BUILDING COACHING CULTURES IN THE FUTURE?

We have observed a trend in coaching and mentoring in the past few years, which we refer to as 'second wave'.[1] This trend is characterised by an increasing focus on the ability to demonstrate return on investment from coaching and mentoring interventions and maximising the value both bring to the organisation and its key stakeholders.

This pragmatic focus on adding value to internal and external stakeholders is already affecting the way organisations go about building and sustaining coaching cultures.

When prompted about future trends in building coaching cultures, the following were mentioned by many of our interviewees.

INTEGRATING COACHING INTO HOW EVERYDAY BUSINESS IS DONE

More and more organisations recognise that as long as coaching is perceived as a 'nice-to-have' or an additional task to be performed, it is doomed to be met with resistance. To prevent that, the trend is to focus on weaving coaching techniques and principles into the way everyday business is done, with the purpose of improving the quality of conversations and hence leading to improved results. Labelling these techniques and approaches as 'coaching' is not a priority. There is a growing tendency to avoid the word 'coaching' in this context because of associations with formal coaching, or with something that didn't work in the past.

PUTTING THE WORK TEAM AT THE HEART OF THE COACHING CULTURE

It is becoming increasingly clear that in order for coaching culture to flourish, developmental conversations, such as coaching and mentoring, need to be happening within work teams. There is a perceived need for these developmental conversations in teams to be multi-directional and for people be able to step swiftly in and out of the role of a 'learner' and a 'coach', sometimes even during a single conversation.

INTEGRATING AND ALIGNING INTERNAL AND EXTERNAL COACHING POOLS

Many organisations have seen the value of integrating internal and external coaching pools and others plan to do this in the future. Using the same criteria, tools and forums for coaches to meet and exchange experiences leads to increased consistency and alignment.

UTILISING TECHNOLOGY

The widespread presence of technology and social media leads many organisations to experiment with using these tools to enhance coaching culture within their organisation. Others are expected to follow suit. Technology is seen as particularly useful in increasing the accessibility of coaching; even if an individual or a team are geographically dispersed, they can still benefit from various forms of coaching or mentoring over the phone with the use of other media.

---

[1] According to www.businessdictionary.com, second wave is 'a stage in the progression or adoption of a new technology when the emphasis shifts from experimentation to result-oriented, commercial application.'

SHAPING EXTERNAL ENVIRONMENT THROUGH COACHING

Some organisations already look at how they can shape or improve their external environment by leveraging their existing coaching capacity. They employ coaching with external stakeholders for mutual benefit. A good example is health coaching in the NHS (described in the 'Stories from the field'), where the organisation's goal is to empower patients to manage their health conditions, something that has the potential to increase the ability of the NHS to respond to increasing demands for health services.

STORIES FROM THE FIELD

HEALTH COACHING IN NHS UK

Contributed by Anthony Owens, Leadership & Organisational Development Consultant, Yorkshire and the Humber Leadership Academy

Background

The increasing prevalence of long-term conditions such as diabetes and musculoskeletal problems increases demands on health services in developed economies. To some extent the well-intended approaches to health care provision have contributed to this picture and created an unhealthy dependency on health services.

Health coaching aims to help patients to self-manage their condition in pursuit of their health goals. In the English National Health Service (NHS) this fundamentally changes a historically paternalistic culture (where health professionals controlled the provision of care) to one of shared decision-making (where patients have a high level of self-efficacy, often referred to as 'patient activation'). Research shows that patients with higher activation have better health outcomes and coaching has been shown to raise patient activation.

The promotion of health coaching offers a means to respond to the escalating demand for health services that will outstrip the capacity of the NHS. More importantly, the approach models a more ethical relationship between care providers and the populations they serve.

Approach

Health Education Yorkshire and the Humber supports the development of sustainable coaching capacity in health systems. Organisations in the region were asked to share what they knew about health coaching to help understand where the baseline was. It turned out that a number of areas had already been working with this approach. Examples included using health coaching by telephone, training members of the public to be health coaches, and training all staff to engage with patients using coaching approaches.

A regional conference was organised in the town of Barnsley, where health coaching was flourishing, and invited the wider region to raise awareness, connection and momentum.

Learning from this experience informed the decision to offer start-up funding and consultancy to areas with good levels of readiness for health coaching. Leeds is a major city in the process of developing integrated approaches to care spanning health and social care. A nationally recognised model, 'The House of Care' (The Kings Fund), had been used to shape initial investment to develop person-centred services.

Health coaching offered an opportunity to instil coaching values and approaches in a townwide workforce. The case for health coaching was quickly recognised by front-line staff and clinical leaders, which created a bottom–up demand for training.

A 'train the trainer' approach was commissioned and delivered by The Performance Coach. The training modelled the coaching approach and was highly experiential. This supported the development of a cohesive cohort, which consisted of credible, passionate individuals from a range of disciplines in health and social care, who later became champions for health coaching and trainers.

Figure E.1 The house of care

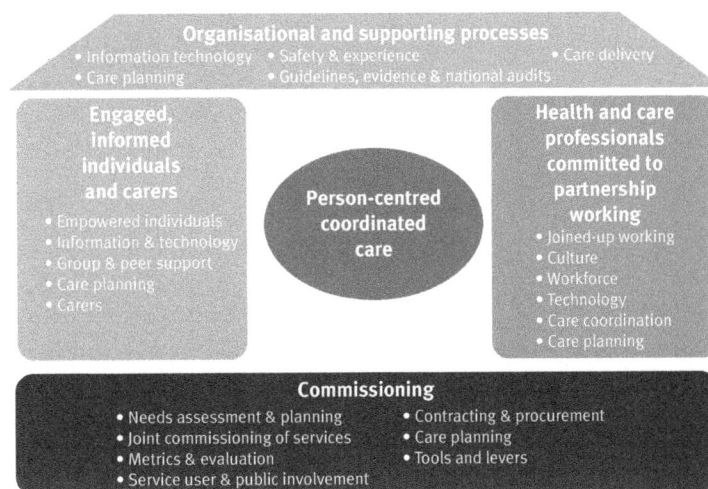

Additionally, an informal group made up of development leads from across the town was formed. The group was encouraged to develop shared purpose and values, appreciate diverse perspectives, form questions and create connections that engaged others. Group members engaged strategic leaders and gradually developed understanding and engagement in health coaching. The group have identified a number of priorities needed to establish health coaching. These include:

- resilience and support for trainers
- priorities for training in neighbourhood teams
- the development of supervision arrangements for practising health coaches
- a townwide workforce development plan that sees health coaching skills throughout the workforce
- gathering evidence and case studies to support learning and future investment.

Impact

Health professionals accessing health coach training are surprised to discover opportunities to be more patient-centred. The programme offers them high support in their resilience and development and reminds them of their reasons for joining the caring professions.

Patients are experiencing higher levels of empathy and engagement in the interactions with those who provide care. This can be a surprise to those who are used to being told what to do. The focus of goal-setting with patients is to shift from 'how we can control your health' to 'how we can help you manage your health and live the life you want'. Some patients report becoming more assertive as a result of health coaching, ensuring their voice is heard and their needs are considered.

At a system level, the evidence for health coaching is growing. A strategic group was formed to create systemic change. The group is set to take an ever more proactive stance in its relationship with formal strategic groups in the town.

Resources and Bibliography

ABBOTT, G.N. (2010) Cross cultural coaching: a paradoxical perspective. In: Cox, E., Bachkirova, T. and Clutterbuck, D. (eds), *The Complete Handbook of Coaching*. London: Sage.

ABBOTT, G.N., STENING, B.W., ATKINS, P.W.B. and GRANT, A.J. (2006) Coaching expatriate managers for success: adding value beyond training and mentoring. *Asia Pacific Journal of Human Resources, 44(3), pp295–317.*

AMERICAN MANAGEMENT ASSOCIATION (2008) *Coaching: a global study of successful practices.* Retrieved from www.amanet.org.

ANDERSON, V., RAYNER, C. and SCHYNS, B. (2009) *Coaching at the sharp end: the role of line managers in coaching at work.* London: CIPD.

ANG, S. and VAN DYNE, L. (2008) Conceptualization of cultural intelligence. In: Ang, S. and Van Dyne, L. (eds), *Handbook of Cultural Intelligence: Theory, measurement, and applications.* Armonk, NY: M.E. Sharpe.

ANG, S., VAN DYNE, L., KOH, C., NG, K.Y., TEMPLER, K.J., TAY, C. and CHANDRASEKAR, N.A. (2007) Cultural intelligence: its measurement and effects on cultural judgment and decision-making, cultural adaptation, and task performance. *Management and Organization Review,* 3(3), pp335–371.

ARAMIAN, C.W. (2009) *Doing business in a multicultural world: challenges and opportunities.* A Joint Report by the United Nations Alliance of Civilisations and the United Nations Global Compact Office. Retrieved from: www.unglobalcompact.org/docs/news_events/9.1_news_archives/2009_04_07/DBMW_Final_Web.pdf

ARMSTRONG, H. (2012) Coaching as dialogue: creating spaces for (mis)understandings. *International Journal of Evidence Based Coaching and Mentoring,* 10(1), pp33–47.

ASAY, T.P. and LAMBERT, M.J. (1999) The empirical case for the common factors in therapy: quantitative findings. In: Hubble, M.L., Duncan, B.L. and Miller, S.D. (eds) *The heart and soul of change: What works in therapy* (pp33–56). Washington, DC: APA Press.

AXELROD, D. (1992) Getting everyone involved: how one organization involved its employees, supervisors, and managers in redesigning the organization. In: Bunker, B.B. and Alban, B.T. (eds), Special Issue: Large Group Interventions. *The Journal of Applied Behavioral Sciences,* 28, pp499–509.

BADER, G. and LILJENSTRAND, A. (2003) *The value of building trust in the workplace.* The Bader Group. Retrieved from http://badergroup.com/the-value-of-building-trust-in-the-workplace/

BARNEY, J.B. (1986) Organizational culture: can it be a source of competitive advantage? *Academy of Management Review,* 11(3), pp656–665.

BERGLAS, S. (2002) The very real dangers of executive coaching. *Harvard Business Review,* 80(6), pp86–93.

BERKE, D., KOSSLER, M.E. and WAKEFIELD, M. (2008) *Developing leadership talent.* San Fransisco: Pfeiffer and Centre for Creative Leadership.

BLESSINGWHITE (2009) *The coaching conundrum report 2009: building a coaching culture that drives organizational success.* Retrieved from http://blessingwhite.com/research-report/2008/12/27/the-coaching-conundrum-report-2009/

BOYCE, L.A., JEFFREY JACKSON, R. and NEAL, L.J. (2010) Building successful coaching relationships: examining impact of matching criteria in a leadership coaching program. *Journal of Management Development*, 29(10), pp914–931.

BRESSER, F. (2010) *The global business guide for the successful use of coaching in organizations.* Cologne: Frank Bresser Publishing.

BRITTON, J.J. (2013) *From one to many: best practices for team and group coaching.* Hoboken, NJ: John Wiley & Sons.

BROOKFIELD GLOBAL RELOCATION SERVICES (2015) *Global mobility trends survey.* Retrieved from http://globalmobilitytrends.brookfieldgrs.com/#?q=5

BROWN, S.L. and EISENHARDT, K.M. (1998) *Competing on the edge: strategy as structured chaos.* Boston: Harvard Business School Press.

BRUNNER, R. (1998) Psychoanalysis and coaching. *Journal of Management Psychology*, 13(7), pp515–517.

BULJAC-SAMARDZIC, M. (2012) *Healthy teams: analyzing and improving team performance in long term care.* Erasmus Universeit, Rotterdam. Retrieved from http://repub.eur.nl/res/pub/31784/Proefschrift_Martina_Buljac%5B2% 5D.pdf

CAIN, S. (2012) *Quiet: the power of introverts in a world that can't stop talking.* New York: Crown Publishers.

CAMERER, C.F. (2003) *Behavioral game theory: experiments in strategic interaction.* Princeton: Princeton University Press.

CAMERON, K.S. and ETTINGTON, D.R. (1998) The Conceptual Foundations of Organizational Culture. In: Smart, J.C. (ed.), *Higher Education: Handbook of Theory and Research.* Springer: London.

CAMPBELL, J. (1972) *The hero with a thousand faces*, Princeton, NJ: Princeton University Press.

CARR, C. and SETO, L. (2013) An action research study on coaches' cultural awareness in the public sector. *International Journal of Evidence Based Coaching and Mentoring*, 11(2), August 2013. Retrieved from http://www.business.brookes.ac.uk/research/areas/coachingandmentoring/

CARROLL, L. (1965) *Alice's Adventures in Wonderland.* UK: Macmillan.

CARTER, D. (2008) Diversity in European coaching. *Training Journal*, May, pp6–7.

CARTER, A. (2010) Research update, at *Harnessing the Potential of Coaching*, IES Research Network Conference. London: Royal Institute of British Architects.

CATMULL, E.E. and WALLACE, A. (2014) *Creativity, Inc.: Overcoming the Unseen Forces that Stand in the Way of True Inspiration.* New York. RANDOM HOUSE

CAVANAGH, M. (2006) Coaching from a systemic perspective: a complex adaptive conversation. In: Stober, D.R. and Grant, A.M. (eds), *Evidence based coaching handbook: putting best practices to work for your clients*. New Jersey: John Wiley & Sons.

CHOI, Y.J. (2010) *East and west: understanding the rise of China*. S.l.: Iuniverse

CIPD. (2015) Learning and development 2015 [online]. London: Chartered Institute of Personnel and Development. Available at http://www.cipd.co.uk/hr-resources/survey-reports/learning-development-2015.aspx (Accessed 23 March 2016).

CIPD. (2008) *Coaching at the sharp end: the role of line managers in coaching at work* [online]. London: Chartered Institute of Personnel and Development. Available at: http://www.cipd.co.uk/hr-resources/practical-tools/developing-line-manager-coaching.aspx (Accessed 23 March 2016).

CLAXTON, J., HORSMAN, D. and ZHANG, C. (2015) *Team coaching – passion, purpose and sustainability*. Retrieved from http://www.ufhrd.co.uk/wordpress/wp-content/uploads/2015/10/UFHRD-2015-Passion-Purpose-Sustainability-3.docx

CLUTTERBUCK, D. (1985) *Everyone Needs a Mentor: Fostering Talent in Your Organisation*. London: Institute of Personnel and Development.

CLUTTERBUCK, D. (2007) *Coaching the Team at Work*. London: Nicholas Brealey International.

CLUTTERBUCK, D. (2011) *Why mentoring programmes and relationships fail*. Retrieved from http://www.gpstrategiesltd.com/downloads/Why-mentoring-programmes-and-relationships-fail-v2.0-June-2011[34].pdf

CLUTTERBUCK, D. (2013) *Making the most of developmental mentoring*, 1st ed. Liverpool: Wordscapes.

CLUTTERBUCK, D. (2013) *The competencies of an effective team coach*. Retrieved from https://www.davidclutterbuckpartnership.com/the-competencies-of-an-effective-team-coach/

CLUTTERBUCK, D. (2013) *The future of team coaching*. Retrieved from http://www.pbcoaching.com/future-team-coaching-david-clutterbuck/

CLUTTERBUCK, D. and MEGGINSON, D. (2005) *Making coaching work: creating a coaching culture*. London: CIPD Publishing.

CLUTTERBUCK, D. and MERRICK, L.(2014) *What every HR director should know about coaching and mentoring strategy*. Retrieved from https://www.davidclutterbuckpartnership.com/what-every-hr-director-should-know-about-coaching-and-mentoring-strategy/

COUTU, D. and KAUFFMAN, C. (2009) What can coaches do for you? *Harvard Business Review*, 87(1), pp91–97.

COX, E., BACHKIROVA, T. and CLUTTERBUCK, D. (2010) *The complete handbook of coaching*. London: Sage.

CREATIVITY, INC. (2014) *Overcoming the unseen forces that stand in the way of true inspiration*. S.l.: Random House.

DE BONO, E. (1985) *Six thinking hats*. Boston: Little, Brown.

DEAL, T.E. and KENNEDY, A.A. (1988, 2000) *Corporate cultures: The rites and rituals of corporate life*. Harmondsworth: Penguin Books, 1988; reissue Perseus Books, 2000.

DE HAAN, E. (2008) I doubt therefore I coach: critical moments in coaching practice. *Consulting Psychology Journal: Practice and Research*, 60(1), pp91–105.

DENISON, D.R. (1990) *Corporate culture and organizational effectiveness*. New York: John Wiley & Sons.

DI STEFANO, G., GINO, F., PISSANO, G.P. and STAATS, B.R. (2014) *Learning by thinking: how reflection aids performance*. Harvard: Harvard Business School.

DOWNEY, M. (2003) *Effective Coaching: Lessons from the Coach's Coach*. London: Thomson.

EVERED, R.D. and SELMAN, J.C. (1989) Coaching and the art of management. *Organizational Dynamics*, 18, pp16–32.

FEHR, E. and FISCHBACHER, U. (2004). Social norms and human cooperation. *Trends in Cognitive Sciences*, 8(4), pp185–190.

FELDMAN, D.C. and LANKAU, M.J. (2005) Executive coaching: a review and agenda for future research. *Journal of Management*, 31(6), pp829–848.

FERRAR, P. (2006) *The paradox of manager as coach: does being a manager inhibit effective coaching*. Unpublished master's dissertation, Oxford Brookes University.

FOX, K. (2008) *Watching the English: the hidden rules of English behaviour*. Boston: Nicholas Brealey Publishing.

FRANKE, R. and MILNER, J. (eds) (2013) *Interkulturelles coaching: coaching-tools für 17 kulturkreise*. Bonn: ManagerSeminare Verlag.

GARVEY, B., STOKES, P. and MEGGINSON, D. (2008) *Coaching and mentoring: theory and practice*. Los Angeles: Sage.

GARVIN, D.A., BERKLEY WAGONFELD, A. and KIND, L. (2013) Google's Project Oxygen: Do Managers Matter? Case study. *Harvard Business Review*, April. Retrieved from https://hbr.org/product/google-s-project-oxygen-do-managers-matter/313110-PDF-ENG

GAY, B. and STEPHENSON, J. (1998) The mentoring dilemma: guidance and/or direction? *Mentoring and Tutoring*, 6(1), pp43–54.

GLOBAL TRENDS 2030 (2012) *Alternative worlds: a publication of the National Intelligence Council*. Retrieved from https://globaltrends2030.files.wordpress.com/2012/11/global-trends-2030-november2012.pdf

GODIN, S. (2000) *Unleashing the idea virus*. New York Do You Zoom.

GOLDMAN SACHS (2008) *BRICs and beyond*. London: Goldman Sachs.

GOLDSMITH, W. and CLUTTERBUCK, D. (1997) *The Winning Streak Mark II*. London: Orion Business Books.

GOLEMAN, D. (2000) *Leadership that gets results*. Boston: Harvard Business Review.

GOLEMAN, D. (2006) *Social intelligence: the new science of human relationships.* New York: Bantam Books.

GOLEMAN, D., BOYATZIS, R. and MCKEE, A. (2002) *Primal leadership: learning to lead with emotional intelligence.* Boston, MA: Harvard Business School Press.

GOODMAN, M. (2002) *The iceberg model.* Hopkinton, MA: Innovation Associates Organizational Learning. Retrieved from http://citeseerx.ist.psu.edu

GURVEN, M. (2004) Reciprocal altruism and food sharing decisions among Hiwi and Ache hunter/gatherers. *Behavioral Ecology and Sociobiology,* 56(4), pp366–380.

HACKMAN, J.R. and WAGEMAN, R. (2005) A theory of team coaching. *Academy of Management Review,* 30, pp269-287.

HANDIN, K. and STEINWEDEL, J.S. (2006) Developing global leaders: executive coaching targets cross-cultural competencies. *Global Business and Organizational Excellence,* 26(1), pp18–28.

HARDING, C. (2013) The transitional space provided by coaching and mentoring. *International Journal of Evidence Based Coaching and Mentoring,* (7), pp56–72.

HARDINGHAM, A. (2004) *The coach's coach.* London: Chartered Institute of Personnel and Development.

HART, E.W. (2003) *Developing a coaching culture.* Centre for Creative Leadership. Retrieved from http://citeseerx.ist.psu.edu/viewdoc/download?doi=10.1.1.197.234&rep=rep1&type=pdf

HAWKINS, P. (2006) Coaching Supervision. In: Passmore, I.J. (ed.), *Excellence in Coaching.* London: Kogan Page.

HAWKINS, P. (2008) The coaching profession; some of the key challenges. *Coaching: An International Journal of Theory, Research and Practice,* 1(1), pp28–38.

HAWKINS, P. (2011) *Leadership team coaching.* London: Kogan Page.

HAWKINS, P. (2012) *Creating a coaching culture: developing a coaching strategy for your organization.* Maidenhead, Berkshire: McGraw-Hill Education.

HAWKINS, P. and SMITH, N. (2006) *Coaching, mentoring and organizational consultancy: supervision and development.* Maidenhead, Berkshire: Open University Press.

HAWKINS, P. and SMITH, N. (2007) *Coaching, mentoring and organizational consultancy: supervision and development.* Maidenhead: McGraw-Hill International.

HAY GROUP'S LEADERSHIP 2030 RESEARCH (2014) Retrieved from http://www.haygroup.com/downloads/MicroSites/L2030/Hay_Group_Leadership_2030%20whitepaper_2014.pdf

HERSEY, P. and BLANCHARD, K.H. (1969) Life cycle theory of leadership. *Training & Development Journal,* 23(5), pp26–34.

HOFSTEDE, G. (1980) *Culture's consequences.* Beverly Hills: Sage.

HOLLENBECK, G.P. (2002) Coaching executives: individual leadership development. In: Silzer, R. (ed.), *The 21st century executive: innovative practices for building leadership at the top,* pp77–113. San Francisco: Jossey-Bass.

HOMAN BLANCHARD, M. and MILLER, L.J. (2008) *Coaching in organizations: best coaching practices from the Ken Blanchard Companies*. Hoboken, NJ: John Wiley & Sons.

HOUSE, R.J. et al (2004) *Culture, Leadership, and Organizations: The GLOBE Study of 62 Societies. Thousand Oaks, CA: Sage Publications*.

HUGHES, J. (2003) *A Reflection on the Art and Practice of Mentorship*. Institutional Investor plc.

HUNT, J.M. and WEINTRAUB, J.R. (2007) *The coaching organization: a strategy for developing leaders*. Thousand Oaks: Sage.

HUNT, J.M. and WEINTRAUB, J.R. (2011) *The coaching manager – developing top talent in business*. Thousand Oaks, CA: Sage Publications.

ICF (2014) *Building a coaching culture report.*

INTERACTION ASSOCIATES (2009) *Building trust in business*. Cambridge, MA: Interaction Associates.

JACOBS, R.W. (1994) *Real time strategic change*. San Francisco: Berrett-Koehler Publishers.

JEHN, K.A. (1998) Managing workteam diversity, conflict and productivity: a new form of organizing in the twenty-first century workplace. *University of Pennsylvania Journal of Labor and Employment Law*, 2, p473.

JOHNSON, B. (1998) *Polarity management: a summary introduction*. Polarity Management Associates.

JONES, G. and GORELL, R. (2014) *How to create a coaching culture*. London: Kogan Page.

KAHANE, A.M. (2012) *Transformative scenario planning: working together to change the future*. San Francisco: Berrett-Koehler Publishers.

KAMPA-KOKESCH, S. and ANDERSON, M.Z. (2001) Executive coaching: a comprehensive review of the literature. *Consulting Psychology Journal: Practice and Research*, 53(4), pp205–228.

KANTER, R.M., STEIN, B. and JICK, T. (1992) *The challenge of organizational change: how companies experience it and leaders guide it*. New York: Free Press.

KATZENBACH, J.R. and SMITH, D.K. (1999) *The wisdom of teams: creating the high performance organisation*. London: Harper Business.

KEDDY, J. and JOHNSON, C. (2011) *Managing coaching at work: understanding, delivering and assessing coaching in organizations*. London: Kogan Page.

KOTTER, J.P. (1995) *Leading change: Why transformation efforts fail*. Boston: Harvard Business School Publishing.

KOTTER, J.P. and COHEN, D.S. (2002) *The heart of change: real-life stories of how people change their organizations*. Boston, MA: Harvard Business School.

KOTTER, J.P. and HESKETT, J. (1992) *Corporate culture and performance*. New York: Free Press.

KOZLOWSKI, S.W.J. and BELL, B.S. (2003) Work groups and teams in organizations. In: Borman, W.C., Ilgen, D.R. and Klimoski, R.J. (eds), *Handbook of psychology (Vol. 12): industrial and organizational psychology* (pp333–375). New York: Wiley-Blackwell.

KRAM, K.E. and CHANDLER, D.E. (2005) Applying an adult development perspective to developmental networks. *Career Development International*, 10(6/7), pp548–566.

KROHN, D. (1998) Four indispensable features of socratic dialogue. In: Saran, R. and Neisser, B. (eds), *Enquiring Minds: Socratic Dialogue in Education*. Stoke on Trent: Trentham Books.

LEAN ENTERPRISE ACADEMY (2009) *Doing the wrong things*. Retrieved from http://danieljoneslean.blogspot.co.uk/2009_07_01_archive.html

LEGGE, K. (1995) *Human resource management – the rhetorics, the realities*, 2nd ed. London: Macmillan.

LEVITT, T.C. (1960) *Marketing myopia*. Boston: Harvard Business Review.

LINDENMANN, W.K. (1997, 2003) *Guidelines and standards for measuring and evaluating PR effectiveness*. Retrieved from http://www.instituteforpr.org/wp-content/uploads/2002_MeasuringPrograms.pdf

LINDVALL, P. (2005) *Coachologi, laganda, lust & lönsamhet*. Stockholm: Performance Management AB.

LIU, C.Y., PIROLA-MERLO, A., YANG, C.A. and HUANG, C. (2009). Disseminating the functions of team coaching regarding research and development team effectiveness: evidence from high-tech industries in Taiwan. *Social Behaviour and Personality: An International Journal*, 37(1), pp41–57.

LUECKE, R. (2003) *Harvard business essentials: managing change and transition*. Boston: Harvard Business School.

LYMAN, A. (2003) *Building trust in the workplace*. London: Melcrum Publishing Ltd.

LYMAN, A. (2012) *The trustworthy leader: leveraging the power of trust to transform your organization*. San Francisco: Jossey-Bass.

MARTIN, J. and SIEHL, C. (1983) Organizational culture and counterculture: An uneasy symbiosis. *Organizational Dynamics*, 12(2), pp52-64.

MASLOW, A.H. (1954) *Motivation and personality*. New York: Harper and Row.

MASLOW, A.H. (1966) *The psychology of science; a reconnaissance*. New York: Harper & Row.

MATTHEWS, J. (2010) Can Line Managers Ever Be Effective Coaches? *Business Leadership Review*, 7(2), pp1–10.

MCCLELLAN, D. (1989) *Human motivation*. Cambridge: Press Syndicate of the University of Cambridge.

MCKENNA, D.D. and DAVIS, S.L. (2009) Hidden in plain sight: the active ingredients of executive coaching. *Industrial and Organisational Psychology: Perspectives on Science and Practice*, 2(3), pp244–260.

MELAMED, T. (2010) *Five monkeys, a banana and corporate culture*. Clearwater A and D. Retrieved from http://clearwater-uk.com/MyBlog/2010/02/28/five-monkeys-a-banana-and-corporate-culture/

NANGALIA, L. and NANGALIA A., (2010) The coach in Asian society: impact of social hierarchy on the coaching relationship. *International Journal of Evidence Based Coaching and Mentoring*, 8(1), p51.

NICOLS, F. and LEDGERWOOD, R. (2005*) The goals grid: a new tool for strategic planning*. Retrieved from http://www.nickols.us

NORTHOUSE, P.G. (1997) *Leadership: theory and practice*. Thousand Oaks, CA: Sage.

NY TEKNIK (2009) *Scanias 3 hemliga framgångsrecept*. Retrieved from http://www.nyteknik.se/nyheter/fordon_motor/bilar/article696139.ece

O'BROIN, A. and PALMER, S. (2006) The coach-client relationship and contributions made by the coach in improving coaching outcome. *The Coaching Psychologist*, 2(2), pp16–20.

OFFERMAN, L.R. and SPIROS, R.K. (2001) The science and practice of team development. *Journal of Management Development*, 16(3), pp208–217.

O'NEILL, M.B. (2007) *Executive coaching with backbone and heart: a systems approach to engaging leaders with their challenges*. San Francisco: Jossey-Bass.

OUCHI, W.G (1981) *Theory Z: how American business can meet the Japanese challenge*. USA: Addison-Wesley.

OWEN, H. (1993) *Open space: organization for the new millennium*.

PASCALE, R.T. and ATHOS, A. (1981) *The Art of Japanese Management: Applications for American Executives*. New York: Simon and Schuster.

PASSMORE, J. (2009) *Diversity in coaching: working with gender, culture, race and age*. London: Kogan Page.

PELTIER, B. (2009) *The psychology of executive coaching: theory and application* (2nd ed). New York: Routledge.

PETERS, T.J. and WATERMAN, R.H.(1982) *In Search of Excellence: Lessons from America's Best-run Companies*. New York: Harper & Row.

PETERSON, D. (2007) Executive coaching in a cross-cultural context. *Consulting Psychology Journal: Practice and Research*, 59(4), pp261–271.

PETERSON, D.B. and LITTLE, B. (2008) Growth market: the rise of systemic coaching. *Coaching At Work*, 3(1), p44–47.

PHILLIPS, P.P., PHILLIPS, J.J. and EDWARDS, L.A. (2012) *Measuring the success of coaching*. Washington, DC: The American Society for Training and Development.

PLAISTER TEN, J. (2009) Towards greater cultural understanding in coaching. *International Journal of Evidence Based Coaching and Mentoring*, Special Issue 3. pp64–81.

PLAISTER TEN, J. (2013) Raising culturally-derived awareness and building culturally-appropriate responsibility: The development of the Cross-Cultural Kaleidoscope. *International Journal of Evidence Based Coaching & Mentoring*, 11(2), pp53–69.

PROSCI, INC. (2014) *Best Practices in Change Management*. Prosci, Inc. Available at www.prosci.com/best-practices-in-change-management-2014-edition.html

QUAST, L. (2011) *Reverse mentoring: what it is and why it is beneficial*. Forbes Magazine. Retrieved from http://www.forbes.com/sites/work-in-progress/2011/01/03/reverse-mentoring-what-is-it-and-why-is-it-beneficial/

REINA, D. and REINA, M. (2007) *The HR executive's role in rebuilding trust*. Human Resource Executive Online. Retrieved from http://www.hreonline.com/HRE/view/story.jhtml?id=12160414

RIDLER REPORT (2013) Retrieved from: http://www.ridlerandco.com/executive-coaching/ridler-report-2013-executive-coaching-rides-recession/

RILLING, J.K., GUTMAN, D.A., ZEH, T.R., PAGNONI, G., BERNS, G.S., and KILTS, C.D. (2002) A neural basis for social cooperation. *Neuron*, 35(2), pp395–405.

ROGERS, E.M. (1995) *Diffusion of Innovations*. 4th ed. New York: Free Press.

ROJON, C. and MCDOWALL, A. (2010) Cultural orientation framework (COF) assessment questionnaire in cross-cultural coaching: a cross-validation with wave focus styles. *International Journal of Evidence Based Coaching and Mentoring*, 8(2), pp1–26.

ROSINSKI, P. (2003) *Coaching across cultures: new tools for leveraging national, corporate and professional differences*. London: Nicholas Brealey Publishing.

ROSINSKI, P. (2010) *Global coaching: an integrated approach for long-lasting results*. London: Nicholas Brealey Publishing.

SANDBERG, S. (2013) *Lean In: women, work, and the will to lead*. New York: Alfred A. Knopf, a Random House Company.

SCHEIN, E.H. (1984) Coming to a new awareness of organizational culture. *Sloan Management Review, 25(2), p3*.

SASTRY, A. and PENN, K. (2014) *Fail better: design smart mistakes and succeed sooner*. Boston: Harvard Business Review Press.

SCHEIN, E.H. (1985) *Organizational culture and leadership: a dynamic view*. San Francisco: Jossey-Bass.

SCHEIN, E.H. (1992) *Organizational culture and leadership*. San Francisco: Jossey-Bass Publishers.

SCHEIN, E.H. (1999) *The corporate culture survival guide: sense and nonsense about cultural change*. San Francisco: Jossey-Bass Publishers.

SCHWARZ, R., DAVIDSON, A. and CARLSON, P. (2011) *Skilled facilitator fieldbook: tips, tools and tested methods for consultants, facilitators, managers, trainers and coaches*. San Francisco: John Wiley & Sons.

SENGE, P.M. (1990) *The fifth discipline: mastering the five practices of the learning organization*. New York: Doubleday/Currency.

SHERMAN, S. and FREAS, A. (2004) The wild west of executive coaching. *Harvard Business Review*, 82(11), pp82–90.

STANFORD UNIVERSITY'S ROCK CENTER FOR CORPORATE GOVERNANCE, AND THE MILES GROUP (2013) Executive coaching survey. Center for Leadership Development and Research at Stanford Graduate School of Business.

STAPLEY, L.F. (2006) *Individuals, groups, and organizations beneath the surface: an introduction*. London: Karnac Books.

STEPHENSON, G.R. (1967) Cultural acquisition of a specific learned response among rhesus monkeys. In: Starek, D., Schneider, R. and Kuhn, H.J. (eds), *Progress in Primatology* Stuttgart: Fischer, pp279–288.

SUE-CHAN, S. and LATHAM, G.P. (2004) The relative effectiveness of external, peer, and self-coaches. *Applied Psychology: An International Review*, 53(2), pp260–278.

TAYLOR, C. (2005) *Walking the talk: building a culture for success*. London: Random House Business Books.

TESTA, M.R. and SIPE, L.J. (2013) The organizational culture audit: countering cultural ambiguity in the service context. *Open Journal of Leadership*, 2(02), pp36–44.

THORNTON, C. (2010) *Group and Team Coaching: The Essential Guide*. London: Routledge.

TOOTH, J.A. (2014) *Experiencing executive coaching*. Saarbrucken: Scholars Press.

TOWERS WATSON (2013) *2013–2014 Change and communication ROI survey*. Retrieved from https://www.towerswatson.com/en/Insights/IC-Types/Survey-Research-Results/2013/12/2013–2014-change-and-communication-roi-study

TRICE, H.M. and BEYER, J.M. (1993) *The cultures of work organizations*. New Jersey: Prentice Hall Inc.

TROMPENAARS, F. (1993) *Riding the waves of culture*. London: Nicholas Brealey Publishing.

TROMPENAARS, F. and HAMPDEN-TURNER, C. (1997) *Riding the Waves of Culture: Understanding Cultural Diversity in Business*. London: Nicholas Brealey.

UTTAL, B. (1983) The corporate culture vultures. *Fortune*, 17 October, pp66–72.

VAN DE VEN, A.H., POLLEY, D.E., GARUD, R. and VENKATARAMAN, S. (1999) *The innovation journey*. Oxford: Oxford University Press.

VAN DEN BERG, P.T. and WILDEROM, C.P.M. (2004) Defining, measuring, and comparing organisational cultures. *Applied Psychology: An International Review*, 53(4), pp570-582.

VERHULST, M. and SPRENGEL, R. (2009) Intercultural coaching tools. In: Moral, M. and Abbott, G. (eds), *The Routledge companion to international business coaching*. New York: Routledge.

WAGEMAN, R., NUNES, D.A, BURRUSS, J.A. and HACKMAN, J.R. (2008) *Senior leadership teams: what it takes to make them great.* Boston: Harvard Business School Press.

WAGNER, J. and HOLLENBECK, J. (2010) *Organizational Behavior: Securing competitive advantage.* New York: Routledge.

WARNEKEN, F. and TOMASELLO, M. (2007). Helping and cooperation at 14 months of age. *Infancy*, 11(3), pp271–294.

WEISBORD, M. and JANOFF, S. (1995) *Future Search: An Action Guide to Finding Common Ground in Organizations and Communities.* San Francisco: Berrett-Koehler.

WEST, M. and THE WORK FOUNDATION (2012) *Effective Teamworking: Practical lessons from organisational research.* 3rd ed. Chichester: BPS Blackwell, John Wiley & Sons.

WEST, M., ARMIT, K., LOEWENTHALl, L., ECKERT, R., WEST, T. and LEE, A. (2015) *Leadership and Leadership Development in Healthcare: The Evidence Base.* London: Faculty of Medical Leadership and Management.

WHITMORE, J. (2002) *Coaching for performance: GROWing human potential and purpose.* London: Nicholas Brealey.

WHITMORE, J. (2009) Business coaching international: unlocking the secrets and the power. *Coaching: An International Journal of Theory, Research and Practice*, 2(2), pp176–179.

WINTER, J. P. (1985) Getting your house in order with internal marketing: a marketing prerequisite. *Health Marketing Quarterly*, 3(1), pp69–77.

WOLPERT, D. and FRITH, C. (2004) *The neuroscience of social interactions: decoding, influencing, and imitating the actions of others.* Oxford: Oxford University Press.

ZACHARY, L. (2005) *Creating a mentoring culture: the organization's guide.* San Francisco: Jossey-Bass.

ZEUS, P. and SKIFFINGTON, S. (2000) *The Complete Guide to Coaching at Work.* Sydney: McGraw-Hill.

Index

ABC-DE model
  generally, 49–51
Accessibility
  coaching and mentoring strategies, 82–83
Action plans
  workshops, 91–92
Administration
  coaching and mentoring managers,
    188–189
Aspirations
  ABC-DE model, 50
Assessment
  coaching pools, 106
Attentiveness
  coaching culture model, 11
Audits
  audit report template, 76
  data analysis, 67–68
  demographics, 66–67
  implementation, 67
  introduction, 65
  preparation and design, 66–67
  project teams, 65–66
  reports and recommendations, 67–68
  tools, 66

Baseline and context assessment
  ABC-DE model, 50
  audits
    data analysis, 67–68
    demographics, 66–67
    implementation, 67
    introduction, 65
    preparation and design, 66–67
    project teams, 65–66
    reports and recommendations, 67–68
    tools, 66
  case studies, 76–79
  cultural context, 63–64
  drivers and barriers, 64–65
  introduction, 63
  marketing plan, 201–202
  measurement levels, 64
  summary, 79
  tools and templates
    audit report, 76
    coaching relationship assessment, 70–71
    development stages of coaching culture,
      73–76
    generally, 66, 68
    interview/focus group template, 68–69

  team leader assessment, 71–72
  top management interview, 69–70
  visible manifestations questionnaire, 73
Behaviours
  coaching culture model, 11
Budget
  marketing plan, 203
Business cases
  sponsors, 190
Business need
  support from key influencers, 47–48

Cascade mentoring
  generally, 171–172
Centralised selection
  management of coaching engagements,
    112
Champions
  coaching and mentoring strategies, 84
  roles, 191–194
Charting the course
  see also **Coaching and mentoring
    strategies**
  ABC-DE model, 50
Clarity
  formal mentoring, 173–174
Coach assessment centre
  coaching pools, 109–110
Coaching and mentoring strategies
  components
    accessibility, 82–83
    integration, 86–88
    introduction, 81–82
    measurement, 88
    support and reinforcement, 83–86
  integration
    HR strategies and systems, 87
    introduction, 86
    value chains, 87–88
    work teams, 87
  introduction, 81
  summary, 97
  support and reinforcement
    champions and sponsors, 84
    infrastructure, 85
    introduction, 83
    marketing and communication, 85–86
    rewards and recognition, 85
    skills base, 84
    structure to facilitate coaching, 84
    systemic constraints, 86

workshops
  action plans, 91–92
  case studies, 95–97
  design and content, 90–92
  evaluation, 94–95
  implementation, 93
  introduction, 88
  objectives and expectations, 88
  outputs, 93
  participants, 89
  pre-reading, 92
  roadmaps, 94
  style, 93
  venues, 92–93
Coaching culture (general)
  case studies, 15–17
  coaching, 7
  coaching culture model
    behaviours, 11
    beliefs and mindsets, 13
    core principles, 11–13
    introduction, 9–10
    processes and structures, 10
    skills, 11
    visible manifestations, 10–11
  culture
    definition, 5–6
    introduction, 3–4
  definition, 7–9
  definitions of coaching, 103–104
  developmental conversation model, 8
  future developments
    case study, 220–222
    generally, 219–220
  mentoring, 7
  stages of coaching culture development,
    13–14
  summary, 18
Coaching culture vision
  coaching and mentoring managers, 187
  definition, 55–56
  effectiveness, 56–57
  introduction, 55
  summary, 62
  visioning process
    case study, 60–62
    consultation, 59–60
    format identification, 58–59
    implementation, 59
    introduction, 57
    key stakeholder identification, 58
    preparation, 58
    process design, 58–59
Coaching pools
  assessment and selection, 106
  coach assessment centre, 109–110
  continuing professional development, 110
  evaluation, 107–108

  feedback, 109
  internal coaches, 137
  interviews, 108
  introduction, 104–105
  observed sessions, 108–109
  request for proposal, 106–107
  requirements, 105–106
  support and development, 110–111
  usage and awareness, 111
Coaching relationship assessment
  tools and templates, 70–71
Collaboration
  coaching culture model, 12
Collective contracting
  team coaching, 154–155
Commitment from organisation
  coaching and mentoring managers, 187
Commonality
  matching clients with coaches, 111
Communication
  coaching and mentoring managers, 188
  coaching and mentoring strategies, 85–86
  marketing plan, 203–204
Community of practice
  internal coaches, 138
Community setting
  mentoring, 168–169
Compatibility
  matching clients with coaches, 112
Complex adaptive systems
  systemic thinking, 23–26
Confidentiality
  coaching and mentoring managers, 187
Conflict resolution
  team coaching, 150
Consultation
  visioning process, 59–60
Context assessment
  see **Baseline and context assessment**
Continuing professional development
  coaching pools, 110
  internal coaches, 138
Continuous learning
  preparation, 44–45
Credibility
  matching clients with coaches, 112
Cross-cultural coaching
  case study, 217–218
  cultural differences, 214–216
  implementation, 216–217
  introduction, 209–210
  skill development, 213–214
  skills and characteristics, 211–213
  summary, 218
  Western origins of coaching, 210–211
Culture
  see also **Cross-cultural coaching**
  baseline and context assessment, 63–64

cultural awareness, 212
definition, 5–6
introduction, 3–4
Curiosity
coaching culture model, 12

Data analysis
audits, 67–68
Demographics
audits, 66–67
Developmental conversation model
generally, 8
Developmental mentoring
developmental coaching compared,
167–168
generally, 166–167
Diversity
preparation, 43
Doing the work
ABC-DE model, 50–51
Drivers
baseline and context assessment, 64–65

Education
mentoring, 169
sponsors, 190–191
Embedded stage
coaching culture development, 14
Ethics
coaching culture model, 12
Evaluation
ABC-DE model, 51
coaching and mentoring managers, 188
coaching pools, 107–108
external coaches, 113–114
marketing plan, 204–205
workshops, 94–95
Expectations
coaching and mentoring managers, 188
coaching by managers, 126
workshops, 88
External coaches
alignment
definitions of coaching, 103–104
introduction, 103
policy and guidelines, 104
purpose and scope, 103
approaches, 102–103
benefits and drawbacks, 102
case studies, 116–121
coaching pools
assessment and selection, 106
coach assessment centre, 109–110
continuing professional development,
110
evaluation, 107–108
feedback, 109
interviews, 108

introduction, 104–105
observed sessions, 108–109
request for proposal, 106–107
requirements, 105–106
support and development, 110–111
usage and awareness, 111
evaluation and measurement, 113–114
evolution, 101–102
introduction, 101–102
management of coaching engagements
introduction, 111
matching clients with coaches,
111–112
selection, 112
three-way contracting, 112–113
organisation development,
115–116
summary, 122
External systems
individual level, 21
introduction, 21
organisation level, 22–23
team level, 22

Facilitation
team coaching, 150–152
Fact-finding
team coaching, 154
Feedback
coaching and mentoring managers, 188
coaching pools, 109
Financial control
coaching and mentoring managers, 188
Focus group template
generally, 68–69
Formal mentoring
see **Mentoring**
Format identification
visioning process, 58–59
Free selection
management of coaching engagements,
112

Goals
team coaching, 154
Group mentoring
generally, 171
Growth
coaching culture model, 12
preparation, 44–45

'Hard' change
generally, 197
High-leverage points and solutions
systemic thinking, 30–32
Honesty
coaching culture model, 12
preparation, 43

HR strategies and systems
coaching and mentoring strategies, 87
Human resources
generally, 186

Implementation plan
marketing plan, 204
Informal mentoring
formal mentoring compared, 172–173
generally, 176–177
Infrastructure
coaching and mentoring strategies, 85
Integration
HR strategies and systems, 87
introduction, 86
value chains, 87–88
work teams, 87
Internal capacity for coaching
coaching by managers
case study, 129–133
coaching leadership styles, 125–126
expectations, 126
introduction, 123–124
managers as professional coaches,
124
mindset, 126
rewards, 128–129
skill development, 126–128
systemic barriers, 128
internal coaches
case studies, 138–143
coaching pools, 137
community of practice, 138
introduction, 138
job descriptions, 138
training and continuous development,
138
introduction, 123
summary, 143
team dynamics
case study, 135–136
changes, 133
introduction, 133
line managers, 134
mindset, 134
practical applications, 134–135
support, 134
team-based learning, 135–136
Internal systems
individual level, 21
introduction, 21
organisation level, 22–23
team level, 22
International standards
formal mentoring, 174, 176
Interviews
coaching pools, 108
interview template, 68–69

Job descriptions
internal coaches, 138

Learning
see also **Skills**
preparation, 44–45
team coaching, 150
Lifelong mentoring
mentoring, 169–170
Limited selection
management of coaching engagements,
112
Line managers
team dynamics, 134
Linear thinking
systemic thinking compared, 19–21

Managers
coaching by managers
case study, 129–133
coaching leadership styles, 125–126
expectations, 126
introduction, 123–124
managers as professional coaches, 124
mindset, 126
rewards, 128–129
skill development, 126–128
systemic barriers, 128
roles, 187–189
team dynamics, 134
Marketing
case studies, 205–206
coaching and mentoring strategies, 85–86
coaching needs, 198
'hard' and 'soft' change, 197
introduction, 197–198
marketing plan
baseline and context assessment,
201–202
budget, 203
communication methods, 203–204
evaluation, 204–205
implementation plan, 204
introduction, 199–201
messages, 203
objectives, 202
target audience, 202
modalities of coaching and mentoring, 199
summary, 207
Matching clients
cross-cultural coaching, 214
external coaches, 111–112
formal mentoring, 174–175
Measurement
coaching and mentoring strategies, 88
external coaches, 113–114
formal mentoring, 176
levels, 64

Mentoring
see also **Coaching and mentoring strategies; Roles**
applications
case study, 170
community setting, 168–169
educational setting, 169
introduction, 168
lifelong mentoring, 169–170
organisational setting, 168
case studies, 177–181
definition, 7
developmental mentoring
developmental coaching compared, 167–168
generally, 166–167
formal mentoring
clarity, 173–174
informal mentoring compared, 172–173
international standards, 174, 176
introduction, 173
level of direction or instruction, 174
matching clients with mentors, 174–175
pitfall avoidance, 175–176
history, 165–166
informal mentoring
formal mentoring compared, 172–173
generally, 176–177
international standards, 174, 176
introduction, 165
summary, 181–182
types of mentoring, 170–172
Multicultural coaching
see **Cross-cultural coaching**
Multifocal perspective
cross-cultural coaching, 212–213

Nascent stage
coaching culture development, 14
Networking
champions, 193–194
network mentoring, 171

Observed sessions
coaching pools, 108–109
'On the edge'
systemic thinking, 23–26
Openness
coaching culture model, 12
Organisation development
external coaches, 115–116
Organisational setting
mentoring, 168

Paradoxes
cross-cultural coaching, 213
Peer coaching
cross-cultural coaching, 214

Peer mentoring
generally, 170
Perceived need
team coaching, 153
Performance improvement
team coaching, 150
Pitfall avoidance
formal mentoring, 175–176
Polarity management
systemic thinking, 26–27
Pools
see **Coaching pools**
Positive experiences
sponsors, 190
support from key influencers, 49
Preparation
ABC-DE model, 49–51
diversity, 43
expected returns, 45–47
formal mentoring, 175
growth, 44–45
honesty, 43
introduction, 39
relevance, 39–41
stakeholders, 51–53
summary, 53
support from key influencers, 47–49
supportive climate
dimensions and key indicators, 44–45
encouragement for taking initiative, 42
generally, 41–42
taking initiative, 42
trust, 43
Pre-reading
workshops, 92
Problem solving
event level, 28
introduction, 27–28
mental model level, 29
pattern level, 28
structure level, 28–29
Process design
visioning process, 58–59
Process ownership
formal mentoring, 175–176
Project teams
audits, 65–66

Readiness
team coaching, 153–154
Reflection
coaching culture model, 12
Relevance
preparation, 39–41
Reports and recommendations
audits, 67–68
Request for proposal
coaching pools, 106–107

Resource provision
    coaching and mentoring managers, 188
    cross-cultural coaching, 214
Respect
    coaching culture model, 12–13
Reverse mentoring
    generally, 170–171
Review
    team coaching, 156
Rewards
    champions, 193
    coaching and mentoring strategies, 85
    coaching by managers, 128–129
Roadmaps
    workshops, 94
Role models
    champions, 192
Roles
    case studies, 194–196
    champions, 191–194
    coaching and mentoring managers,
       187–189
    human resources, 186
    introduction, 185
    sponsors, 189–191
    summary, 196

Selection
    coaching pools, 106
    formal mentoring, 175
    types of selection, 112
Self-awareness
    team coaching, 149
Shadow boards
    mentoring, 171
Skills
    see also **Cross-cultural coaching**
    coaching and mentoring strategies, 84
    coaching culture model, 11
    development, 126–128
    team coach's competencies, 151–152
'Soft' change
    generally, 197
Speed mentoring
    generally, 171
Sponsors
    coaching and mentoring strategies, 84
    roles, 189–191
Stakeholders
    case studies, 51–53
    introduction, 51
    visioning process, 58
Storytelling
    champions, 192–193
Strategic stage
    coaching culture development, 14
Strategies
    see **Coaching and mentoring strategies**

Supervision
    team coaching, 156–157
Support
    champions and sponsors, 84
    coaching and mentoring managers, 188
    coaching pools, 110–111
    infrastructure, 85
    introduction, 83
    marketing and communication, 85–86
    network and initiatives, 187
    rewards and recognition, 85
    skills base, 84
    sponsors, 190–191
    structure to facilitate coaching, 84
    supportive climate
       dimensions and key indicators, 44–45
       encouragement for taking initiative, 42
       generally, 41–42
    systemic constraints, 86
    team coaching, 150
    team dynamics, 134
Systemic barriers and constraints
    coaching and mentoring strategies, 86
    coaching by managers, 128
Systemic thinking
    complex adaptive systems, 23–26
    five whys, 30–31
    high-leverage points and solutions, 30–32
    internal and external systems, 21–23
    introduction, 19
    linear thinking compared, 19–21
    'on the edge', 23–26
    polarity management, 26–27
    problem solving, 27–29
    summary, 35–36
    systems theory, 21
    'why tree', 30–31
    working smarter
       case study, 32–35
       high-leverage points and solutions,
          30–32
       introduction, 30
       'why tree', 30, 31

Tactical stage
    coaching culture development, 14
Taking initiative
    preparation, 42
Target audience
    marketing plan, 202
Team coaching
    applications, 149
    benefits, 146–147
    case studies, 158–163
    coaching sessions, 155–156
    definition of team, 145–146
    definitions, 147–148
    facilitation, 151–152

future developments, 157–158
introduction, 145
process
  coaching sessions, 155–156
  collective contracting, 154–155
  goals and timescales, 154
  introduction, 152
  preparation, 153–154
  review, 156
  scoping and contracting, 154–155
review, 156
summary, 163
supervision, 156–157
team coach's competencies, 151–152
team coach's role, 149–151
Teams
see also **Team coaching**
audits, 65–66
coaching and mentoring strategies, 87
definition, 145–146
dynamics, 133–136
team leader assessment template,
  71–72
Three-way contracting
external coaches, 112–113
Timescales
team coaching, 154
Tools and templates
audit report, 76
coaching relationship assessment, 70–71
development stages of coaching culture,
  73–76
generally, 66, 68
interview/focus group template, 68–69
team leader assessment, 71–72
top management interview, 69–70
visible manifestations questionnaire, 73

Top management interview
tools and templates, 69–70
Training
see also **Skills**
formal mentoring, 175
internal coaches, 138
Trust
preparation, 43

Value chains
coaching and mentoring strategies, 87–88
Visible manifestations
questionnaire template, 73
visioning process implementation, 59
Vision
see **Coaching culture vision**

'Why tree'
systemic thinking, 30–31
Work teams
coaching and mentoring strategies, 87
Workshops
action plans, 91–92
case studies, 95–97
design and content, 90–92
evaluation, 94–95
implementation, 93
introduction, 88
objectives and expectations, 88
outputs, 93
participants, 89
pre-reading, 92
roadmaps, 94
style, 93
venues, 92–93